BLOOD ON THE LEAVES

BLOOD ON THE LEAVES

Real Hunting Accident Investigations—And
Lessons in Hunter Safety

Rod Slings, Mike Van Durme, and B. Keith Byers

Guilford, Connecticut

An imprint of Rowman & Littlefield

Distributed by NATIONAL BOOK NETWORK

British Library Cataloguing in Publication Information Available

Library of Congress Cataloging-in-Publication Data

Blood on the leaves : real hunting accident investigations—and lessons in hunter safety / Rod Slings, Mike Van Durme, and B. Keith Byers.
   pages cm
   Includes bibliographical references.
   ISBN 978-1-58667-157-0 (pbk.) — ISBN 978-1-58667-158-7 (e-book)
   1. Hunting accidents. 2. Hunting—Safety measures. 3. Firearms—Safety measures. I. Hunting and Shooting Related Consultants.
   SK39.5.B56 2015
   639'.10289—dc23
                                                                    2015004136

First of all, I would like to dedicate this to my late parents, who inspired my love of the outdoors, Art and Hattie Slings, Pam Slings along with our daughter, Shelby, and our "grands," Cooper and Kelsey. I would also like to acknowledge the victims and the families of hunting related shootings I have investigated for their strength and willingness to cooperate in finding the truth for the sake of prevention. A special shout-out and thank you to all the volunteer hunter education instructors who have continued to make hunting the safe activity it has become over the years. Thank you as well to the professional natural resources staff members and wildlife officers who have guided the volunteer efforts and shared their passion through the International Hunter Education Association.

Lastly, I would like to thank God for the strength and passion He has instilled in me as I have dedicated my life's work to the prevention of hunting-related incidents. Being able to reach out to Him each and every time to deal with tragic events I have encountered has saved me. He has given me the guidance to focus my efforts as well as blessing me with two great partners: Michael Van Durme and Keith Byers. We share in our faith and to do the next best right thing to prevent tragedy and pass on the lessons we have learned.

—Rod Slings

I would like to dedicate my works in this book to my loving wife, Daryl. She put up with my life as a wildlife law enforcement officer for thirty-one years. Without her support and understanding of the job, I could not been successful in a career field that I dearly love.

Also I would like to dedicate my works in this book to Captain Denny Hill for believing in me and seeing potential where others did not. Without his support, insight, and giving me the opportunity, my partners, Rod Slings and Mike Van Durme, would be writing this book with someone else.

And last but certainly not least, I would like to dedicate my works in this book to Rod Slings and Mike Van Durme. They have made my life's journey a richer and more colorful place. Our friendship holds no bounds. "I'm at the place I need to be."

—B. Keith Byers

I would like to dedicate my efforts here to my family, who helped form me and have supported me in every endeavor. My parents and grandparents, my siblings, and especially my wife, Mary, and children, Ben, Jessica, and Jordan, have always been behind me, even when they had no idea where I was going. This book would not have been possible without Rod Slings and Keith Byers, my partners, my friends, and my companions on the journey.

—Michael Van Durme

Special Dedication from the Authors
And finally, we would all like to dedicate our work to the game wardens everywhere, no matter what title is on their uniforms. They are the backbone of protecting both the wildlife and the people who go afield to enjoy it. One of the greatest game wardens of all was Mike Bradshaw, Texas Game Warden, a dear friend and coworker who left us too soon. He embodied the passion and professionalism that characterizes real game wardens.

CONTENTS

If you go to hunt, take a solemn oath never to point the shooting end of your gun toward yourself or any other human being.

In still-hunting, swear yourself black in the face never to shoot at a dim, moving object in the woods for a deer, unless you have seen that it is a deer. In these days there are quite as many hunters as deer in the woods; and it is a heavy, wearisome job to pack a dead or wounded man ten or twelve miles out to a clearing, let alone it spoils all the pleasure of the hunt, and it is apt to raise hard feelings among his relations

—"Nessmuk," George Washington Sears,
Woodcraft and Camping, 1884;
Dover Publications, Inc., New York

INTRODUCTION OF ROD SLINGS

The incident scene will speak to you; you must listen for the sake of prevention.

FOR MANY YEARS, MY QUOTE ABOVE HAS BEEN MY SIGNATURE line, while the philosophy of "Find something you love to do and get paid for it, you will never have to work a day," has been very close to describing my career.

I was raised in a family where hunting was something everyone did. It was not so much a rite of passage as it was just part of life. Sunday afternoons were spent plinking at cans or shooting clay birds. I can remember my dad and uncles using a rifle to shoot the metal ring off old metal coffee cans as the cans were thrown in the air. They were all very good shots. Every fall they shined, or what was also called "jacklighting": illegally shining a spotlight into trees to locate raccoons. The shot would be made from the car, which was also illegal. I stayed at the car holding the light so they could go retrieve the raccoon, all the while watching out for the game warden. The raccoons would be skinned and their fur sold. These outings even occurred while driving the back roads on the way to and from the grocery store with the family on a Saturday night.

For me, growing up provided almost daily lessons on how to hunt, but as you can tell, not all the methods were legal or ethical. Later in my life these events provided valuable knowledge, helping me catch those who hunted illegally. My occupation as a protector of wildlife made me the black sheep in the family.

I took a little guff at times when the family got together, but I always knew they respected me and loved me for my passion for wildlife.

I began my career with Iowa State Parks as an assistant park ranger in 1973. My family always camped, fished, and hunted, so getting hired for an outdoors job was fantastic. As time went on, I worked my way up the ladder and continued my education.

I worked in state parks for the first years of my career while also working navigation enforcement on the lake. The best part of my job came every fall, when I worked alongside the local conservation officers. In 1984 I was approached by the chief of enforcement about him creating some new law enforcement positions dealing with safety. Once the positions were approved, I interviewed for and became one of six new conservation officers assigned to the Recreational Safety Officer Unit. The unit was responsible for working with the department's safety education programs, boat crash investigations, and hunting incident investigations in addition to working enforcement.

As officers in the unit, we were sent to a number of training opportunities, including advanced boat crash investigation from the Coast Guard and Underwriters Laboratories and training from the National Association of Boating Law Administrators.

In 2001 I was promoted as a law enforcement supervisor to oversee the Recreational Safety Officer Unit. Having well-trained investigators in Iowa helped us reduce hunting-related shootings. Looking back, the impact Wisconsin DNR had on me became my life's work and focus.

The Wisconsin DNR inspired me to focus on hunting-related shootings. The late Homer Moe, Wisconsin conservation warden and Hunter Education Administrator, along with his team, created the initial science for these investigations. Homer and his team saw the need for specialized training to find out exactly how and why these hunting accidents were happening.

Homer began his career as a Wisconsin state trooper from 1955 to 1961. His investigative work with the patrol inspired him take a closer look at each of the many deaths Wisconsin was having during the fall deer season.

In 1987 I attended a four-day training session in Prairie du Chien, Wisconsin, put on by Wisconsin conservation wardens Homer Moe, Bill Hoyt, Bob Tucker, Larry Keith, Rick Wolf, Gary Homuth, and Bill Engfer. Craig Jackson, Rick McGeough, Randy Edwards, and I were all Iowa officers. We went back to Iowa and began investigating the hunting-related incidents that were taking place. Craig Jackson and I joined forces with four other Iowa officers assigned to the Recreational Safety Officer Unit. A curriculum was created based on the Wisconsin model, and every Iowa CO was trained.

In 1993 Homer Moe asked me to assist him at Central Missouri State University (CMSU) in Warrensburg, Missouri, for the first Hunting Incident Investigation Academy. This was a collaboration of Homer Moe, Dr. Leanna Depue at the CMSU Safety Center, and Bob Staton of the Missouri Department of Conservation. At the time, Missouri was having a number of turkey-hunting incidents during their spring season and hoped to reduce them.

The four-day course covered a number of topics, including managing the scene, locating evidence, ballistics, diagramming, photography, evidence collection, and report writing. This first academy brought together about twenty-eight wildlife officers from around the United States.

The academy continued at CMSU until eventually we took it on the road, moving from Warrensburg, Missouri, to Lindenwood University near Troy, Missouri. The academy has since traveled to

Connecticut, Florida, Georgia, Iowa, West Virginia, and back to Wisconsin. Over time the attendance has increased to include wildlife officers from the United States, Canada, Mexico, and South Africa. Academy participants have been commissioned, active wildlife officers, while the instructor cadre has comprised officers from Iowa, Missouri, New York, Georgia, Wisconsin, Connecticut, and Florida.

The International Hunter Education Association has been the primary sponsor of the academy since its beginning back in 1993, and I am honored to say that I am the only instructor who has taught at every academy since its inception.

States that have sent officers have had an amazing improvement in the quality of the data collected and incident reports generated. Each incident is now treated as a research project. The data collected is shared with Hunter Education administrators around the country. In turn, the curriculum development is adjusted based on the lessons learned from each incident. The data collected has also been used by wildlife agencies in their prevention efforts prior to specific hunting seasons.

Notices in the annual *Game Guide* and press releases, TV, radio, websites, and social media efforts are all used to get the message out to remind hunters to be safe. With these efforts, the number of hunting-related incidents continues to decline and is at an all-time low.

Shortly after the beginning of the academy, I met students Michael Van Durme of the New York Department of Environmental Conservation and Keith Byers of the Georgia Department of Natural Resources. It didn't take long for the three of us to share our stories and passion for the "need to know." Michael and Keith soon became academy instructors, sharing their passion, skill sets, and leadership with wildlife officers from all over.

These talents, together with many case studies of investigations the three of us had worked from different parts of the country, helped us quickly move from mere colleagues to true friends.

When I retired from the Iowa DNR in 2008, I began to consult on my own. Later that business blossomed into a consulting business when I joined forces with Michael and Keith as they retired from their respective agencies.

During our individual careers, integrity had been an important factor in our daily lives. Our solid faith, along with our respect for one another, has made this an amazing and rewarding collaboration. When I called Michael and Keith about starting the business, they did not hesitate. Now we share our knowledge, skills, and experience as we provide a number of services to both agencies and individuals. We serve as subject matter experts, litigation support for hunting-related incidents and tree stand falls, public speakers, and now authors—all with the same intention of listening, working, and preventing hunting incidents.

It's been a long time since I heard the shots ring out from the car on those dark nights when I was a kid, but those memories laid the foundation for my work to this day!

Introduction of Keith Byers

As a young boy, the outdoors was my playground. I quickly became fascinated with all of nature, particularly the animals. And so my quest began.

Shortly before I entered the first grade, I acquired my first BB gun. I had been born into a family of bird hunters, specifically bobwhite quail and mourning dove. It seemed only fitting that I follow in that same path. Just a little encouragement and direction—and that BB gun—and a hunter was born.

Gun in hand, I hunted in the yards and woods around our home and my grandparents' home in my preschool years. Nothing that crawled, flew, slithered, or walked was safe. This continued through my early school years, and when I entered the fifth grade, I was finally trusted with a .22 caliber rimfire rifle and a .410 shotgun. I felt as though I had stepped up to the big leagues.

I never will forget the first gray squirrel I bagged; it was on my grandparents' farm. I had been walking around the wood line of the pasture, and there sitting on an old stump was a squirrel. Trembling, I quickly raised the single-shot .22 to my shoulder, took aim, and fired. I can still taste the squirrel dumplings my grandmother cooked that night.

These experiences as a youngster molded me into an outdoor person and gun advocate. When it came time for a career, I was at a loss for a couple of years. Then fate struck. I read an article about game wardens in *Georgia Sportsman* magazine. From that moment on, I made it my quest to become a game warden.

Six months after my twenty-first birthday, that quest ended when I was hired by the Georgia Department of Natural

Resources, Law Enforcement Section. I would learn how to hunt new quarry—one said to be the most dangerous animal on earth—man.

I quickly learned how to apply my woodsman's knowledge to the job of game warden. In addition to hunting animals, which I still loved doing in my time off, I was now hunting poachers.

Early on I realized I would not be present when some of these violations of the law took place. Long before I went through my first investigative course, I began to notice that these lawbreakers would leave something at or take something away from a scene. Using this evidence, I began to piece cases together, much like a puzzle, to see what picture developed.

There was huge satisfaction in figuring out one of these whodunits. The highlight was knocking on the door of a perpetrator and placing him under arrest. The look on the face of someone who had thought he had gotten off scot-free was indeed priceless.

My talent in solving investigative cases did not go unnoticed in my department. Capt. Denny Hill, in particular, was aware of my growing talent and began sending me to a few investigative courses. These only made me thirsty for more and strive to be the best I could be.

Before long I began instructing mandate classes at the Georgia Police Academy in "The Fundamentals of Investigation" and "Crime Scene Processing." One evening in 1997, the course of my life and career changed forever. I received a telephone call; on the other end of the line was Capt. Denny Hill.

Captain Hill had been assigned to a new position as Col. Joel Brown's chief assistant. The colonel was organizing a new team of investigators that would investigate and reconstruct hunting and boating accidents across the state, and Captain Hill wanted to know if I would be interested in taking on this assignment. Corp.

Eddie Hall would be joining me on the team, and the captain made it clear that there would be a lot of training involved. This was a dream come true; I cannot express the excitement I felt about this new assignment and opportunity.

In 1998 two more team members and I, along with Corporal Hall, were sent to the Central Missouri State University in Warrensburg, Missouri, to attend the Hunting Incident Investigation Academy. This was a profound and eye-opening experience. What I learned during that course would alter the course of my life forever and set me on a career path that is still being realized today. There I met instructor Rod Slings and fellow student Mike Van Durme, and our friendship began.

When my coworkers and I arrived back in Georgia, we immediately began applying our newly gained knowledge and investigative skills in the field. We relayed our information back to Colonel Brown, and we slowly began to change how hunting incident investigations were handled throughout the state. Thus the Critical Incident Reconstruction Team (CIRT) was born and immediately put to work. The deer season after we attended the national academy found us working several high-profile hunting incident cases, and we never looked back.

Along the way I became supervisor of the CIRT, and the two-man team grew to four and then to seven. Over the years the team grew to a fifteen man unit tasked with investigating and reconstructing the state's most tragic hunting incidents and boating accidents.

In 1999 I was sent to an International Hunter Education Conference in Buffalo, New York. There I met up with Rod Slings and Mike Van Durme again, and Rod asked if we would be interested in becoming instructors at the national academy. His request made another of my dreams come true, so of course my answer was, "Yes!" My first year as an instructor was in 2000 in Warrensburg, Missouri.

After this academy class, the friendship between Rod, Mike, and me strengthened. Every subsequent class we instructed together only deepened our friendship and bond. We were all approaching retirement and all knew we did not want to give up our passion for hunting incident investigations just because we retired.

Out of this passion and friendship, Hunting and Shooting Related Consultants, LLC, was born. I want to believe we have made a difference in the way these types of incidents are investigated across the United States and worldwide. It is our mission as instructors, investigators, and reconstructionists to continue to instruct game wardens, conservation rangers, and wildlife officers to share our passion on how to investigate and reconstruct a hunting incident scene properly. The information derived from these investigations goes a long way toward correcting safety concerns in the hunting world and provides justice where it is due. Our beloved sport of hunting and concern for all hunters demand no less.

Introduction of Michael Van Durme

My father was my teacher. But most importantly he was a great dad.

—Beau Bridges

The American model of wildlife ownership and management is much different from most of the rest of the world. In the United States wildlife is owned by all the people, and with a proper license, and within the regulated seasons, all citizens are allowed to hunt. Proper training is required and there are many laws to regulate the dates and means and methods, but rich and poor alike are granted equal opportunities to hunt.

In Europe, as in many other places, it is not that way and never has been. In times past, the lands and its inhabitants—both human and animal—were owned and controlled by the reigning ruler, or someone designated by the ruler, and while many places no longer have a monarchy or similar ruling system, wildlife is still owned and controlled by the landowner. In times both past and present, only the wealthy, the nobles, and the landowners have been allowed to hunt. Hunting was and is reserved for the upper classes alone. Gamekeepers were employed to manage the land and the wildlife but also to keep the common folk from taking game. Poaching, or unlawfully taking game, has been going on for as long as there have been rules to break.

In 1905 in the town of Waarschoot, Belgium, a young man, Henry by name, made his living hunting the abundant wild hares that lived throughout the area. He got quite good at it and found a ready buyer at the butcher shop in the nearby town of Sleidinge, about four miles away. He also came to like the cute little red-headed daughter of the owner, which made his visits to the shop all the more pleasant.

As often happens, the local gamekeeper eventually caught him. He was reminded, physically, that lower-class people were not allowed to hunt; only the wealthy landowners could. Henry was brought before the judge and given the standard sentence for poaching at the time. He was ordered to return to court in thirty days, when he would be put in jail for his crime. Instead of returning to court and going to jail, Henry gathered his meager possessions and boarded a boat to America to seek his fortune.

Upon arriving in the land of opportunity, Henry found employment and saved all his money. In late 1910 he returned to Belgium to marry that cute little red-haired girl from the butcher shop. Henry Van Durme and Clara Martens were married in Belgium in January 1911. They found passage aboard the RMS *Mauritania* and arrived at Ellis Island, New York, the next month. They first moved to Rochester, New York, and soon took up residence in the nearby valley town of Dansville as farmers. They settled in to grow grapes on the east hill of the valley.

They would go on to have eleven children, one of whom was my dad, Nicholas. Henry continued to hunt and taught all his boys to hunt as well. A local newspaper article about their twenty-fifth wedding anniversary described my grandparents as two of "the most thrifty, prosperous and patriotic citizens in the valley" despite the fact that (or because of it) they had continued to make and sell wine throughout Prohibition.

When my grandmother first told me this story, I was in awe. I barely knew my grandfather, as he passed away when I was eight years old, but knowing he was a poacher, a hunter, an adventurer, and a romantic who returned across the ocean to claim his young love made him a hero in my eyes.

I was proud of my heritage as an outdoorsman, and right out of college I started working at the Department of Environmental Conservation's Bureau of Wildlife Management, waiting to take the test to become a conservation officer or game warden. At this time I met Frank Ely, chief of the conservation officers, who had been around for a long time and knew just about everyone. When I introduced myself, his ears perked up. "Van Durme?" He asked which one of the Van Durme boys my dad was, and I told him it was Nick.

He smiled and said that while he had arrested most of the Van Durme boys, he had never arrested Nick. He spoke highly of my grandmother. Anytime he stopped by the house, he would say, "Clara, I am going to need Dick (or Phil, Ray, John, etc.) and the deer (pheasant, rabbit, etc.) he shot."

My grandmother would think for a minute and then send one child off to fetch the poached animal and another to fetch the poacher of the day. Warden Ely would tell her he needed twenty-five dollars for the fine and then take the child, one of my not-quite-yet uncles, off to see the judge. After a bit he would return with the errant hunter and often leave the poached animal behind, knowing it would be eaten.

Captain Ely was happy to tell me that he never got any grief, games played, or lies with these encounters. He could testify that the Van Durmes were stand-up people who respected the law—even if they did break it once in a while.

When I became an environmental police officer, I remembered that conversation and tried to give every person the chance to stand up and account for his or her actions. Most of the time, if given the chance, people were honest and admitted they made a mistake. If I treated them with respect, they ended our contact by shaking my hand and saying, "Thanks." I always considered that handshake a sign that I was doing a good job.

But in too many cases violators are not normally upright people who made a mistake. They are people who decide to lie, cheat, and steal for their personal gain and pleasure. These are the people whose capture requires real investigative police work. These are the people who, even when caught in the act, will lie and blame others. You needed to put together an ironclad case to convict these criminals, but I never minded the work. In fact, these were the ones I got the most pleasure from catching and convicting.

I read every book I could find and volunteered to go to every class I could, including Fingerprinting, Interview and Interrogation, Written Statement Analysis, Crime Scene Photography, and Evidence Collection. I also volunteered to teach these skills to new recruits, as nothing forces you to become better at a skill that having to teach it to others. Through this ongoing process, I came to attend the National Hunting Incident Academy in Missouri, where I met and became fast friends with Rod Slings and Keith Byers. Over the years we became co-instructors at the academy, eventual business partners, and now cowriters of the book.

And while my grandfather may have come to this country because he broke the law, I know his blood and legacy run through my veins. With every step I take, every conviction I was and am a part of, and every story I tell, I know I do both him and my father proud.

INTRODUCTION

THANK YOU, AND WELCOME TO OUR COLLECTION OF SHORT STORIES based on actual investigations we have supervised, investigated, consulted on, and/or reviewed. The names and places have been changed to protect those involved in these cases, but the details have not.

The intent of this book is to share actual events that took place, to learn from these events, and to continue to enhance the prevention of hunting-related incidents. As a result of thorough investigations by us and other trained investigators around the country, and by learning from the information collected, hunting remains safe and is getting safer every year. Sharing this information with you and the vast army of over fifty-seven thousand noble volunteers who teach hunter education only helps to increase hunter safety.

This is not an antihunting book and is certainly not intended to scare anyone away from hunting. We, the authors, are all active and dedicated hunters. We share and pass on our knowledge, skills, and experiences of hunting with family, friends, and those who want to learn safe and ethical hunting methods. By sharing our experiences with you, the readers, it is our hope that the lessons we learned continue to educate and impact the decisions of current and future hunters.

Our families and friends have always been curious about our work and regularly asked us to tell our stories. Our passion for hunting and our investigative skills make these sometimes tragic stories unique.

If you are a *CSI* buff and love to read mystery novels, whether you hunt or not, these stories will tug at your heartstring. They will bring you to tears or laughter as a result of the decisions people make. You will find these true-life, human-interest stories to be unlike any others you have read. After reading our stories, you likely will look at the definition of the word "accident" differently than you did before. As you see each story unfold, you should ask yourself, *How could this be prevented?* We have included "Lessons Learned" with every story to help you understand how the incident could have been prevented.

Each story will differ based on the landscape, the species of the game animal, and the state of mind of the hunters involved, as well as their age or experience. What they all have in common is that one day a person went hunting, alone or with friends, and on that day their life changed forever.

1

The First Time I Got Shot . . .

The hardest thing to see is what is in front of your eyes.
—JOHANN WOLFGANG VON GOETHE

THE FIRST TIME I GOT SHOT, I WAS SURPRISED. IT HAPPENED SO fast, and, like everyone else, I thought it would never happen to me.

Through most of my career I have been a police officer and a firearms instructor. I also taught Street Survival. I was well trained in the proper use of firearms, as well as when and how to respond with deadly physical force. Early in my career I rarely had to draw my sidearm. I remember the first time distinctly: Two vicious dogs and a homeless man with a brick attacked me, and I pulled my gun as a deterrent—it worked.

I was also careful to always practice good *situational* awareness, always very conscious of who had a firearm and where it was pointed. As a conservation officer, I knew that every hunter and fisherman I checked would have at least one knife, and many would have firearms. I was sure I would always be able to see trouble coming and be able to respond properly to protect myself and anyone else—or so I thought.

I was on patrol as a New York State environmental conservation police officer when I got the complaint—someone was using a rifle to hunt ducks on one of the State Wildlife Management Areas near me. Anyone hunting ducks in July, with a rifle, was a different call indeed, and I was anxious to catch the poacher in the act.

When I got to the area, I found a car parked near the dike of a large impoundment. As I got out of my patrol car, I clearly heard a gunshot from a long way into the marsh and saw a flock of ducks take to the air, confirming what had been reported.

The challenge was to catch the poachers in the act before they could destroy any evidence. I didn't waste time putting on hip boots; I just hurried across the hummocks and through the cattails in the direction of the shots. I could stay out of the water most of the time, but often there was no choice but to wade knee-deep through the muck as I stalked closer. They were clearly moving, probably in a canoe, and soon I got close enough to study them through my binoculars.

Sure enough, there was a canoe with older men in the bow and stern, along with a younger boy in the middle. While I was glad to see the youngster was wearing a bright orange life jacket, I still needed to investigate the shots. They had .22 rifles and were paddling along and then raising their rifles to shoot at . . . frogs!

Now the shots made sense! It was indeed frog season, and they were just hunting frogs. The person calling in the complaint had heard the shots, seen the ducks fly away, and just assumed someone was hunting ducks.

I understood the confusion. Frog hunting was not real popular in this area to begin with, and most frog hunters used spears rather than firearms. I found myself getting excited—I had never checked a frog hunter before.

According to New York state law, you can only hunt frogs from sunrise to sunset; and as it was getting close to sunset, I could tell they were headed back toward their car. I decided to circle around to the road and check their licenses when they came ashore.

But I was not ready to give myself away just yet. I stayed just over the back side of the dike, out of sight, in case they had something to hide. Soon they were paddling across the open water toward my position. As they drew closer, I stepped on top of the dike, about fifteen feet above the water line.

I had my Stetson tipped smartly forward, hands on my hips, with the fiery sun just beginning to set behind me. Anyone watching would have been impressed by such a striking sight!

The occupants of the canoe continued toward me. When they were about thirty yards away, the gentleman in the front put his paddle down and slowly raised his rifle in my direction. A little shocked by his unexpected actions, I just stood there, looking at him and wondering, *What the heck is he doing?*

I wasn't afraid at all—nobody would just up and shoot at the game warden. All of a sudden there was a *bang* and a *zip* past my left ear! Before I could even react, I was brought to my knees, seeing stars and grabbing my ear, which now hurt like heck!

I pulled my hand away and there was blood! What the?! I couldn't believe it—Hey! He just shot me . . . in the ear!

They could certainly see me now as I quickly jumped up and ordered them to shore. As they beached the canoe, I grabbed their rifles, first from the man in the front of the canoe and then from the one in the back. I told them to stand aside and then I informed the man in the front that he had just shot me!

I demanded both their hunting and driver's licenses. With those in hand, I walked down the bank, headed back to my car, and got on the radio to call for backup. I was able to get in touch with my partner, who was not far away. I told him where I was and that I had just been shot. My attempts to reach the state police were unsuccessful.

After making those quick calls, I checked my ear again. Although it still hurt, the bleeding had almost stopped. By the luck of genes and Godly design, I have unattached earlobes; apparently the bullet just ripped through the end of my lobe.

At the same moment, though, I was struck by the thought that this bullet had passed within an inch of my carotid artery! If I had attached earlobes, or if the bullet was just one inch closer, I could have been dead!

I also realized that the shooter must have seen a frog at the edge of the water in front of me. When he shot at the frog the bullet ricocheted off the water and hit my ear. He hadn't looked up and hadn't seen me, despite my being in plain sight on top of the dike, just a short distance away. I was just above his line of sight.

I finally got through to the state police via my radio. I explained where I was, that I had been shot, and that I needed to run a file check on the firearms. I was giving them the make, caliber, and serial numbers as my partner arrived. When he stepped out of the car, I was pleased to see he was wearing the new bulletproof vest he had just been issued. I was junior to him, so my vest would be delivered later, but even if I had it, it could not have protected my ear.

The state police radio response to my request was unexpected, to say the least. Apparently the rifle that had been used to shoot me had been stolen—in Los Angeles! This put a whole new spin on everything. My partner and I went back up the dike to question the hunters and get to the bottom of this stolen rifle report.

After informing the shooter of the charges being considered against him, the guy became indignant.

He said, "You can't accuse me of shooting you! I have been hunting for almost fifty years and never shot anybody!"

I responded that the goal in hunting is to go your *whole* life without shooting anybody! Having a perfect record for fifty years did not give anyone permission to shoot anybody, much less me!

He became even more upset when I informed him that his .22 was apparently stolen. He insisted he had purchased it new in Pennsylvania about thirty years ago and had owned it ever since. Taking a look at the gun, I agreed it did look to be about thirty years old, but the information from our statewide criminal database reported it as stolen. We returned to the car to follow up on that important detail and finally got the troopers to call LAPD for more information.

It turned out that the stolen rifle was actually a newer model Winchester bolt action, while the one I was holding was an older model Winchester pump action. Apparently Winchester had just reused the serial number. The NYSPIN computer database only records the make, caliber, and serial number, not the model number, so the "stolen" claim was an honest mistake.

I formally charged the shooter with Assault, Reckless Endangerment, and Discharging a Firearm across a Roadway, as the bullet that hit my ear had continued on across the road behind me. Obviously not happy with these charges, the shooter explained he was the head of a statewide sportsman's group!

"Shouldn't that count for something?" he asked.

I told him he should ask all his members if being their leader made it okay to shoot a game warden.

When I met with my boss the next day, he was not exactly happy; he thought I had been a little heavy-handed with the charges. However, he would support me and we would see what the courts would do. But he made it quite clear that he did not want me to file a hunting accident report. After all, I was "not really shot that bad."

It was now my turn to be unhappy. I was frustrated with his decision but had to concur. After all, in those days the report was just two pages long, and we really did not put a lot of effort into filling them out. A hunting accident report was more of a data collection form for the Hunter Education Program run by the State of New York. Most states followed similar protocols. Even though the law required all other police agencies to report all hunting accidents to us, most agencies did not. As a result, we would often read about hunting accidents as reported in the newspaper, many days after the incident.

When he appeared in court, the hunter was allowed to plead to lesser charges, but his hunting license was suspended for two years and he was ordered to retake the Hunter Education course before he could buy another license.

While I was told not to take the time to fill out a report on the shooting, the shooter took the time to file a personnel complaint against me. In the complaint he listed several grievances: I had been hiding in the cattails when I was shot; therefore, it was my fault. My partner had shown up wearing a flak jacket. The shooter had been accused of having stolen the rifle when in fact it was not stolen. Perhaps worst of all—I had yelled at them.

After a brief internal investigation, it was determined that only the last charge might have been true, and all my bosses agreed it might be okay to yell at someone, especially after he shot you.

My first personal experience as a victim of a hunting accident made for some good cocktail stories and office banter, but it also started a real fire within me; it created a passion for the truth that was to be fueled again and again.

Knowing how frustrated I felt, as a professional I knew we needed to do better when we responded to these incidents for everyone else—other law officers, hunters, and innocent bystanders. I also knew I never wanted to be shot again—even if was just a nick to one of my too long ears!

Lessons Learned

- Identify your target and what is beyond it. The frog hunter saw what he was hunting for but never took the time to look beyond that target to see if it was safe to fire in that direction. I was in plain sight just beyond his target.
- Never shoot at anything unless you are sure you have a safe backstop. There was a road just over the dike, in the direct line of fire. The shooter was too caught up in the excitement of the shot to ensure the safety of the shot.
- Bullets can ricochet off water, so be very careful when shooting toward water. Shooting straight down at a frog will not result in a ricochet, but shooting across the water at a low angle will almost always cause a ricochet.

2

A Trip to a Local Sporting Goods Store Brings Back Vivid Memories

The pain of parting is nothing to the joy of meeting again.
—CHARLES DICKENS

FREQUENTING SPORTING GOODS STORES TO PURCHASE TACTICAL gear for an upcoming training academy is something pretty common in my work investigating hunting incidents. But bumping into someone who has any familiarity with a specific incident is not common—at all.

During one shopping expedition, I approached the checkout counter with the items I needed. The older lady at the cash register asked if I had found everything okay.

Taking a look at what I had laid out, she then said, "Haven't I seen these items before?"

I told her I was a retired wildlife law enforcement supervisor and was using the items for an upcoming training. I went on to explain that my specialty was investigating hunting incidents and that I had a consulting business with two partners from other states. I told her our business provided litigation support, we could be called as subject matter experts, and that we also trained wildlife officers in hunting incident investigation techniques.

Her face brightened at my explanation. She said, "Oh, my husband had a hunting accident about twenty years ago. He was very lucky the gun didn't go off."

She went on to say, "Two wildlife officers came to the hospital to interview him about the accident."

I immediately pointed under my chin and asked, "Is this where the injury was?"

She was a bit surprised. "Why, yes!"

I responded, "I investigated a case where the hunter slipped and fell on the muzzle of his 20-gauge shotgun barrel; acting much like an 'apple corer,' it entered under his chin and thrust up into his sinuses."

With a puzzled look on her face, she looked me over and then exclaimed, "Yes! That was my husband!"

I reminded her that the accident had happened south of there about forty miles and that he had two sons with him.

She shook her head in agreement. "Yes, our son and grandson were hunting with him."

Her memories stirred my own. It was late January, and the father, son, and grandson were quail hunting in the southern part of the state when the incident occurred. The ground was covered with snow, and a recent ice storm had coated the snow with a slick, hard crust. The group had split up after a covey break and were searching for the individual quail that had scattered.

The father was walking up a steep hill. Due to the icy, slick conditions, he sometimes was using the fence to pull himself up the hill. He was using a "two-handed carry," where the 20-gauge shotgun is held in a vertical position, when all of a sudden he slipped.

As he fell to his knees, the muzzle slipped under his chin. He was quickly impaled as the muzzle was driven up and in by the force of his fall.

The shotgun's barrel went up into his throat at such a specific degree that it barely missed his spinal cord. Fortunately, the impact of the butt of the shotgun hitting the hard ground did not cause the gun to discharge. The safety was *on*, and it worked! However, his wound was pretty severe, and he began to bleed profusely.

When he attempted to yell, not much sound came out due to the location of the injury. Luckily his son and grandson thought they heard something just over the hill and walked toward the sound. They saw him on the slick hillside, lying in pool of blood, which was soaking the snow. They worked their way to his side to render aid and used a cell phone to call 911.

Due to the remote location, rescue seemed to take forever, but he was eventually flown to the nearest trauma center, where he underwent several surgeries to repair the damage caused by the muzzle.

His wife, the cashier who just happened to wait on me, told me that after one of his surgeries, she spent the night at his bedside. When she woke up, his hospital bed was covered in blood and his skin was very cold to the touch. She ran out to the nurses' station and summoned help.

Soon about nine doctors and nurses were in the room working on him due to the large amount of blood loss. He survived but did lose sight in one eye, as the shotgun muzzle had severed the optic nerve.

I was pleased to hear that he was living a comfortable life with his family and very thankful the outcome had not been worse.

I left the store thinking about coincidences of running into someone directly related to an incident from my own past, and the providence that this incident had ended well for all.

Lessons Learned

- Always keep the safety finger out of the trigger guard until you are ready to fire.
- When on difficult or steep terrain, always unload your firearm.
- The "carry" you choose to use is very important. A two-handed carry is a good carry; however, always remember that holding the firearm in a horizontal position allows the firearm to point left or right—away from your body but possibly in the direction of another hunter. *Never* point the muzzle toward your hunting companions when using this carry.
- Many hunters use a "sling" on their firearm. In this case, a sling would have allowed the hunter to use both hands to pull himself up the hill. Even so, it is prudent to unload the firearm, even with a sling, especially on difficult terrain. This type of injury would not have happened if either of these options had been practiced.

3

He Loved His Boys

Tragedy makes you grow up.

TOM WAS TOTALLY COMMITTED TO HIS FAMILY, HIS JOB, HIS OLD black Lab, Holly, and, yes, hunting. He was a member of several hunting-related organizations and contributed much of his time to his passion for the great outdoors. He planned to raise his two boys, Jake, age eleven, and Brian, eight, with the same principles. In fact, Tom could not wait to introduce his boys to hunting. He had worked with both of them at a friend's farm, shooting the 20 gauge shotguns he had bought each of them shortly after their births. Jake was big for his age and caught on quickly. Due to Brian's size and age, he was struggling with the shotgun's recoil, even when the shotgun was rested on the shooting bench. Nevertheless, Tom felt the boys were ready for their first hunt.

It was late in January, and quail season wouldn't close until the end of the month. They lived in the northern part of the state and had to drive about four hours south to reach quail country. Tom had hunted this farm a number of times over the years and knew the boys would have a chance to get a shot at a quail, so he called ahead to get permission to hunt.

Early on Saturday, Dad and the boys were all dressed in their camouflage, head to toe. The boys kissed their mother good-bye. Her last words were "Please, be careful!"

They loaded up the family SUV, along with Holly the Lab, and headed south on their great new adventure. Both the boys and Holly slept most of the way on the long drive. Once they reached the farm, they checked in with the farmer and talked about the best place to find a covey of quail. The boys couldn't wait to get started. The farmer opened the gate, and then Dad and the boys drove down into the field where some wooded drainage draws were located between the picked cornfields.

As they got out of the SUV and uncased their guns, Dad gave them "the safety talk" about keeping their guns pointed in a safe direction and keeping the safety on. Then Dad, Holly, and the boys began their hunt. They followed Holly as she worked back and forth in front of them, sniffing the ground like she had for many years before.

As they approached a large brush pile about six feet tall and twenty feet across, Dad could tell Holly was getting "birdy." She knew there must be quail hiding in this large pile of dead trees and brush. As they gathered around, Holly began sticking her nose into the pile. Dad told the boys to get ready.

Jake took his safety off, as did Brian. Dad walked up to where Holly was and gave the pile a kick—nothing happened. Suddenly, Holly ran around to the backside of the pile.

Once again, Dad asked, "Are you ready boys? There's got to be birds in here!"

Dad followed Holly around the pile. Once again Holly stuck her nose into the pile. Immediately a quail exploded up, flying near Holly and then up and straight toward Brian. Brian had his gun raised already and *boom!* He shot at the quail, missing it. The quail had flown right toward him.

It just so happened that Dad was directly across the brush pile when Brian took the shot. Due to Brian's height, the height of the brush pile, and Dad being in full camouflage, Brian could not see where his father was. With that single shot, Dad was struck with one pellet that entered his right eye, passed through his brain, and severed his brain stem.

Dad went down. Hearing the crash of his body, the boys ran to see if he was okay, only to find his lifeless body.

Jake said, "I'll go get the farmer; you stay here with Dad!" Jake ran as fast as he could.

Brian began to sob, trying desperately to wake his dad up. Jake found the farmer, who called the ambulance. The first responders arrived and attempted to save Dad's life. It was too late. That single pellet had cut Dad's brain stem, ending his life.

Even before this hunt began, we could reflect on this terrible tragedy and identify a number of things that went wrong, including Dad's perhaps overanxious desire for his boys to become hunters. This, along with other easily avoided mistakes, resulted in this father never being able to see his boys grow up and their not having a dad. But perhaps the greatest tragedy is that Brian will always have to live with the fact that he was the one who pulled the trigger that day.

Lessons Learned

- Direct supervision is crucial when starting any young hunter. The law in the state in which this incident occurred requires a *one-on-one* ratio of direct supervision; this means one responsible adult to supervise each young hunter. It also requires the adult to remain within arm's reach of the youth so the adult can communicate with the young hunter at all times.

- The right age to start a youngster hunting differs with each child as he or she is introduced to the responsibility of the hunt. Maturity, size, and ability to follow directions are all important factors. Starting young hunters out with an empty BB gun is one way to begin. This allows them to make mistakes, be corrected, and learn about safe muzzle control without fear of injury—or worse.
- Hunter education is a must for gaining the knowledge and skill sets required for a safe hunt. Remember, hunter education is just the beginning, learning the basics. Hunting requires a lifetime of being a safe and ethical hunter. With every hunt you learn a bit more; as time goes on, you acquire the knowledge of every aspect of the hunt.
- A basic rule of every hunt remains: As a hunter, you want to see others and be seen by everyone. Camouflage is the type of clothing you wear when you want to be concealed, such as for waterfowl or turkey hunting. Upland game hunting, such as for quail or pheasant, in most states requires wearing blaze orange. This is a proven color that will help keep you, your family, and your friends safe.
- Always know where all other hunters are and where your "safe zone of fire" is. Sometimes you do not have any safe zones at all, and no shot can be taken. At this point in the described hunt, having another adult assisting and supervising, as the law required, would have prevented this tragedy.
- Also, never move out in front of another hunter's muzzle. This puts you in a dangerous position, no matter how experienced your hunting companions are.

4

Hunting Giant Squirrels

Look before you leap for as you sow, ye are like to reap.
—SAMUEL BUTLER

ON THE MORNING OF OCTOBER 29, JOHN SEABRIGHT HAD NO
idea what the day was going to bring. He had only decided to go
hunting the night before, but as he got his equipment together, he
was looking forward to being out in the woods the next morning.

Now John did not put a lot of thought into his hunting. As
usual, he was going to keep it simple. Upon waking and having
some breakfast, John picked up his Harrington & Richardson
single-shot shotgun, breeched it open, and loaded it, all the time
hoping he would get a shot this morning.

Well after daylight, he walked out the door of his home and
decided he would just slip through the woods, quietly still-hunting.
John hoped he could sneak up on his quarry and get a shot.

As John left his yard, he began to get into stealth mode. He
slowed his pace and just eased along a trail that ran through the
woods away from his house. He had not gone far down the trail
when all of a sudden there was his quarry, just the game he had
been looking for! Much to his dismay, his quarry also saw him
and bolted through the woods. Excited, John made a decision

that would affect him for the rest of his life; in a matter of seconds, his life would be changed forever.

This same morning, Wardens Brian Cree and Paul Johnson had met up in Cree's assigned county and been patrolling the state wildlife management area (WMA) for illegal activity. After a couple hours, they had had no action and had not run into anything of interest or concern, so they decided to drive over into the adjacent county and patrol along its northern border.

Cree and Johnson had not been in the area long when they received a call from Warden Vance Griggs, who advised them he was en route to the hospital to check on a subject who had been involved in a hunting incident. Cree asked Griggs to let him know the status of the victim and the location where the incident had occurred. Griggs responded that he would be in contact when he knew more.

Warden Cree was the supervisor of the Critical Incident Reconstruction Team (CIRT), which was assigned the task of investigating and reconstructing the state's most serious hunting incidents and boating accidents. Since this incident occurred in his work section, he knew he would be taking the lead in the investigation. He waited impatiently to hear from Griggs.

When Griggs reached the hospital, he was immediately led back to the emergency room area. They had already put the victim, John Seabright, in a private room, and Griggs was told it was all right to go inside. He found the victim in bed with a large bandage around both his left hand and the lower part of the arm. Griggs introduced himself and told the victim why he was there. Griggs needed to know what had happened this morning and how Seabright's injuries had occurred.

Seabright began by saying that he stumbled and fell, then the gun went off and he shot himself. Saying that he needed more details than that, Griggs asked Seabright to just start at the beginning and tell him what had happened.

Seabright told Griggs he had left his house that morning to go squirrel hunting. He walked out the door and went behind his house into the woods. He stated that he was walking along a trail and saw a squirrel, which then took off through the woods. He began running after the squirrel, trying to get a shot.

He again stated that he tripped and fell while running, and when he fell, the gun fired, shooting off about half his left hand, including three fingers. He told Griggs he had left his gun in the woods at the scene.

After writing down all this information, Griggs contacted Cree and filled him in on his conversation with the victim; it appeared the wound was self-inflicted, meaning the victim had shot himself. Griggs then gave Cree all the other pertinent information, including the victim's address. Cree told Griggs that he and Johnson would be en route to the incident scene and the victim's home.

Cree and Johnson pulled up at the address Griggs had given them. Cree went up to the front door and knocked. Nobody came to the door, and it appeared nobody was home. He figured everybody was probably still at the hospital with the victim. Cree went back to his vehicle to get a few pieces of investigative equipment, including a camera.

Cree and Johnson then headed behind the house to the backyard and began trying to find where Seabright had left the yard to enter the woods. It was not long before they found a trail with fresh footprints and a few drops of blood. They followed the footprints and blood drops for about a hundred yards and discovered a single-shot shotgun with a green stock lying on the trail.

Cree advised Johnson to just leave it where it was for now, and they continued to search the area on down the trail. The trail turned sharply to the left, and just as it turned, Cree saw flies buzzing low to the ground, just a few yards off the trail. Upon closer inspection, he could see a bit of flesh and some blood on the ground. It appeared that fire ants had already claimed most of the flesh for food.

Just a few feet back from the bloody mess, the wardens also saw an old woven-wire fence sticking up about six to eight inches off the forest floor; the fence had apparently collapsed from age. Out about ten feet beyond the fence, in the same direction the blood and flesh were scattered, Cree noticed an oak tree; at the base of this tree were strike marks.

Cree immediately recognized these marks as buckshot pellet strikes. He knew the victim had stated to Griggs that he had been hunting squirrels, but something was not right.

Cree turned to Johnson and said, "Let's go check the firearm. Before we move it, we need to take photographs of it."

Locating the gun, Cree took a series of photographs of the firearm. He then marked its location and picked it up. Cree immediately noticed there were leaves and dirt between the hammer and firing pin. He opened the breech and inside found a fired Winchester 00 buckshot shell.

Taking note of its size, Cree turned to Johnson and jokingly said, "There must be some mighty big squirrels in these woods."

Cree just shook his head. The spent shell told the wardens that the victim had lied about what he had been hunting.

The 00 buckshot Seabright had used was illegal ammunition for hunting squirrels; you might even say it was overkill. Buckshot that size is normally used to hunt deer. If Seabright had shot a squirrel with that size buckshot, the squirrel would have been torn to shreds.

Cree went back to the oak tree and used his knife to dig a buckshot pellet out of one of the pellet strikes. He photographed the scene and bagged the fired 00 buckshot shell and pellet for evidence. Warden Cree knew what had caused the hunting incident by the story the evidence told at the scene. It was now time to find out why the victim had lied about what he was hunting.

Cree and Johnson's investigation work came to one conclusion: Seabright was still-hunting for deer that fateful morning. He knew his hunt would take him onto property owned by someone else, property he did not have permission to hunt. He even decided he would not wear a fluorescent orange vest where he would risk being seen. A fluorescent orange safety vest is required by law if you are hunting deer. So is a big game license, and Seabright also failed to have one of those in his possession.

As Seabright was easing along still-hunting, he jumped a deer. He immediately pulled the hammer back on his shotgun, cocking it, and began running through the woods in order to try for a clear shot. As he was running, he failed to notice the old woven-wire fence sticking above the ground. His feet got tangled in the fence, and he tripped and fell forward.

As he was falling forward, his left hand passed in front of the shotgun's muzzle as he landed on the ground. Something caused the shotgun's hammer to drop on the firing pin, discharging the firearm when it struck the ground. This fact was clear, because leaves and dirt were found between the hammer and the firing pin.

Cree thought it was more than likely that Seabright's right trigger finger had still been inside the trigger guard while all this was taking place and had caused the firearm to discharge. Upon discharging, the gun sent the load of 00 buckshot pellets through his left hand at point-blank range, causing the massive damage to Seabright's hand.

Seabright said he was squirrel hunting. He did not tell the truth about what he was hunting because he was violating two state laws: "Hunting Deer without Wearing Fluorescent Orange Clothing" and "Hunting Big Game (Deer) without a Big Game License."

In addition, the victim had also violated three of the basic standards of firearm safety: "Watch your muzzle. Keep it pointed in a safe direction at all times." "Never climb a fence or tree or jump a ditch with a loaded firearm; this includes running." And finally, "Keep your finger off the trigger until you are ready to shoot."

Beyond the charges and their legal consequences, the victim's damaged hand would be a daily reminder of what can happen when you don't put a lot of thought into hunting—an activity worthy of a great deal of thought.

Lessons Learned

This victim violated three of the basic commandments or rules of firearm safety:

- Watch that muzzle! Be able to control the direction of the muzzle at all times.
- Never climb a fence or tree or jump a ditch with a loaded gun.
- Keep your finger off the trigger until your sights are on target (and you have made the decision to shoot).
- Running with the firearm cocked and your finger on the trigger and not watching for obstacles in the woods is a surefire recipe for disaster.
- If he had not lied about what he was hunting and had been outfitted with the proper safety gear and proper license, he would not have been charged.

5

That's Not Possible

Never let the facts get in the way of a good story.
—Too many sources to list

The Department of Natural Resources (DNR) lieutenant was almost home when the local evening news came on the radio. Deer season was in full swing, and this was the earliest he would get home in more than a week. The lead story on the news opened with, "The Madison County Sheriff's Office today reported that a Smithville man had been injured in a hunting accident. The unidentified man had fallen and shot himself in the buttocks. Sheriff Kevin Williams reports that it was just an accident and no charges would be filed."

The lieutenant was completely amazed. Still driving toward home, he tried to imagine the contortions someone would have to go through to accomplish that. How on earth could you possibly shoot yourself in the buttocks? It seemed impossible. When he got home, he called the local wildlife agent and asked him to look into it.

First thing the next morning, the agent was at the hospital to interview Dale Grove, who was still in a lot of pain. He was lying on his side to take the pressure off his wounds. It seems the bullet had gone in one side and out the other, leaving him with both entrance and exit holes. Dale's story was that he was hunting mule deer in the foothills along the river. He was walking uphill just before sunset when he slipped in the snow and fell. Somehow his gun went off and he shot himself. He had managed to crawl up to the roadside, where a neighbor eventually saw him and called 911.

The agent tried his best to get a better explanation as to how the injuries happened, but there was none to be had. The agent thanked Dale and headed off to the scene to begin his investigation. The location was right along a main highway, well marked with tire tracks, footprints, and bloody snow, along with some of the litter left behind when the ambulance squad had treated the victim the day before. From this point of the investigation, the story was incredibly simple and clear.

Looking across the fence into the overgrown pasture, the agent could see two sets of footprints in the snow. They were side by side, as though one person was helping the other. The footprints came up from the river bottom, directly to the fence. One set of footprints looked clear and firm; the other set was from someone dragging his feet and bleeding. It was clear the wounded man had either stepped or been lifted over the fence and then had lain in the snow at the roadside. In addition, the firm set of prints went off to the left and then returned.

The agent stayed on the road side of the fence as he looked at the footprints, which went about thirty yards along the fence and then turned around and came back. Right where the tracks stopped, there was the imprint of a shotgun in the snow, under a bush. There were also footprints from someone who had come from across the road, leaned over the fence, and removed the shotgun.

Back at the scene, the agent crossed the fence to backtrack the footprints down into the pasture. He stayed well off to the side so he would not compromise any evidence as the backtrack led him down over the hill and into a densely overgrown area. Just into the overgrowth, the tracks led to a "breakdance" area—the place where someone had clearly fallen down, spun around, and bled a lot. One set of tracks had come from the left, under a leaning tree and vines, while the other set had come from a big oak tree off to the right. Walking over to the tree, the agent could see where the snow was all tromped down. There he could clearly see several cigarette butts and one spent shotgun shell.

It did not take the wisdom of Sherlock Holmes to figure this one out. One person had been standing next to the big oak, tromping down the snow and smoking his cigarettes, when Dale came walking toward him through the thickest overgrowth along the river. Dale was dressed in brown coveralls, and he had to bend over at the waist to go under the tree that blocked his way.

Seeing movement, the person waiting at the tree shot at something that was about the size, shape, and color of a deer—the victim—striking Dale directly in the buttocks. Realizing what he had done, the shooter helped Dale up to the road and across the fence before hiding his gun under the bush.

Sometime later he returned to retrieve the hidden shotgun. The agent had investigated many complex shooting scenes and was adept at sorting through all the evidence and statements to get to the truth. He had encountered mistaken memories, foggy details, and outright lies from both victims and shooters. But today he was almost overwhelmed with how much the facts conflicted with the sheriff's report and just how far from the truth the story traveled.

The response to the scene the night before had included the sheriff, the chief of detectives, several deputies, and the Crime Scene Unit. They had talked to the victim at the roadside as he was treated and transported by the ambulance squad. However, none of them had so much as looked across the fence to investigate. After all, it was just another hunting accident, and they were finished before they even started.

The agent returned to the hospital with all the facts from the scene and gave Dale another chance to explain what really happened. Faced with the facts, his story changed. This time he explained he had been hunting by himself and been shot by some guy he had never seen before. The guy then helped him up to the roadside and told him he had better claim he shot himself or else the guy would come back and beat him up. Dale said he did not want to lie but was afraid of the guy who shot him.

The agent listened patiently and took detailed notes. Being an experienced and skilled interviewer, he knew it was best to just let the story roll on. When this new version was over, the agent looked Dale in the eyes and spoke in a calm voice. "Okay, now, how about this time we try the truth? I know you were pushing deer toward your friend, and I know he did not mean to hurt you at all. But we both know that you know who shot you, and you know I am going to find him. I will find his gun, and the real truth is all going to come out."

Fighting back tears, the real story finally arrived. It was his friend, Nathan Johnson, who had done it—a friend who did not have a hunting license. Worse yet, Nathan was a convicted felon who could not legally possess a firearm.

It was true that Nathan had threatened him, and Dale took that threat seriously. Nathan had said he was sorry, that he did not mean to hurt him, but he also was not going back to jail. He insisted that Dale claim he shot himself or he would be left in the woods to bleed. The agent took a new signed statement that clearly detailed what had really happened. As he left the hospital, he called the lieutenant to bring him up to date.

Together they decided that stopping by the sheriff's office to bring them up to speed on the new details of the case would be the most politically correct action. They would offer to let the sheriff's office join in the investigation. The agent drove to the sheriff's office and was stunned by the response. Instead of thanking him for his excellent investigative work and for giving them the chance to save face by helping document the real story, he was reprimanded.

The overwhelming theme of the conversation was, who the heck did he think he was, second-guessing them? This was their case, and he had no right even being involved. They had finished their investigation, and he needed to stay out of it.

They were really mad, and they made it clear that a formal complaint about his interfering would be filed with his chief. After this response, both the agent and the lieutenant were a bit surprised by the next morning's newspaper story updating the status of the case.

The story explained that after further investigation, the Madison County Sheriff's Office had arrested Nathan Johnson, age thirty-four, in the shooting of Dale Grove of Smithville. Johnson was charged with criminal possession of a firearm, assault in the second degree, and hunting without a license. No further charges were expected.

Lessons Learned

- Always identify your target. The longer you wait for something, the more you expect it to happen soon. If you are deer hunting and know there are deer in the area and know your friend is going to chase some deer toward you, the anticipation builds. Every sound or sight could be that deer, and your brain can jump to conclusions. This is called "premature closure." Seeing something brown was enough to get the hunter to jump to the conclusion that it must be a deer. He fired, even though he knew his friend was wearing brown and would be coming toward him soon.

- Do not wear colors that are similar to what you are hunting. Avoid colors like brown (like a deer) or black, white, red, or blue (like a turkey's head) that can lead to being mistaken for game.
- Hunting with people you know have broken the law a lot is not a good idea. Is that the kind of person you really want to be in the woods with? People who disregard laws tend to disregard safety rules as well.
- Lying to skilled investigators is rarely successful. They probably already know what really happened and are just checking to see if you will tell the truth. Many times the act of lying to the police is a more serious crime than the wildlife offense the person is trying to hide.

6

Coyote Hunting

While we are free to choose our actions, we are not free to choose the consequences of our actions.

—STEPHEN R. COVEY

ON THE ONCE WIDE-OPEN SPACES AND ROLLING GRASSY PLAINS of the Midwest, the land is now sectioned off with roads, fences, and homesteads. Instead of the major prairie grasses of the rolling tallgrass prairie, such as big bluestem, little bluestem, Indian grass, and switchgrass, all blowing in the wind, the rich black fertile soil now nurtures row crops such as corn, soybeans, oats, or wheat. The crops located on this vast landscape are feeding all of us and, in turn, feeding the world.

Coyote hunting seems to offer unique challenges on this once tall prairie landscape. As predators, they threaten farm animals, such as newborn calves, and pets, not to mention the threat to other wildlife. Meanwhile, the methods of harvesting these elusive animals vary; some choose to hunt, while others select trapping.

On one particular coyote hunt, a group of hunters were covering several square miles of harvested cropland on a cold mid-December day with a light covering of snow on the ground. The group had spotted a coyote, so one of the hunters drove his pickup into a field to see if he could get a shot at it. Two other hunters had stopped just south of a T intersection, down a bit between slight ditches on both sides of the road.

All of a sudden the coyote came running from the east, crossing the gravel road in front of them. As soon as the hunters saw the coyote, they focused on the animal; their shots rang out, aimed to the southeast and south. The coyote was hit and crossed the road, dying in the field just west of the road. The two shooters retrieved the coyote and headed home for supper.

Gathering later that evening, the hunters were talking and realized no one had heard anything from Rick, the hunter who had driven out in the field. All attempts to call him had been unsuccessful.

One of the hunters returned to the last place they had seen Rick to see if something might have happened. It had grown dark as the hunter entered the field, and he followed pickup tracks to Rick's truck. As he pulled up alongside, it was clear the driver's window had been shattered. There was Rick, slumped over in the driver's seat. Rick had been shot and had no pulse; he had been hit by one of the shooters with a .243 rifle round.

The investigators found empty cartridges lying on the gravel road just north of where blood from the coyote was also found. Based on analysis of the slug by the state crime lab, the shooter was identified, but both individuals were charged with shooting from the road. Although charges against both men were later dropped, their friend and hunting companion remained dead.

Lessons Learned

- Many times on this type of pursuit for coyotes, a number of hunters are involved, driving in and out of fields or casting dogs to chase coyotes into view. This can cause confusion about where everyone is located. However, shooting from a road or vehicle remains illegal in many states, including the state where this incident occurred.
- In this case, the hunters shot not only from a roadway but also down the road to the south, where a farmhouse was located. Luckily, there were no reported injuries from the farm.
- Taking shots down, from, or across roadways or shooting toward the horizon is never a good idea. The distance in which a center-fire rifle projectile might travel may be up to several miles, and you may not even see what your shot strikes.
- Never shoot unless you are sure there is a safe backstop behind your target. This can be very difficult in flat, open country, but each person is always responsible for every bullet he or she fires—there is no way to bring it back once the trigger is pulled.

7

Speak Now, or Forever Hold Your Peace

If there's something wrong, speak up!

—PETE SEEGER

AN OUT-OF-STATE HUNTER WAS VISITING FAMILY IN MAY SO that he could hunt the spring turkey season, when only bearded turkeys are legal and the limit is one per day and two per season. He had hunted the same area for years and always had success. Over time, he had built a simple ground blind at the base of a big tree. It was just a bunch of fallen branches and limbs, but it worked well and allowed him to move a little bit without being seen.

Five days into the monthlong season, he had seen and heard a few birds but had not been able to call any of them in close enough for a shot— yet. He wasn't too worried. His full set of camouflage clothes and the ground blind kept him well hidden, and the turkeys were not at the peak of breeding yet. The male "toms" were sometimes answering, but they were not ready to commit and come in to his calls. He even tried some "gobble" calls, hoping one of the toms would come out to chase away the perceived competition.

About 8:00 a.m. he saw something coming toward him through the big, open hardwoods. He leaned both left and right to get a better look and finally saw that it was another hunter, about eighty yards away, walking right toward him.

As his hat was reversible to blaze orange, he slowly took it off and held the inside forward, thinking the hunter would see the blaze orange, realize there was another hunter already there, and leave.

Meanwhile, the other hunter stopped, slowly raised his binoculars, and looked right at the blind. He was sure he had seen the red head of a mature male turkey, but now it was gone. He lowered his binoculars and kept slowing stalking forward, closer to where he knew he had heard a turkey gobble just a little while ago.

In the blind, the hidden hunter again tipped the orange lining of his hat toward the approaching hunter, slowly moving it back and forth. The stalker stopped again and raised his binoculars. He was sure he had seen the turkey again, somewhere just into the thick brush ahead. As he studied the area carefully, he could see the characteristic red head of a mature tom turkey moving slowly back and forth.

He needed to get closer to get a shot, so he kept some large trees between him and his turkey and slowly moved to within sixty yards of the hiding spot. As he leaned out from behind a tree, he clearly saw the red head again and fired!

The big tree shielded the man in the blind from most of the damage, but the hidden hunter was still hit in the face and neck with twenty-five pellets, taking one directly in his right eye.

He was rushed to the hospital by the man who shot him and ended up losing sight in his right eye, along with two teeth. He endured additional painful procedures to remove and repair the damage from the other pellets.

In this case, both the victim and the shooter faced multiple charges. The victim was charged with Hunting without a Valid License and Making a False Statement on a License Application. Not wanting to pay the higher price for a nonresident license, he had been claiming his relatives' local address as his own. The man who shot him was charged with Reckless Endangerment and Assault for causing serious physical injuries to the other hunter.

Investigation of the incident made it clear that this was not "just an accident." When the victim's hat was first examined at the hospital, the lining was clearly bright orange. The shooter's story of seeing red did not make sense. Was he color blind?

When the facts in hand do not match with the statement, it is easy to assume the person is lying or, at least, confused. To be as close to the original incident's conditions as possible, another re-creation was done the next day at 8:00 a.m., the same time as the original incident. The victim insisted that he could clearly see the hunter who shot him, while the shooter claimed he saw only the red of the turkey's head. When the measurement of visibility device was placed into the blind and observed from the shooter's position, it was noted that the visibility was, at best, 20 percent. The investigator then held the hat in the same location, and another investigator stood where the shot had been fired. The lining was very hard to see at all. Surprisingly, when the lining was seen, it was clearly red—the same red as a turkey's head in spring—and not the expected blaze orange.

Even waiting a few hours longer in the day will change everything. By noon the sun was overhead and the hat lining was much more visible; this time it was clearly bright orange!

Each man made serious mistakes that contributed to life-changing injuries for one and a lifetime of regret for both hunters.

Lessons Learned

- Any movement may cause another hunter to react and shoot. Remember, only humans talk; and there is no mistaking the sound of a human voice in the woods. If another hunter has walked in on you, accept the fact that the game has already left the area.
- When you see another hunter, speak up—clearly and loudly. "Hello, Hunter!" or "Over here!" will protect both of you from making a dangerous, even deadly, mistake.
- All blaze orange will fade over time. Dirt and repeated washing will make it fade faster.
- Sunlight on blaze fabric will be reflected, which creates the hunter orange effect. But in the darkness of dawn and dusk or the shade of deep woods, the color will not provide the same level of protection.
- Using a gobble call in spring brings additional concerns. Another unsafe hunter may try to stalk close enough to shoot the "gobbler." In this case, the shooter violated one of the most basic rules of turkey hunting: "Do not try to stalk a turkey, and never stalk the sound of a turkey." He should have made sure there was a turkey and then made sure it was a bearded turkey. Finally, he should have decided if he had a safe and ethical shot before pulling the trigger. The shooter merely saw something that looked red and took a shot. He skipped all three of these vital steps before he fired.
- This case also demonstrates the importance of doing a thorough investigation and re-creation with every incident. Investigators can never perfectly re-create any scene because of changes in environmental conditions, such as weather. Leaves and branches can fall and shift during the time between an incident and the investigation. The best investigators strive to come as close as possible to the incident conditions so they can best understand what the shooter could or would have seen when the incident occurred.

8

Victim, No Shooter?

Before everything else, getting ready is the secret of success.

HENRY FORD

ON DECEMBER 17, WARDEN BRIAN CREE HAD JUST EATEN SUPPER and was settling in for a quiet evening at home when the telephone rang. He got up out of his chair, hoping it would not be someone with an in-progress complaint. The warden picked up the telephone receiver and said, "Hello." On the other end of the line, he heard a familiar voice from headquarters: "We have a problem in Greene County. About dusk there was a hunting incident; a hunter was found dead. All preliminary reports indicate he was shot in the head. No shooter has come forward at this time, and we have no suspects."

Cree asked for all the available information and began taking notes. The headquarters person asked for the earliest time of arrival for him and the Critical Incident Reconstruction Team (CIRT). Cree advised headquarters that, late as it was, nothing could be done tonight. He would make all contacts and arrangements for everyone to meet at the Greene County Sheriff's Office first thing the next morning. He hung up the telephone.

Warden Cree knew this was the worst kind of hunting incident possible for an investigator—a victim with no known shooter. When no known suspects have stepped forward or stand out, it's hard work for an investigator to figure out who fired the fatal shot.

Cree began to notify the other CIRT members: Wardens Ken Gillis, Hank Folly, and Joe Hunt. He gave them the preliminary information he had obtained from headquarters and the time and place to meet. After making the necessary calls, Cree checked over his equipment and got ready for bed. It would be a restless and short night for him. The incident scene was a four-hour drive away.

The alarm went off at 3:30 a.m. Cree got up and turned it off, put on his uniform, checked to make sure all his equipment was packed, and then pulled out of his driveway and pointed his vehicle north. During the long drive, he ran over in his head a checklist of things he wanted to do—what would be first and how it would be best to proceed with this type of investigation. He hoped maybe someone would have come forward during the night; that is what a responsible hunter should do. Or maybe the sheriff's department had developed a suspect. That sure would make things easier.

Cree arrived at the sheriff's office at around 8:30 a.m. and found Warden Hank Folly already there. Cree and Folly met with Investigator Matt Sims of the sheriff's office. Much to Cree's dismay, no known suspects had been identified.

A short time later, the other CIRT members began to arrive. A meeting was held to find out what was known so far about the incident, what information they could use, and what evidence was collected from the scene. Investigator Sims gave Cree about ten photographs that had been taken of the scene and of the victim. He also produced the victim's rifle, which was found at the scene.

Investigator Sims then filled the team in. "This is all we know so far. The victim was hunting on his hunting club property on the evening of December 17 with a friend. He was hunting out of a two-piece climbing tree stand that he found on the property. The stand did not belong to him, and he did not know whom it belonged to. The victim's hunting partner stated that the victim had liked the hunting location and the stand so much that he had considered leaving a note on the stand to the owner offering to purchase it. At around 5:30 p.m., the victim called his friend on his cell phone and told him that he had not seen anything, would be climbing down soon, and would meet him back at the vehicle. The friend arrived back at the vehicle a little after dark. When the victim did not show up, the friend began to worry. After a while he tried calling the victim's cell phone but didn't get an answer. The friend called the victim's cell phone several times. After more than an hour had passed, the friend went looking for the victim and found him on the ground at the base of the tree, dead. The friend immediately called 911."

When the sheriff's deputies arrived on the scene, they were met by the victim's hunting partner. He directed them to the location of the body. The first responding officers found the victim lying face up with his left shoulder up against the base of the tree he had been climbing. The climbing stand he had been using was located by his right side. The arms of the top piece of the climbing stand (the section he was sitting in) were lying directly to his right. The arms were tilted on the ground, and the victim had his right leg stuck between them.

Looking at the photographs, Cree could see a large entrance wound in the forehead of the victim, just above the bridge of the nose. The exit wound appeared to be on the back side of the head. The bullet appeared to have passed clean through the entire skull of the victim. Also, examination of the victim's firearm revealed cracks in the stock and a bent scope. This seemed odd to both Cree and Folly. They discussed the possibility that the victim must have fallen on his firearm for it to be damaged in that manner.

With all the information made available to the CIRT, it was time to go to work. Cree held a team meeting and a plan of action was discussed. Sims informed Cree that the victim's body had been sent to the state crime lab. The warden called the crime lab to ask the technician to give him the height of the victim and the exact location and measurements of the entrance and exit wounds on the victim's head. He also was going to ask the technician to run a rod through the victim's skull to get the angle of trajectory of the bullet's path through the skull. Warden Cree was going to use this information, along with the laser trajectory finder at the scene, to possibly locate where the shooter was standing when the fatal shot was fired. Maybe, just maybe, the shooter left behind some kind of evidence at that location.

You can imagine Cree's surprise when the technician stated that a bullet had not caused the wounds on the victim's head. Astonished, Cree asked the technician what had caused the wound. The technician stated that it was possibly some kind of tubing. Shaking his head in amazement, Cree hung up the telephone and told the CIRT members and Investigator Sims what the technician had relayed. You could see a shocked expression on all their faces.

Cree turned to Sims and asked, "Where is the deer stand?"

Sims replied, "It's in the back of one of our trucks, parked out back."

Warden Cree looked at his team. "Let's have a look at it."

The CIRT members and Investigator Sims went to the back parking lot of the sheriff's office and retrieved the two-piece deer stand. After an examination of the stand, blood was found on the seat portion, on the left upper armrest, tubing that sticks out beyond the blade that attaches around the tree.

Upon closer examination, the team discovered particles of bone and brain matter. They could see where the paint had scraped off when it passed through the victim's skull, and there was also brain matter in the end of the tubing.

The mystery about what caused the wound in the victim's head was solved: It was the tree stand! Now the question that remained was how?

This type of stand had a V-shaped metal blade that went around the back of the tree and was attached to the two upper arms. Further examination revealed that a bolt was missing where one end of the blade attached to the arm of the stand. Did it come unbolted, or did it break or shear in two? Those were the new questions that needed to be answered.

A series of photographs were taken of the tree stand and of the victim's firearm to document all the evidence involved with the case. After this was finished, it was time to visit the scene and all CIRT members and Investigator Sims headed out.

Folly brought out the metal detector, and after a few passes around the tree the victim had climbed, the metal detector signaled a metal object under the leaves. Warden Folly carefully pulled back the leaves and there found the answer to the lingering questions—the top part of a bolt. The bolt had either broken off or sheared off at the first threads.

Pulling together all the data, Cree and the team knew what had happened. The victim had gone hunting on the evening of December 17 with a friend. At approximately 5:30 p.m., the victim called his friend on his cell phone, stating that it would not be long before he came down from the stand and to meet back at the vehicle. Sometime after this call, the victim started his descent from the tree. At some point early on in his descent, the bolt attaching the blade to the left arm of the seat portion of the tree stand broke or was sheared in two. This sudden failure of the bolt, along with the victim's weight on the seat portion of the tree stand, caused the victim to plunge violently to the ground. The tree stand landed first, hitting the ground with the left arm of the upper portion of the tree stand pointing upward. Milliseconds later, the victim's head struck the tubing of the upper arm at a point just above the bridge of the nose on his forehead. The impact sent the upper arm through the victim's brain and out the back of his skull. It was clear that at some point the victim was able to pull himself off the arm of the tree stand before he fell to the ground. That was the position in which his friend found him.

Lessons Learned

- Falls from trees and tree stands are more common than many realize. It is becoming the most common cause of injury and death to hunters. While most falls result in nothing more detrimental than a bruised ego or broken bones, tragedies like this can occur.
- Checking all equipment is important before every season and every hunt, especially equipment left in the elements, such as a tree stand or duck blind. Make sure all bolts, screws, securing lines, and ropes are in working condition. Replace anything that shows signs of wear, especially anything your life depends on.
- If the victim had been wearing a tree stand safety harness or Fall Arrest System, he probably would be alive today. These devices attach the hunter to the tree while allowing enough freedom of movement to hunt. A harness would have saved his life.

9

Caught on Video

In general, pride is at the bottom of all great mistakes.
—JOHN RUSKIN

IT WAS A SUNDAY MORNING IN MAY, MOTHER'S DAY, AND THE last day of the spring turkey season—a beautiful time to be in the turkey woods. A band of brothers, four US Army Rangers, had finally returned home from tours in the Middle East. They had been friends since high school. Their bond was strong: They hung out together, fished together, drank beer together, and hunted together; they were truly inseparable.

On this particular Sunday morning, the last day of the season, three of the four friends headed out early, hoping to fill two of the hunters' remaining turkey tags. The property they would be hunting on belonged to the mother of Donnie, the fourth member of the group, who was running late. The three parked their trucks near the farmhouse on the southwest corner of the farm. They began their hike through the row crop field surrounding the farmhouse up to the hardwood timber. The three hunters began their hunt by setting up against trees near one another where one of them had harvested a nice tom turkey the day before. Though unspoken, the peer pressure had increased for the two hunters who had not yet harvested. The competition and bragging rights were strong with this band of brothers.

After an hour or so with no activity, the three became bored and began to drive, or "stalk," looking for a bird. This method is not always a safe or recommended technique because you spread out from one another, not really knowing where your companions may be as you move through the timber. But, as luck would have it, one of the hunters was able to ambush a young jake turkey. The group reunited with the successful hunter to watch him tag the bird, have a cigarette, take a break, and celebrate the harvest.

Back at the farmhouse, Donnie had arrived to say a quick hello to his mother on this Mother's Day morning. Pulling on his camouflage coveralls and black stocking-cap face mask and then lifting his video camera to his shoulder, he laughed as he told his mother his plan: "I'm going to go shoot them, unless they shoot me first."

Donnie's plan was to sneak up on his buddies, secretly videotape them in action, and then retreat to show them the video later—thus proving he was the better Army Ranger. As Donnie stepped out the back door of the farmhouse, he heard the gunshot to the northeast of the house. The shot came from the timber where the jake had just been harvested.

Heading out, Donnie began to sneak up the hill; keeping low he began to belly crawl in the direction of the shot. Finally he began to hear his buddies, laughing and talking. Donnie hit the record button on his video camera. Tiny dewdrops began collecting on the camera lens from his crawling through the grass. Donnie whispered into the video camera, "They don't know I'm here yet; they don't know I'm here yet."

As Donnie moved steadily toward his buddies, he looked into the cameras viewfinder and then looked up the hill, where he could see movement. Donnie's head and face, covered with his black face mask, bounced up and down, up and down as he continued his quest.

As Donnie got closer, the movement of his head and face covered in black was noticed by one of his buddies. It was Nick, who had not yet bagged his bird. Focusing on the movement through the grass and trees, Nick raised his new camouflage shotgun with a super-full choke.

This choke would create a very tight pattern of shot pellets and was popular for striking a turkey's head for a clean kill. An instant after mounting the shotgun to his shoulder, Nick pulled the trigger. Immediately a groaning sound was heard coming from the direction of his shot.

Running to where the noise came from, Nick saw Donnie lying flat—face down on the ground, already covered in blood. Nick immediately reacted, reverting to his military training as he yelled, "*E-VAC! E-VAC!*"

Stunned by what had just happened, Donnie began yelling expletives. "#$%^&! . . . Don't let me die! I'm not going to die! Get me out of here!"

As the other two buddies joined Nick, they picked up Donnie and headed toward the trucks as though they were rescuing their fellow Ranger from the battlefield.

As this all played out, the video camera continued to record as it lay in the deep spring grass. Once the shotgun discharged, the camera had tumbled to the ground. Even though the camera had been struck with six pellets, it continued to capture the audio of the events taking place. There were the sounds of Donnie's moans from being shot, the change in his breathing, the unnerved pitch of each voice involved, and the reactions of concern of this band of brothers for one of their fallen.

Donnie's buddies carried him toward the truck. As they moved away from the camera left lying in the grass, their voices began to fade into the distance; voices of desperation were replaced by the sounds of birds singing on that beautiful spring morning in May.

Although struck with twenty-six pellets of a duplex shotgun load, sizes #4 and #6, from a distance of thirty-three yards, Donnie survived the incident. The wounds covered his upper chest, fingers, and face. Donnie lost one eye and underwent several surgeries on the other to save his sight. One of the many pellets indicated by X-ray had elongated on Donnie's forehead. The pellets that hit his chest created superficial wounds due to the layers of clothing he was wearing and the angle at which he was struck from being in the prone position.

Donnie's safe return home from serving our great country was tragically followed by this preventable incident. Both recently honorably discharged and newly married, he had a seventeen-year-old wife and six-month-old baby waiting for him at home. Donnie had also just begun a job as a construction laborer. Fortunately, even though he had a long recovery time, Donnie was able to return to work. And the incident did not divide this band of brothers but actually brought the group closer together.

Lessons Learned

- When hunting turkeys, it's your responsibility to properly identify your target before you shoot. Did you see the beard of the legal bird? Did you see the spurs of the male turkey, another physical feature that can be used to confirm a legal shot?

- Assess your shot from all angles. What is beyond your target? Is it now safe to take this shot? You *must* be sure of all these things *before* you pull the trigger. Remember, once that trigger is pulled, you can never call that shot back!

- The people we choose to hunt with are usually our family and closest friends. The hunting field is no place for competition among hunting companions. Peer pressure can push a person into making a rash decision. Hunting requires knowledge, skill, and solid decision making. Not following these principles can result in a lifetime of guilt.

- The person who pulls the trigger usually carries the greater degree of comparable negligence when someone is injured. However, sometimes the victim shares some of the blame. In this case, you can't help but wonder whether Donnie contributed to his own injuries by sneaking up on his friends. His movements, black face mask, and failure to communicate with his friends were contributing factors in this incident, but what percentage of responsibility victims share is usually left to the courts to decide.

10

The Bait and Switch

The ends do not justify the means.

—ANONYMOUS

WARDEN THAD THOMAS HAD BEEN ON ROUTINE PATROL IN HIS
county on December 27 when he received an urgent call from
his district office at approximately 10:19 a.m. A hunting incident
had occurred in Lacy County. The district office gave Warden
Thomas the few details they had and then gave him directions to
the incident scene.

When Thomas got to the road that led to the property where
the incident had occurred, he was stopped by Tim Brantley.
Brantley informed the warden that local law enforcement and
emergency medical services (EMS) personnel had already left the
scene, but he gave him directions to the location and the telephone number of the man who leased the property where the
victim had been hunting.

Arriving at the scene, Warden Thomas contacted Lacy
County dispatch, which then connected him with the sheriff's
deputy who had responded to the call. The deputy informed
Thomas that the victim had shot himself in the foot. Learning
this, Thomas contacted EMS to find out which hospital the victim had been transported to.

Thomas also contacted Warden Sam Pippin, a member of their agency's Critical Incident Reconstruction Team (CIRT). He gave Pippin contact information for the man who leased the property where the incident occurred. Warden Pippin told Thomas he would be en route to the scene and told him to go to the hospital and see if he could interview the victim for more information as to what had taken place. Thomas replied that he would go to the hospital and shortly thereafter met up with his supervisor, Warden Sid Wilkes. Thomas and Wilkes proceeded to the hospital to interview the victim.

Warden Pippin had just pulled up into his residence's driveway when he got the call from Warden Thomas. He began packing his CIRT equipment in his vehicle, making sure he had everything needed to reconstruct an incident scene. Once the equipment was packed and in order, he headed to the area where the incident had taken place. While Pippin was en route, Warden Thomas informed him that the victim's name was Terry Adams, a white male, sixteen years of age. Thomas further reported that the victim had shot himself in the foot while attempting to lower his gun out of his tree stand. Pippin contacted the man who leased the property where the incident had occurred. He told the warden that he would need to contact Jamie Adams and passed along Jamie's cell phone number.

Wardens Wilkes and Thomas arrived at the hospital, where they spoke to the victim and his father, Steve Adams. The father stated that he had taken his three sons, Jamie, Tate, and Terry, hunting. He said his youngest son, Terry, had shot himself in the foot while preparing to climb down from his tree stand. The victim, Terry, was then asked to describe what had happened.

Terry told the wardens he was hunting and saw three deer and shot one. He told them he waited about thirty minutes after shooting the deer and decided to climb down out of his deer stand. He pulled up the haul line he used to raise and lower his gun in and out of the tree stand, put the end of the line through the trigger guard on his firearm, and then used the hook snap to attach the line back to itself. From a standing position up in the tree stand, he grabbed the haul line. When he felt the weight of his rifle on the line, the rifle fired, shooting him in his left foot. Terry was then asked if he had a hunting license and if he had taken a Hunter Education course.

The victim replied, "No," to both.

Thomas recorded all their contact information and then proceeded to the incident scene.

Meanwhile, Pippin called the victim's brother, Jamie Adams. He told Jamie he was about ten minutes away, and Jamie let Pippin know he would meet him at the gate that led into the hunting club. He also told the warden he had been hunting for the deer his brother had shot.

Pippin arrived at the hunting club gate at approximately 12:17 p.m., but Jamie was not there. His absence concerned the warden a little. After their telephone call just minutes earlier, and the seriousness of the situation, Pippin had fully expected Jamie to be at the gate to meet him.

Finally, at 12:36 p.m. Jamie and Tate Adams, the victim's brothers, showed up at the gate from inside the hunting club. They got into the back of Warden Pippin's truck and directed him a very short distance to the end of the road, close to the incident scene.

Everything that had taken place over the past half hour or so caused Warden Pippin's game warden sixth sense to begin working overtime. Now seeing that the scene was only a short distance behind the gate, the fact that they were not at the gate as expected, along with their demeanor and actions, made Pippin believe the young men were trying to hide something.

Jamie took the lead and guided the warden to the tree where the incident allegedly had taken place. At the location, Pippin found a climbing tree stand attached to a tree with climbing marks up and down the tree trunk. On the foot piece of the stand, he observed what appeared to be a bullet hole through the bottom of the stand. On the ground around the base of the tree where the stand was attached he could see blood on the leaves and a single glove.

Pippin took a few initial photographs of the scene and GPS coordinates of the location. All the while, he could not shake the very strong feeling that the brothers were not telling him the truth and were trying to cover something up.

Warden Pippin began to question the brothers, and eventually the questioning got around to the deer Terry had shot. They told him they had already looked for it and could not find it. They both acted as though they did not want to look for it anymore.

Pippin was blunt. "I do not like game that has been shot to go to waste. I think we need to search the area one more time for the deer."

Reluctantly, the brothers agreed.

Jamie halfheartedly pointed directly in front of the tree stand and replied, "The deer went in this direction."

While Jamie and his brother Tate began to move in that direction, Pippin's game warden sixth sense again took over. He reasoned that if the brothers were trying to hide something, they would probably try to lead him away from whatever they were hiding. So he decided to search in the opposite direction.

As the warden started walking away from them, Jamie called out, "The deer went this way. You are going in the wrong direction."

Heading almost directly behind the tree stand, Pippin said, "I am going to search in this direction anyway."

After walking a short distance, he found a small, dim trail. He followed the trail and there, on the trail, found the mate to the glove lying on the ground under the tree stand. Pippin now knew his instincts had been correct—something was definitely not right.

He continued down the trail and found corn scattered all over the ground; Pippin had just stumbled into an illegally baited area. He called out to Jamie and asked him to come over to his location.

Pointing down to the corn on the ground, Pippin was blunt again: "Jamie, it is time to be honest about this situation. I know you are trying to hide something, and it is just a matter of time before I find out what it is."

Jamie hung his head down, realizing they were caught. Pointing to a tree about twenty feet away, he said, "The tree my brother was in is over there."

Warden Pippin examined the tree and found tree stand climbing marks up and down this tree trunk as well. He had just found the actual incident scene.

By this time, Warden Thomas arrived at the incident scene and learned from Pippin that the scene had been moved. Pippin took photographs of the correct scene, GPS coordinates, and bait sample of the corn. Jamie and Tate were arrested and transported to the Lacy County Jail. Once there, Tate was charged with "Nonresident Hunting without a License," "Hunting without Hunter Education Certification," and "Interference with a Warden's Duties." Jamie was also charged with "Interference with a Warden's Duties."

During questioning, Pippin learned that after Terry had shot himself in the foot, his father, Steve, had told his brothers to move the tree stand because of the bait they were using. Jamie and Tate followed their father's instructions and moved the tree stand 247 feet from where the incident actually had taken place. They attached the climbing tree stand to another tree and climbed up and down the tree twice to leave climbing marks. The two brothers then picked up the bloody leaves around the base of the tree and their brother's gloves from the actual incident location. They carried this evidence to the second location and scattered it around the base of the tree under the tree stand. They managed to place one of their brother's gloves on the ground under the stand, but during the switch they dropped the other glove in the trail between the two locations.

On December 29, Wardens Pippin and Thomas went back to the incident scene. They searched the scene for the shell casing and projectile (bullet). A .30-06 caliber spent shell casing was found at the base of the tree at the baited site. The projectile/bullet could not be located.

After searching the incident scene, the wardens went to the father's residence to meet with him and Terry, the victim. They were both advised of their Miranda rights, and both agreed to waive their rights to an attorney and speak to the wardens.

The father told the wardens that he wished he had not put out corn for his son to hunt over because he knew it was wrong; he just wanted his son to kill a deer. The father was charged with placing bait out where his son was hunting. After this admission, the father retrieved his son's left boot, which had a bullet hole through it, and gave it to the wardens. He also did not object to the wardens taking the tree stand his son had been using. Both of these items were taken for evidence and photographed by Warden Pippin. The discussion that followed filled in the details the investigators didn't already know.

Steve Adams had taken his three sons, Jamie, Tate, and Terry, hunting that morning. Directed by his father to the area of the bait, Terry placed a climbing tree stand on a tree within twenty feet of the bait and climbed it to hunt.

The two other brothers and his father also sat on deer stands that morning, waiting for deer to come to their bait. At approximately 9:50 a.m., Terry saw three deer from his stand and decided to shoot one. He pushed the safety on his Mossberg bolt-action .30-06 caliber rifle to the fire position, took aim through the scope, and fired. He quickly ejected the spent shell from the rifle, getting ready for a possible follow-up shot. That case was found by Pippin and Thomas at the base of the tree. The deer ran off, but Terry was sure he had hit it.

Terry sat in his stand for approximately thirty more minutes and then he decided to climb down and look for the deer, but he never put the safety on his rifle back in the safe position. He stood up and, using the same haul line he had used to pull his rifle up into the stand that morning, attached it again to his rifle. His haul line had a dog leash–type clip on the end, and Terry ran the clip through the trigger guard of his rifle and over the front of the trigger and then attached it with the clip back to the haul line itself. He then rested the rifle's barrel on his left foot.

When Terry took the slack out of the haul line to lift the rifle, the weight of the rifle pulled the trigger, sending a .30-06 caliber ballistic silver-tip bullet through Terry's left foot. The bullet entered the top of his boot at a slight forward angle. It traveled through his foot, exiting out the bottom of his boot and going through the bottom piece of his climbing stand, causing major tissue damage to his foot. Despite his injury and pain, Terry climbed down the tree using the climbing stand and managed to get assistance from his brothers and father.

Steve then helped Terry to his vehicle and transported him to meet the EMS unit that had been called. Before leaving, knowing his son was hunting over bait, Steve instructed the brothers to move Terry's tree stand to another location to conceal the facts. Everyone out hunting this day bore some responsibility in the results.

Lessons Learned

- Hunting together as a family is a tradition eons old. Parents teach their children both by their actions and by their words. It is crucial that parents teach their children well, especially in an arena where weapons are used and people can get hurt—or worse.
- In many areas, baiting for game is illegal. Despite the father's best intention to help his son have a successful hunt, he would have been better off teaching him the patience necessary for a successful hunt than how to break the law.
- This case shows how people can be drawn into committing crimes out of family and/or peer pressure. Discovering just who is at fault and to what level is not always easy, but it is always necessary.
- The need for a Hunter Education course cannot be overstated. Such a course would have included instructions on how to properly use a haul line. In addition, a Hunter Education course helps reinforce state laws and the importance of an ethical hunt.
- Unloading and then loading a firearm takes very little time and should always be done when climbing in and out of a tree stand. There is no way to shoot a deer while climbing in or out of the stand, so always unload, climb up or down, and then reload when you are ready to resume hunting.

11

It's Duck Season

*To all those who have suffered us a consequence of our trou-
bled past I extend my sincere thoughts and deep sympathy.
With the benefit of historical hindsight we can all see things
which we would wish had been done differently or not at all.*
                                    —QUEEN ELIZABETH II

IT WAS THE OPENING DAY OF DUCK SEASON, THE DAY PASSIONATE
duck hunters wait for all year long. Picture a chilly fall morning,
camo clothes, chest waders, the bag of decoys, shotguns, duck
calls, and a jug of hot coffee all loaded in a narrow, twelve-foot-
long, flat-bottomed aluminum boat, along with two big duck
hunters and an old Labrador retriever named Tank.

Butch and Sonny were lifelong hunting partners who had
been hunting together since they were kids. On this opening
morning, while it was still dark, they paddled their way out to a
point on a small lake. They had hunted from this spot many times
before. They knew the slight wind that morning would be perfect
to create a lifelike rocking for the decoys on the water.

They maneuvered the small boat about to set out the decoys
one at a time without ever leaving the boat. They carefully finished placing their spread of decoys and then settled back in amid

the cattails, where they poured cups of hot coffee and waited for the shooting hours to begin. Tank, Butch's old dog, was anxious as always to bolt into action, retrieving downed ducks as he had done many, many seasons before.

As it began to get light, the silhouettes of the ducks began to emerge in the early-morning sky. Butch and Sonny had placed their boat as close to the shoreline as possible and had brought along a couple of five-gallon buckets to elevate themselves just above the concealment of the cattails.

Legal shooting time finally arrived just as the mallards began to pour into their decoys! Butch stood up quickly, taking a shot at a drake dropping out of the sky. At that exact moment, Sonny also began to stand up in the small boat, now rocking as a result of the blast of Butch's 12-gauge shotgun.

In the sway of the boat, Sonny fell backwards, falling hard onto the gunwale. With his shotgun pointing toward Butch and his finger inside the trigger guard, Sonny's gun went off. The single shotgun blast hit Butch in the back with the full load of steel #4 shot pellets. The mass of pellets entered into his lower right back, spreading pellets upward throughout his mid- to upper-left torso. The blast damaged many vital organs in its path.

Killed immediately, Butch abruptly fell to the deck of the boat. As Sonny crawled toward Butch's lifeless body, he realized there was nothing he could do. Adding to the confusion, Tank was now bouncing all over the boat, trying to figure out what had just happened to his master.

Once Sonny collected himself, he used his cell phone to call 911. Devastated, he knew emergency medical personnel would be unable to save his friend. How would he explain what happened to Butch's wife and family? How could he live with what had just happened?

The local sheriff's office, emergency medical technicians (EMTs), and wildlife officers responded to the scene. The local medical personnel arrived along with the county coroner, who pronounced Butch dead. The stress Sonny was experiencing from shooting his good friend pushed him into a major anxiety attack. The EMTs moved from the victim to the shooter and focused on helping Sonny.

The officers carefully moved Butch's body from the boat onto the stretcher to be loaded into the ambulance. After this delicate process, both a deputy and a wildlife officer drove to Butch's house to notify his wife. The wildlife officer had loaded Tank into his truck for the ride into town.

As they reached Butch's house, Tank began to whine and became very agitated. The officer talked to Tank, trying to ease his worry, but Tank found it hard to wait. As they approached the door, Butch's wife pulled the curtain back to see who had just pulled into the driveway. She looked at the officers, then at Tank. A very frightened look came over her face. She knew the news she was about to receive was not good. Death notifications are never easy to receive or to give.

Lessons Learned

- Duck hunting requires a lot of specialized hunting equipment in what can be difficult conditions and locations. The gear is usually heavy and bulky, especially in a confined space such as, in this case, a small boat. Adding a dog to your hunt requires additional planning and safety considerations. Planning your hunt and hunting your plan is vital!
- Select and use the right type and size of a boat when duck hunting. This tragic accident is the result of a plan that was actually a

recipe for disaster. The boat was too small for the intended use. It was too narrow, too shallow, and very unstable. The size of the two hunters alone caused the small boat to be overloaded, not to mention the additional weight of the heavy clothing and the dog. Choosing to sit on buckets was another mistake. When the shooting began and the men stood up, they caused the small boat to become even more unstable. It is vital to make sure your boat meets or exceeds the capacity of the intended use.

- Safe and successful waterfowl hunting means remembering that birds may come in from any direction. Being on a stable, safe platform is crucial for making a safe and accurate shot.
- Always point your firearm's muzzle in a safe direction, and know where your hunting companions are at all times.
- Communicating who has the shot is not only good hunting etiquette but also a necessary safety practice.
- When you start to slip or trip while carrying a firearm, the most important thing to remember is to keep the muzzle pointed in a safe direction. Keeping your finger off the trigger until you are ready to fire is equally important. Following those two rules would have turned this tragedy into a simple fall and a bruised backside.

12

Seven Years to the Day

*I am a firm believer in the people. If given the truth, they can
be depended upon to meet any national crisis. The great point
is to bring them the real facts.*

—ABRAHAM LINCOLN

WHEN WILDLIFE OFFICERS GATHER AT OUR HUNTING INCIDENT
Investigation Academy, no matter what state they hail from, the
individual contributions they bring are amazing. The stories are
always very engaging. The sharing of these experiences not only
impacts the other students but the instructors as well. There is no
question we all learn from one another. One shared story stands
out about the importance of not only finding out the truth but
also making it known, no matter how difficult it may seem.

A few years ago, a game warden by the name of Lon was
attending the academy. We were talking about the importance
of telling everyone in a hunting party that was involved in an
incident who the shooter turned out to be. Usually the shooter is
already aware of his or her culpability, but the person may be in
denial. In some cases, several hunters may have fired at the same
herd of running deer in the area of the victim, and nobody really
knows who the shooter was. In all cases, the hunters involved wait

anxiously for the investigators to tell them what really happened. They need to know the truth.

Lon told of an investigation he had worked on a number of years earlier. He had received a call from the sheriff's radio dispatcher that a hunter had been shot; the sheriff was requesting his assistance. Emergency medical technicians (EMTs) had been dispatched, and the sheriff and a couple of his deputies were also headed to the scene.

At the scene, the officers and EMTs determined that the victim, Bob Anderson, had died immediately from a single gunshot wound. The hunters involved in the incident were using a barn as a gathering place as they awaited the authorities. The deputies met them there and began to interview and take statements from them.

As the story unfolded, the deputies discovered that the group was completing a deer drive—when a number of hunters spread out and walk through the woods, pushing or driving the deer out of the timber. These groups of hunters are called the "drivers." Waiting on the other end of the timber are the hunters referred to as the "standers," or "blockers." The goal is to move the deer out to these standing hunters. This type of hunting party can become an annual event for family and friends of all ages.

After the deputies shared the hunters' interview information with the sheriff and Game Warden Lon, they both headed up into the timber with Jim and Dave, the two hunters in the party who had admitted to shooting at deer during the drive.

Together, Lon and the sheriff followed Jim and Dave up to the location where they said they had each fired their shotguns. The officers were not only looking for physical evidence but also listening to the exact details Jim and Dave were sharing with them. An empty yellow 20-gauge shell was found where Dave said he had taken his shot, and an empty red 12-gauge shell was located where Jim said he had taken his shot. The sheriff and Lon told Jim and Dave to return to the barn where the other hunters were waiting.

Lon and the sheriff took photographs and measurements and then worked up a field diagram of the scene. The empty shells were collected and tagged as evidence. Once they were finished, they headed to the barn, where an even larger crowd of family and friends had assembled. When Lon and the sheriff walked into the barn, the sheriff announced to those grieving that it appeared to be "just a hunting accident." Everyone seemed to be very relieved. They all headed home after a long and difficult day.

An autopsy was performed on Bob the next day, as per state law; both Lon and the sheriff attended. The single projectile removed by the medical examiner was a somewhat deformed, but still intact, 12-gauge shotgun slug. The empty shotgun shells at the scene, along with the statements provided during the interviews, were all consistent with the location of Bob, the victim. The gauge of the retrieved slug proved that it had come from Jim's shotgun.

Knowing the truth, Lon, the sheriff, and his deputies gathered at the sheriff's office that afternoon to discuss how to proceed. The sheriff shared his sympathy for the loss of the family involved. The discussions led up to how to explain to the two shooters, Jim and Dave, about the evidence and results of the autopsy, and how to let Jim know he was, in fact, the shooter.

The sheriff said, "Look, these are both good families; they both contributed to my last campaign for sheriff. We are not going to do this to these two guys!"

The sheriff insisted that the best way to handle the situation was to withhold the truth. Jim would never know his guilt.

It would be better that way. The one-page report was filed as *A Hunting Accident, Shooter Unknown.*

Lon was very upset with this decision. He felt the truth was always the best route to take, but he was unable to convince the sheriff that sharing the truth was the best for all involved.

Seven years to the day of the incident, Dave was found in his pickup truck near the area where Bob had died all those years before. Dave had shot himself. A note in the truck read, "I can no longer live with the fact that I shot Bob."

Lon heard the news of Dave's death from one of the deputies who had also been on the scene seven years earlier. Lon felt sick when he heard of yet another tragedy. He had been plagued over the years, knowing that the truth had been withheld.

Dave had *not* shot Bob; Jim had!

If the investigating officers had only told the truth seven years ago, a tragic suicide could have been avoided. Telling Dave and Jim who had actually caused the death might have eliminated the guilt Dave harbored inside for those many years. The sheriff's expectation that Jim and Dave would be spared any pain proved fatally incorrect. Dave could have been treated, along with Jim, for the mental wounds they both most likely had, along with the additional burden that Jim harbors thanks to two deaths he feels responsible for.

Lessons Learned

- Deer drives can be very productive but also very dangerous. As the drivers get closer to the standers, the deer that have been sneaking ahead of them will often start running and zigzagging through the woods. Everyone can become so excited to finally see the deer that they might not take time to see the other hunters and may even forget where those other hunters are. Focusing first on the safety of each and every shot is far more important than getting a shot off at a running deer.

- Investigators need to recognize that there can be both physical and additional psychological wounds for those involved in a traumatic event such as a deadly firearm incident. Every hunter in the group and the officers involved become part of the story, and it impacts each one in different ways.
- Based on our experience, we personally feel that the person responsible for the shooting needs to be told of his or her responsibility in a private, controlled situation. Professional counseling support needs to be present to help the person cope with this difficult news.
- Charges of Negligent or Reckless Use of a Firearm or even Involuntary Manslaughter can cause additional stress for all involved. The entire group—from the investigators to the victim's family and the responsible shooter—need to be aware of the necessity to resolve the anguish that a shooting creates. The people involved also need to be supportive of one another, to find some type of resolution in all of this.
- People involved in a hunting-related shooting incident need to be told about resources that are available to them. The Red Cross, county mental health office, and many private counseling services offer treatment for the posttraumatic stress these situations create. Letting those involved know about these resources is a vital aspect of any hunting-related shooting investigation.

13

The Decoy in the Road

We are all ready to be savage in some cause.
The difference between a good man and a bad one is the choice
of the cause.

—WILLIAM JAMES

WARDEN TOM LENDER PAUSED MOMENTARILY AND GAZED DOWN the sandy, two-path road at the turkey hen decoy. Taking the maps in his right hand, he looked at them one more time. He knew this area was not marked on the maps to be baited. However, bait had been found on this hunting club property just days before. One of those sites was nearby, so it was very likely this area could also be baited.

The warden knew there had to be a hunter down this road, hunting near the decoy. He had heard "calling" earlier but could not determine the hunter's exact location. With bait scattered in several areas on the hunting club, Lender decided to do a license check on the hunter and continue to check the area for bait. Warden Lender had no way of knowing that his decision would change his life and the people around him forever.

He began walking down the road toward the decoy, intently scanning the woods on each side of the road for the hunter as he eased along. Step by step he came closer to the decoy and his fate. When he got within sixteen yards of the decoy, the unthinkable would happen. He was about to be shot.

But going back to the beginning would be best. Back on March 16, Wardens Dan Odum and Tom Lender met up in Moore County to look for turkey bait. It was likely illegal to hunt turkeys over bait in their state, and their agency made it a priority to locate baited sites prior to the season opener.

Baiting for turkeys was not only illegal but also unethical.

It was eight days before the season opened, and they knew most hunters who hunted over bait had been baiting their hunting sites for several weeks. They had decided to concentrate their search efforts in Moore County, although it was not their assigned county. It was in their work section, and Warden Lender was second in command.

Lender and Odum had not notified the warden assigned to Moore County that they would be looking for bait in his county. In fact, they did not want Warden Leo Neely or his running partner, Warden Dave Peters, to know they had found bait. Neely and Peters were what you call, for lack of a better term, "good ol' boys." They had issues with the department they worked for and did not mind voicing their opinions to those who would listen.

The wardens decided to search a property that belonged to the Sheffield family. The Sheffields were the largest landowner in Moore County and leased out most of their lands to hunting clubs. A few hours into searching, the wardens finally hit pay dirt. They found several baited sites, and Lender drew a map of the area on two pieces of five-by-four-inch notepad paper. He marked the baited sites so he would not forget where they were when he came back to check them on opening day. Lender and

Odum immediately left the baited area undetected and did not tell anyone about what they had found.

On the night of March 23, Lender told Wardens Neely and Peters to meet him along with Wardens Odum and Jack Madden at 5:30 the next morning at Hopewell Church, near the Logan County line. This is all the information Lender would give Neely and Peters. He said he would brief them on the rest of the information for the work detail the next morning. As you can imagine, this did not sit too well with Neely and Peters, and they wondered what was in the works.

It was a short night for Tom Lender, who was a true game warden at heart. He loved his job, and this was his twentieth year of service. He had the reputation of a warden who would go to great lengths to apprehend game law violators. So proficient was he at catching violators, he had earned the tag "Chicken Hawk."

It is said he would swoop down on the violators like a chicken hawk and catch them in the act of breaking the game laws of his state. His fellow wardens respected him, but he was also somewhat of a jokester. When he was around, there was never a dull moment.

The night was also short because he was anxious and he enjoyed apprehending lawbreakers. Wild turkey hunting season opened in the morning, and there was bait on the ground. Along with bait come illegal hunters taking advantage of the resources. He left his residence long before daylight in order to meet the other wardens at the rendezvous point. He arrived a little before 5:30 a.m. at Hopewell Church. Being the supervisor of this work detail, Lender briefed everyone on what was going on and about the baited sites he and Odum had found in Moore County.

It was decided that he, Neely, and Peters would check the sites he had mapped out on March 16 and Wardens Odum and Jack Madden would check other areas. The game plan was laid out, and Lender, Neely, and Peters climbed into Lender's truck and began driving toward the baited sites in Moore County while Wardens Odum and Madden rode together to other baited sites.

All the wardens left Hopewell Church at approximately 6:30 a.m. and headed toward the baited sites to see if anyone was hunting turkeys over bait. When Lender, Neely, and Peters arrived at the Sheffield property, they turned onto a two-path road and observed a vehicle parked in the roadway. They drove about three hundred yards and came across two hunters walking down the road. The wardens checked the hunters' licenses and guns and found them to be in compliance with all laws.

Lender then drove out to the main road and turned south. Lender was familiar with this area and told Neely and Peters that he and Odum had found bait on this part of the hunting club. They traveled about three quarters of a mile and observed a set of vehicle tracks turning east onto another two-path road. They turned onto the road and followed the tracks for approximately two hundred yards until they came up behind a truck parked in the road. He pulled up behind the truck, parked, and the wardens got out and began walking. All the wardens were in their uniforms, which included dark green pants. Lender had on his black flight jacket, over which he wore a camouflage-brown, bug-tamer mesh jacket for protection from mosquitoes.

The wardens walked past the parked truck about two hundred to three hundred yards. As they walked, they began to hear a hunter using a turkey call. The wardens made their way silently toward the calling hunter. As they eased around a curve in the road, the three wardens spotted a hen turkey decoy set up in the middle of the road about forty yards from their position. They eased back around the curve a little to keep out of sight until they could figure out exactly where the hunter was located. Neely scanned the area with his binoculars, trying to locate the hunter. The wardens decided to stay at this position until the hunter made another call. This decision paid off—in ten to fifteen minutes the hunter began calling again.

Carl Fowler and his daughter Pam had planned to go turkey hunting on the opening day of the season. Carl was excited because his daughter had never before expressed interest in going with him. But Pam had been getting more interested in hunting as she went through high school. She had watched turkey-hunting videos with her father and listened to him practice with his calls. With all this exposure to turkey hunting, she finally decided to give it a try.

On March 24, the opening morning of the state wild turkey season, she met her father at his house at 5:00 a.m. Carl and Pam got into his truck and drove toward the hunting club. Pam was a little hungry, so Carl stopped at a Stop 'n' Shop and got her chocolate milk. They continued to the hunting club and arrived at approximately 5:45 a.m.

They got out of the truck, put their gear together, and began walking down a two-path road to the place her father wanted to hunt. When they arrived at the location, her father began looking for a place to set up and call. After choosing a setup spot, he set up a hen turkey decoy in the middle of the road. Carl then went back to his setup position and got his call out. The hunters made their guns ready; it was going to be an exciting hunt this morning.

Opening day, hunting with his daughter for the first time—what could be more special? Carl loved to hunt turkeys and had bagged thirty-three in his long turkey-hunting career. Needless to say, he was an experienced turkey hunter.

The two hunters settled in and waited for daybreak. Right around daylight they heard a turkey gobbling; they just sat and listened to the bird for a few minutes. It was just before 7:00 a.m. when Carl made his first call using a slate turkey call. He wanted to draw the gobbling turkey out to the road, where it could see the decoy after it flew down.

This first call is what the wardens heard as they walked down the road. Afraid of spooking the turkey, Carl decided to wait a while before he made another call. He looked at his daughter seated to his left and thought how good it was to have her here with him today. He also thought how great it would be if they harvested a turkey. After quietly waiting awhile and not hearing the gobbler again, Carl decided to make another call. He carefully scratched out a few notes with his slate call. This is the call the wardens heard while positioned around the curve forty yards from the decoy. After this call, Carl laid the call down and waited.

From their position around the curve, the wardens tried to determine on which side of the road the hunter was set up by listening to their calling. They thought he was on the west side of the road but could not be sure. After waiting a few more minutes and listening carefully, the wardens began to discuss the best way to approach this hunter. They could not see him or definitely pinpoint his location and did not realize they were already on his back side.

The wardens decided that one of them should circle back around and come in behind the hunter. Lender decided he would do it because he had been on this part of the hunting club before and he knew the area.

When Lender circled around to come in on the other side of the decoy, he would be approaching from the direction the hunter was facing. Lender told the other wardens to wait at their present position and stay out of sight. He circled the block of woods, using a road that went around the block. It took him several minutes to walk to where the road he was on intersected the road the decoy was on. When he turned the corner at the intersection, it was not long before the hen decoy came into view.

As he walked down the road toward the hen decoy, he paused and looked at the maps he held in his right hand. Even though this area was not marked on the maps, it was very close to a baited site he had located a few days earlier. State law dictates that a hunter had to be at least two hundred yards away from any bait while in the act of hunting turkeys; and depending on where this hunter had set up, they were going to be cutting it close to the two-hundred-yard mark. Lender began easing down the road, scanning the woods on both sides for any sign of the hunter.

Carl was the first to see the movement through the under-growth just beyond the decoy. He got his daughter's attention; she too saw something moving out in the roadway, easing toward the decoy. Neither doubted that it was a turkey gobbler. Their excitement grew, and before they ever thought to identify what the movement was, the shooter eased the firearm into position.

The white object they were sure was the gobbler's head was getting closer to the decoy. Through the brush, they could see the head bobbing up and down as it got closer. The hunter waited until the supposed gobbler was within thirty yards of their setup position. The shooter took careful aim with a Remington 870 pump-action 12-gauge shotgun and fired, sending the load from a Winchester #5 three-inch magnum through the brush toward the target.

Lender felt the impact from the #5 shot shell pellets, trav-eling at thirteen hundred feet per second, milliseconds before he heard the muzzle blast. Hit in his legs, abdomen, and groin, Lender cried out in pain. He stumbled around to his left and fell face down on the side of the road, with his head lying in the direction he had come from. Lender had been critically wounded. The shot shell pellets had taken out about a six-inch section of his left femoral artery.

Hearing Lender cry out, both hunters jumped up and hurriedly made their way out to the roadway. Carl saw someone lying facedown on the ground and realized someone had been shot. He raced to the victim and sent his daughter to get their truck. Kneeling down beside the victim, Carl realized it was a wildlife officer. Lender cried out in pain and fell into a semiconscious state.

Around the curve, Wardens Neely and Peters had been waiting patiently for Lender to circle the block and come in behind the hunter. Neely had turned on his radio in order to communicate with Lender if he needed them. They had been waiting for about fifteen minutes when they heard a shotgun blast and someone cry out around the curve toward the decoy. Neely looked at his watch and saw that it was 7:02 a.m.

The wardens walked quickly in the direction of the shot. They had only walked a few feet when they heard someone yell, but this time it had a distraught sound to it. Neely and Peters looked at each other, realizing something was very wrong.

They broke into a run down the road toward the shotgun blast and the yells. As they rounded the curve, they saw a person dressed in camouflage kneeling down over another person lying on the ground. Peters yelled repeatedly at the person in camouflage, "Is there anyone else with you?"

As they got closer, the person in camouflage turned and looked up; Neely recognized Carl Fowler, whom he had known for several years. Carl worked at Jim's Boats & Motors, which provided boat repair services for their wildlife agency. By this time, the wardens were almost within touching distance of Carl and realized the person lying on the ground was Tom Lender.

Carl was crying and imploring, "Let's get help, let's get help; I shot him."

Neely immediately attended to Lender, who was still lying facedown on the ground. Neely did not see any blood yet, but Lender was groaning from pain. Peters tried to call 911 dispatch on his mobile radio but could not get through. He then tried to contact Wardens Odum and Madden to advise them of the incident and get their assistance. Still, he could not get through on the radio.

Neely and Peters began running toward their vehicle and got about halfway before seeing a pickup truck heading toward them. They stopped the truck and the driver told them she was Pam Fowler, Carl Fowler's daughter. Neely asked if she had a cell phone and said he needed to use it. The wardens got into the truck beside her, and Neely used Pam's cell phone to call 911 dispatch. Finally reaching someone, he advised them of the situation, their location, and to send an ambulance immediately.

Pam was very upset and crying. "Is my father okay?" she asked.

Neely assured her that he was and advised her to calm down and continue driving to her father's location. When they got back to the scene, everyone immediately bailed out of the truck. Neely and Peters, along with Carl, let down the tailgate of the truck and began carefully moving Lender.

As they did, they could see a large quantity of blood on the ground under where Lender had been lying. Lender had been lying on his right hand, and when they moved him, Neely noticed he still had the two maps in his right hand. Neely took the maps and placed them in his pocket.

The wardens and Carl took hold of Lender and placed him in the back of the truck. But it was their next action—made by either luck or divine intervention—that might have saved Warden Lender's life. When they closed the tailgate it pushed

Lender's legs up closer to his torso, putting him in an almost fetal position. This action may have been enough to stop some of his blood loss from the damaged femoral artery.

With Lender loaded in the back of the truck, Neely jumped in the driver's seat. Pam sat in the passenger seat, while Peters and Carl rode in the back to help hold onto the injured warden. Driving quickly down the road, Neely had to stop at Lender's vehicle; it was blocking the road and there was no way around it.

They retrieved the keys from the injured Warden's pocket, moved the vehicle, and drove out to the main road. They met up with a Moore County deputy, who advised them that an ambulance was on the way. Neely pulled back onto the highway, with the deputy in front, escorting them.

They were still at least eighteen miles from the nearest hospital, in Tomberlin. Driving as fast as he dared, Neely kept pace with the escorting deputy. They had traveled eight to ten miles when they finally met the ambulance. Neely immediately pulled over, and the emergency medical services (EMS) technicians began to work on Lender.

The EMS technicians advised the deputy and wardens that they needed someone to drive the ambulance while they worked on the victim. Neely immediately jumped into the driver's seat and drove toward the South Central Medical Center in Tomberlin.

The Moore County deputy called ahead and advised law enforcement of the dire situation. Immediately law enforcement officers went to every traffic light along the ambulance's route and stopped traffic. Neely did not have to slow down at all en route to the emergency room. This immediate action by fellow law enforcement officers probably helped save Lender's life.

When they arrived at the ER, Dr. David Meeks was waiting. He had been notified that a gunshot victim was coming in critical condition. He took one look at Lender and thought, *I wouldn't give a nickel for his life right now.*

The doctor did a preoperative diagnosis: gunshot wounds to the chest, bilateral groins, femoral arteries, and extremities. His preoperative diagnosis was gunshot wound with multiple injuries to the right femoral artery and femoral vein, with an entire segment, approximately six inches, of the femoral artery blown away with a pulsatile expanding aneurysm. There were also multiple superficial femoral and common femoral vein injuries, right, and superficial femoral and common femoral artery and vein injuries, left. After Dr. Meeks's initial diagnosis, Lender was immediately taken into surgery. The fight to save his life continued.

Warden Brian Cree had taken off the opening day of turkey season. He had enjoyed hunting many game animals and birds throughout his life, but turkey hunting was his favorite. He usually hunted in three to five states a year in pursuit of turkeys and had written several articles in state and nationally distributed magazines about his favorite pastime.

This morning, though, as good a hunter as Cree was, the turkeys were just not cooperating. He had not even heard a gobble. He had spent most of the morning doing a little calling from a stationary position, trying to elicit a gobble from an old tom. All his calls must have fallen on deaf ears, because nothing came to his calls or answered him. He had been sitting with his back against a pine tree for most of the morning and was getting a little stiff. He decided to get up and start easing through the woods, doing some broadcasting with his calls. He had only moved about forty yards from his setup position at the pine tree when his pager began to vibrate. Cree remained a warden even when he hunted, and the pager reminded him of that fact. He read the message: "Warden Tom Lender has been shot by a turkey hunter." It was 8:47 a.m.

Cree was shocked by what he read. He knew Lender well; they worked in the same district. He wondered how this could have happened. Several scenarios went through his mind as he headed out of the woods. Had Lender been shot on purpose in an altercation? Was this a hunting incident? More important, was Tom all right? What was his condition? Just what could have happened?

For now, he had only the message that had been paged out, but Cree had a bad feeling in the pit of his stomach. He had his vehicle in sight when his pager began to vibrate again. This time the message on the pager read, "Call the State Operations Center ASAP."

Cree immediately took out his cell phone and made the call. He was advised to proceed to the area where Warden Lender had been shot, given directions to the location, and advised that other Critical Incident Reconstruction Team (CIRT) members were already in route. It was now 9:00 a.m.

Cree was in charge of the CIRT, which was tasked with investigating and reconstructing all serious injury and fatal boating accidents and hunting incidents throughout the state. He did not waste any time getting out of the turkey woods and back to his residence, where he changed into his uniform, hurriedly organized his equipment, and headed south toward the incident scene.

Dr. Meeks was doing everything humanly possible to save Warden Lender's life. It wasn't easy. He not only had to deal with the gunshot wound but also contend with a stroke that Lender suffered due to major blood loss. Now on the operating table, Lender's life was in the hands of God and Dr. Meeks, along with his surgical staff.

While Dr. Meeks and his team fought to save Tom Lender's life, Cree was in constant radio communication with the other wardens, getting directions and information as it came available.

Warden Dan Williams met him on Highway 225 and led him to the incident scene. It was now 11:00 a.m.

At the scene, Cree met with District Supervisor Darrell Ashe, who was the ranking officer in charge of the scene. Ashe had locked down the scene until CIRT investigators arrived. Supervisor Ashe briefed Cree regarding the circumstances surrounding the incident that were known at the time and took him to the incident scene.

The first thing Cree did was to establish a staging area outside the taped-off area. This would be where all equipment would be placed and assignments given out to CIRT investigators as they arrived on scene. It would also be used for strategy sessions and to bring everyone up to date on developing information.

Cree grabbed several different colors of flagging from his evidence bag. He was now ready to do an initial walk-through of the scene. The first thing that caught the warden's eye was the hen decoy staked in the middle of the two-path road. Taking his time as he eased down the road, he saw scuff marks along with a few drops of blood in the road and a drying pool of blood to the left of the marks on the edge of the road. Cree placed flags at both locations. He then placed a flag by the hen decoy and proceeded past it and into the woods on the right side of the road. There he found the hunters' setup position. Lying on the ground was a camouflaged Remington 870 12-gauge pump shotgun. To the right of that was a slate turkey call and striker. Just a few feet beyond the shotgun, Cree could see that someone had been sitting up against a small oak tree; to his right there was another depression in the leaves at the base of another oak tree, indicating someone had been sitting there as well.

A search of the area revealed no fired/spent shot shell in the immediate area around where the hunters had been. Closer examination of the firearm, without picking it up, indicated that a shot shell was still in the chamber and the safety was in the "off," or fire, position. With the absence of a spent shell in the area and a shot shell visible in the chamber of the shotgun, Cree deducted that the shooter must not have ejected the fired/spent round after firing. Cree flagged all the evidence, including locations of the hunters, shotgun, slate turkey call, and striker.

Cree then sat down at both locations where the hunters had been. From the position closer to the road and shotgun, he noticed limb clips straight out from the location. This is where the shooter had fired the shotgun. Closer examination of the brush out from this location turned up multiple limb clips and pellet strikes on small trees. He marked the limb clips with orange flagging tape and placed yellow glass-headed pins in the pellet strikes in the small trees. He was able to follow the shot shell pellet strikes and limb clips through the brush to the edge of the road. They all led directly back to the scuff marks and blood drops he had found in the middle of the roadway. This confirmed that the scuff marks marked Warden Lender's location when he had become a victim.

Cree then directed his attention and search efforts to locating the shot shell wad. Searching back through the brush toward the shooter's position, he found no sign of it, so he searched the area around the victim's location—still nothing. He expanded his search to the area beyond the victim and the other side of the road. There he found more limb clips, and lying on the ground at the edge of the road, he located the shot shell wad. Cree marked the limb clips with orange flagging tape and placed a flag by the plastic wad.

Cree canvassed the scene once again, taking his time to search all areas but locating no other evidence. Having flagged all the evidence, he went back to the staging area and began assigning each piece of evidence its own number.

Beginning with the shooter location, he assigned it #1 and began to systematically work his way through the incident scene, numbering the rest of the evidence. Cree was in the process of numbering the limb clips and pellet strikes in front of the shooter location when Supervisor Ashe brought State Bureau of Investigation (SBI) Agent Bret Comer onto the scene.

Agent Comer asked whether anyone had interviewed the shooter. When Cree replied, "No, not yet," the agent suggested that he go interview the shooter while Cree continued to work the scene. Then they could get together and share information.

Comer took a few photographs of the scene before heading out to interview the shooter, and Cree got back to numbering the evidence. At approximately 1:30 p.m., fellow CIRT member Warden Sam Pippin arrived at the scene. Cree met him at the staging area and brought him up to date on the situation at hand. They decided to wait for the other CIRT members to arrive before they proceeded any further with documenting and reconstructing the incident scene.

Back in the operating room, Dr. Meeks had just completed his work. Following the extensive surgery, Lender was placed in the intensive care unit (ICU). His right leg was split from the groin down to the knee. There was about an inch left intact, and then another split continued down the leg and stopped just above the ankle. This large incision was approximately one to two inches wide and about an inch deep. It would be packed with gauze and a saline solution and the wound left open to heal from the inside out. This delicate process would be watched carefully until May 2, thirty-nine days after he was shot.

It was approximately 3:00 p.m. when CIRT members

Wardens Ken Gillis and Jack Bozeman arrived at the incident scene. Cree and Pippin met them at the staging area, where Cree briefed them on the situation and advised them that he had the area flagged and had assigned numbers to all the evidence located inside the incident scene. The wardens discussed how they wanted to next proceed with the reconstruction.

Gillis and Pippin were assigned to take photographs of the scene and the evidence. Gillis would take the photographs while Pippin filled out the photographic log, which gave each photograph a number and provided a brief description of what each photograph portrayed.

After all photographs had been taken, the wardens ran a shot line from the shooter's position to the victim's position. Cree tied orange flagging tape along the shot line in order to make it stand out more when photographed. When the shot line was in position, a visibility test was done using a measurement of visibility device (MVD).

Using this device, the wardens were able to estimate the visibility the shooter had through the brush when aiming toward the victim. The shooter's visibility toward the victim was estimated at approximately 65 percent. While Gillis and Pippin finished up the photographs, Cree and Bozeman began to run a baseline through the middle of the scene and to take measurements of evidence locations.

With the location of all the evidence documented by photographs and measurements, it was up to Cree, as lead investigator, to collect and mark all collectable evidence. Bozeman recorded each item that was collected on the agency's evidence collection log.

When the shooter's firearm was picked up and examined, it was determined that a fired/spent shot shell was found in the chamber, along with two live rounds in the magazine. With the fired shot shell still in the chamber, Cree immediately thought that this was something an inexperienced hunter would do.

Usually, an experienced hunter would eject the fired round immediately upon firing to get ready for a follow-up shot, if needed. This action becomes a "muscle memory" response, done immediately so the hunter is always ready for the next shot. This piece of evidence placed some doubt in the team leader's mind as to the identity of the actual shooter. Despite Carl Fowler's admission that he had shot Warden Lender, Cree was skeptical.

More information would be needed before this theory could either be proved or discounted. When Cree advised Agent Comer of his suspicions, Comer said he would be sure to include this information when he interviewed Carl and Pam Fowler.

Cree secured all collected evidence items in his vehicle to be transported to his assigned county's sheriff's office, where it could be locked down in their evidence room. Cree assigned Wardens Williams and Collins the task of using a three-hundred-foot measuring tape to document the distance to the nearest baited site that had been marked on Warden Lender's maps. Since the bait site turned out to be beyond the two-hundred-yard distance limit, the hunters were not considered to have been hunting turkeys over bait.

Things were beginning to wind down at the site as District Supervisor Stu Reid and Agency Supervisor Dick Header arrived. They had just come from the medical center and told everyone that Warden Lender was out of surgery but his condition was listed as critical.

Cree gave both supervisors a walk-through of the scene, describing what evidence had been found and pointing out its location. Supervisor Header thanked Cree and all the CIRT members for their timely response and the work that they had done on the case. It was time to start packing up the equipment and head home.

While all this was happening at the site, SBI Agent Comer located Carl and Pam Fowler at the medical center. He introduced himself and requested a room from the hospital staff to interview both subjects. They were led to a small visitor waiting room on the first floor of the hospital. Agent Comer told both Carl and his daughter that he wanted to interview them regarding the incident that had occurred earlier and advised them of their Miranda rights. Carl stated that if the agent wanted to interview them, he would first need to consult with an attorney.

Comer allowed Carl to place a telephone call to his lawyer, Ed King. The law office informed Carl that Ed King had himself just been released from the hospital and would be unable to represent him and his daughter. However, Will King agreed to represent them.

King arrived quickly at the hospital to consult with his clients, Carl and his daughter Pam. After a brief consultation, the attorney advised Agent Comer that his clients would not be making a statement at this time. The agent then told the attorney he would be consulting with Central Judicial Circuit District Attorney Rick Miles in reference to any future charges against Mr. Fowler.

Not being able to conduct the interviews, Comer located Wardens Peters and Neely at the medical center. The agent interviewed each warden separately. They both detailed the events of that morning—from the moment they had arrived on the hunting club and all their actions up to when the hunting incident had taken place.

Each warden described concisely and clearly what he had seen and his actions after Warden Lender had been shot. The wardens' interviews corroborated each other, with Neely going into more detail than Peters. Neely told Comer that Carl Fowler was in compliance with all state regulations as far as his hunting requirements were concerned.

On March 26, Comer was able to conduct a prescheduled interview with Carl Fowler, with Carl's new attorney, Sam Carr, in attendance.

Comer advised Carl and his attorney of the nature of the interview, which concerned the incident that had occurred on Saturday, March 24. Comer also advised Carl and his attorney of the importance of giving truthful information regarding the person who had actually fired the shotgun.

Carl and his attorney stated that they understood and would tell the truth. Comer also advised Carl of his constitutional rights and had him sign the required waiver. Carl was then asked to relate any information he had concerning the incident. He then began his telling of the story.

On Saturday March 24, he and his daughter went turkey hunting and arrived at the hunting club around 5:45 a.m. He stated that his daughter was not actually hunting but basically observing. They left the truck and walked to the location where the incident happened. Carl indicated that around daylight, he heard a turkey gobbling and that they listened until around 7:00 a.m. He began calling the turkey up, trying to draw it into the area near the decoy. Carl said his daughter was seated to his left, on the ground.

He said he observed a white turkey head coming to the decoy and the turkey head was bobbing. Carl stated that he tapped his daughter and she watched the turkey. He also stated that he saw the turkey blow up as if it were beginning to strut; it looked as though the turkey was getting closer to his decoy and looked like it was fanning. He stated that he shot at this time and soon after realized that he had actually shot a man.

Carl related that he turned and observed Wardens Leo Neely and Dave Peters. He told his daughter to go to the truck, call 911, and get help. He believed that Neely and Peters followed his daughter to the truck. He said they loaded Warden Lender into his truck and had to move another truck out of the way before reaching the highway and eventually meeting the ambulance off Highway 56.

Carl repeated that this was the first time his daughter had been turkey hunting with him. He was working the call, and she was not hunting. He explained he had been hunting for ten to twelve years and considered himself experienced. He then expressed sorrow for what had happened.

After the interview with Carl Fowler, Agent Comer contacted Neely at the medical center in Tomberlin. Neely told the agent that he had the two sheets of notebook paper displaying an assortment of Lender's handwritten notes and diagrams. Neely explained that these items had been in Lender's hands at the time of the shooting. He knew Lender had been carrying the sheets when he was shot because the papers contained shot holes and a quantity of blood. Furthermore, the diagrams depicted the areas where turkey bait was located in the general area of the incident in question. Comer retrieved these pieces of notebook paper from Neely and secured them as evidence.

Warden Cree was not only in charge of CIRT but also one of the agency's most highly trained investigators. He had been trained in many aspects of investigative and forensic techniques, including fingerprint classification and development. He had been in touch with Agent Comer and was made aware of the interview with Carl Fowler and the information obtained during the interview. Carl had indicated that he was the shooter and his daughter was there just as an observer.

But Cree was not sold on the fact that Carl had been the shooter—not just yet. To him, the way the shotgun was found, with the fired/spent shot shell still in the chamber, indicated an inexperienced hunter; Fowler's daughter was twenty-one years old, and this was her first time hunting with her father. The father continued to say that she was not hunting, just observing. This seemed a little odd to Cree and raised more questions than answers—questions that needed to be answered.

On Monday, March 26, Cree contacted Instructor Mike Rusher at the State Police Academy to get permission to use the academy's fingerprint lab. Rusher had been Cree's instructor in many classes, and they had developed a friendship over the years. Cree gave him a brief rundown of the situation and explained that he needed to process the shot shell rounds found in the shooter's gun for fingerprints. Rusher told Cree he could use the lab anytime.

Cree and Rusher agreed to meet at the academy on March 28. Cree did not tell anyone what he had in mind in regard to fingerprinting evidence items. He did not want this information to get out until the daughter, Pam Fowler, had been questioned. Cree also contacted Lender's section supervisor, Warden Bart Harris. Hospital staff had given Harris the articles of clothing Lender had been wearing at the time of the incident, and Cree needed to examine them as evidence. Harris told him that he had thrown all of Warden Lender's clothing away. Cree was furious! Every warden should have known that clothing can be very important evidence in any investigation, and now Lender's was gone. Cree could do nothing to bring back the lost evidence, but he could work diligently with the evidence he had.

As planned, Cree met Rusher in his office on March 28. Cree wanted to use the lab's cyanoacrylate fuming chamber—the best technique available—in order to try to develop a latent fingerprint on the shotgun shells found inside the shooter's firearm. This fingerprint development technique is also known as the superglue fuming process.

Rusher unlocked the cabinets containing the necessary chemical and stood by to assist the warden if needed. A certified dactylographer (a person who studies fingerprints for the purposes of identification), Rusher was also an expert in fingerprint processing and development.

Cree put on a pair of latex gloves and carefully placed the two live shotgun shells and the fired round in the fuming chamber. He then placed a warm cup of water in the chamber to increase the humidity, which helps rehydrate any latent fingerprints that might be present. He squeezed a small quantity of cyanoacrylate fuming liquid (aka superglue) into a small aluminum container. This he placed on a heating element to heat up, at which point the liquid would turn to gas and attach itself to the oils and ammo acids found in any fingerprints, making them visible to the naked eye.

The last thing Cree placed in the chamber was a control—his own thumbprint. He rubbed his thumb down the crease beside his nose in order to make his thumb oilier. Cree then pressed his thumb down onto a black lifted fingerprint print card and placed the card in the chamber. When his thumbprint became visible, he would know that any prints on the shot shells would likely be developed and the shells would be ready to be examined with a magnifying glass.

Cree sealed the chamber, turned on the heating element, and waited. Once the ridges in his print were visible, Cree turned off the heating element, reached into the chamber, and retrieved the three shot shells. Taking a magnifying glass, he slowly began to examine each shot shell for ridge detail of a print. On one of the live shot shell rounds he hit pay dirt—a partial print had been developed on the plastic part of the shell. He could find no other prints. Cree thanked Rusher for his assistance and use of the lab and headed back to the sheriff's office to secure the shot shell evidence in their evidence room.

On March 30, Cree signed the shooter's shotgun out of the evidence room in order to fingerprint the firearm. This particular Model 870 Remington had been dipped in a vinyl-type camouflage coating, which posed a real challenge to fingerprint. Putting the gun into a cyanoacrylate chamber would have been the best method for developing a print, but it would have rendered the gun inoperable. The fumes would have superglued all parts of the gun together. Cree didn't feel like writing a letter to headquarters justifying why he had used this method and that they needed to replace the gun. He had to come up with another method to develop any fingerprints that might be on the gun.

He decided to use fluorescent green powder and a black light to develop any prints. There was just one problem: The process required the vinyl material on the gun to be hydrated, and he did not have a "huffer." Cree knew he would have to improvise, again. His sheriff's office had a room without windows, and he knew he could make that work.

Cree took the shotgun to this room, closed the door, and turned out the lights. Using his flashlight, he put on latex gloves, picked up the shotgun, and placed his mouth about one to two inches from the gun's receiver. He began to huff warm air along the ejection port side of the receiver. This warm air would rehydrate any prints on the vinyl material. Cree then turned off his flashlight and, using the black light for illumination, used a feather fingerprint brush to dust a small amount of florescent green powder along that side of the receiver.

Looking through the amber/orange-tinted Plexiglas attachment on the black light, Cree scrutinized the gun for prints. There were no visible prints on the port side of the shotgun. Cree then repeated the procedure on the other side of the shotgun receiver. Success!

He found a perfect latent fingerprint about dead center on that side of the receiver. Using fingerprint lift tape, he carefully removed the print and placed it on a black lift print card. Cree used this technique to examine the rest of the shotgun but found no other prints.

On April 11, Warden Lender and District Supervisor Stu Reid met with SBI Agents Bret Comer and Ronny George at their office in Loganville to discuss the case and exchange information. At this time, Cree turned in the evidence he had recovered and developed, including the Remington Model 870 12-gauge shotgun, two live rounds of Winchester shot shells, and two lift print cards containing the two fingerprints he had discovered. All this evidence was signed over to Agent George to be processed in the state crime lab.

Cree was careful to let the agents know that no one knew he had fingerprinted the shells and firearm. He had strong suspicions that these prints belonged to Pam Fowler, the daughter. If she had just been an observer, as her father asserted, her prints should not be on either the shotgun or shells.

Agent Comer indicated they were scheduled to interview Pam Fowler the next day with her attorney present. Cree asked the agent to let him know how the interview had gone when they were finished.

The agents gave Cree transcripts of their previous interviews with Carl Fowler and Wardens Dave Peters and Leo Neely, along with a scanned copy of the two pieces of notebook paper Lender had been carrying when he was shot. The agents also provided Cree with copies of all photographs taken by Agent Comer at the incident scene, as well as those taken of Warden Lender. These graphic photos included Lender's visible wounds caused by the shot shell pellets as well as wounds resulting from the surgery.

On April 12, SBI Agent Ronny George met Pam Fowler at attorney Sam Carr's office for the interview. At this time, the attorney told George that Ms. Fowler had prepared a handwritten statement concerning the incident. The statement read as follows:

Met my dad at his house 5:00 a.m.; left for the hunting club. Stopped at Stop 'n' Shop convenience store for some chocolate milk. Arrived at the hunting club about 5:45 a.m. Got out of truck; my dad had to use the restroom, so I held his gun and some calls. I gave them back to him. Walked to place where we were going to hunt. I held his "stuff" while he cleared the ground for me to sit. Then I gave it back to him when I was sitting. Heard turkey and owl about ten minutes after being there. About sunrise, heard turkey again. Then heard something walking; we were watching what we thought was a white turkey head bobbing with fan spread. He was walking toward our decoy. Watched for a few minutes then my dad shot at what he thought was a turkey.

After reading the statement, Agent George asked the attorney if it would be okay to ask his client additional questions about the incident. The attorney permitted Ms. Fowler to answer. Prior to questioning, Ms. Fowler was read her constitutional rights, and she assured the agent that she understood those rights.

Agent George asked about the distance between the turkey and the decoy. Ms. Fowler stated she was not sure of the distance; however, she also stated that when the shot was fired, she did not think the turkey was that far away from the decoy. She stated that she thought she observed what appeared to be a turkey's white head and saw it fanning. When asked if she fired the shotgun at the time, she asserted that "there was no way" she had fired the gun.

Agent George asked her if she ever had the gun in her actual possession on the date in question. She affirmed that when she exited her father's truck, he had used the restroom and she had held the shotgun, she believed, "by the strap." Ms. Fowler added that when they got to the area where they were seated, she might also have held the gun with it facing downward.

After the interview, George obtained fingerprints and palm print impressions of both Ms. Fowler and her father. Upon completion of the interview, Agent George called Cree to let him know what he had found out.

Cree was very frustrated after the telephone conversation with George. It seemed more than a little odd that Ms. Fowler would point out in her prepared statement that she had held her father's shotgun. He had not told anyone other than the SBI agents about his suspicions or his fingerprinting of the shotgun and shot shells, but her statements seemed to take her out of the picture as far as proving she was the shooter.

In her statement, she had managed to give a valid reason for her prints possibly being on the shotgun, and there was no way to prove otherwise. The case would proceed with Carl Fowler listed as the shooter. He had confessed to this fact and had made a sworn statement, but Cree still was not convinced that he was indeed the shooter.

Cree began to organize a time for a reenactment of the incident. Reenactments are very helpful to an investigator because they provide an opportunity to sit in the shooter's position and view things from his or her perspective.

The goal of every reenactment is to re-create the incident as closely as possible from the shooter's perspective. This aids the investigator in the search for answers to the question as to what the shooter may have seen when the trigger was pulled. Cree contacted Neely and Peters and set April 16 as the date. Cree also gave Warden Jim Pierce a call. Pierce was about the same height and build as Warden Lender, and Cree hoped he would be available to assist with the reenactment; Pierce assured him it would not be a problem. Cree asked Pierce to wear the regular uniform and bring his black flight jacket and bug-tamer jacket, just as Lender had done.

Everyone involved with the reenactment was to meet at the incident scene well before daylight to get the equipment set up. Cree planned to videotape the reenactment at the same daylight time the incident had occurred on March 24. He also wanted to record a tom turkey (gobbler) walking down the two-path road, taking the same path as Warden Lender had to the place where he had been shot; but he knew it was unlikely that he could get a live turkey to cooperate. He had to think of another solution to this problem.

Cree suddenly had a brainstorm! He went to the closest Walmart and purchased a remote-control, four-wheel-drive truck. He attached a turkey gobbler decoy over the truck body. Cree now had his very own, and quite realistic, turkey tom that could be videoed *walking* down the road.

On April 16, Cree met Wardens Neely, Peters, and Pierce well before daylight at the hunting club where the hunting incident had occurred. Pierce was dressed exactly like Warden Lender had been. He was given two pieces of five-by-four-inch notebook paper and instructed to hold it in his right hand as he walked down the road. Cree then got out his 35mm camera, video camera, and tripod. Using a flashlight and measurements taken at the incident scene on March 24, he marked Warden Lender's position in the road when he was shot. He then used the measurements to locate and mark the hen decoy position.

Cree found the shooter's position, where he set up the tripod, attached the video camera, and adjusted the tripod to the approximate shotgun aiming height. He sighted the camera at the position Warden Lender was when the shot had been fired by the alleged shooter, Carl Fowler. Pierce was given a starting point back down the road. With all the equipment set up and ready and everybody in his assigned place, all that was left was to wait on the sun and the exact time the incident had occurred.

Looking at his watch, Cree could see that they were just seconds away from the approximate daylight time. He asked his colleagues to get in their places and get ready. Cree had decided to tape the first segment of video without any magnification. He turned on the video camera and yelled, "Action!"

Carrying the two pieces of notebook paper in his right hand, Pierce began to ease down the road toward the shooter's position. Just before Pierce got to the position where Lender had been shot, Cree could see movement through the brush from the shooter's position. As Pierce took a few steps closer, the white notebook paper in his right hand came into view through the underbrush. The closer Pierce got to the shooter's position, the more pronounced the notebook paper became.

Cree continued to videotape Pierce until he reached the area where the hen decoy had been staked. At this position, Pierce came into full view.

Cree taped four more segments with Pierce walking the same route with the notebook paper in his right hand, increasing the magnification of the video camera in each segment. After sitting in the shooter's position and watching the reenactment unfold, Cree knew what had caused the shooter to pull the trigger. Without a doubt, the shooter had fired at the white notebook paper in Warden Lender's right hand. The shooter had associated the white paper with the white on a turkey gobbler's head.

Cree also noted that the shooter had not taken a clear shot but had shot through the brush. If the shooter had waited just a few steps more, Warden Lender would have been in full view when he reached the hen decoy.

After the last segment of video was taped, Pierce and Cree got out the remote-controlled "strutting tom turkey" decoy. They set it up in the road at the position where Pierce had begun his walk down the road and handed the controls to Neely. Cree went back to the shooter's position, turned on the video camera, and once again yelled, "Action!"

As before, the first segment of video with the remote-controlled decoy was taped without magnification. Neely moved the strutting turkey decoy down the road toward the shooter's position. The first thing Cree noticed was that the decoy was not as visible through the brush as Pierce had been, as one would expect with a grown man versus a tom on a truck.

As a result, the white on the tom turkey was considerably lower to the ground than the white notebook paper in Pierce's hand. The white on the decoy's head was also not as pronounced and visible. Cree could not see it or any movement until it was much closer to the hen decoy and past the position where Warden Lender had been shot. He taped one more segment with the remote-controlled turkey gobbler, this time increasing the magnification. Cree was very happy with the results of the reenactment; there was no doubt now as to what had caused the shooter to take aim and shoot at Warden Lender.

Cree took a few more measurements that had not been taken on the day the incident occurred. With the assistance of the other wardens, he measured the distance from the shooter's position to the edge of the road as 8 feet; from the observer's position to the edge of the road as 15 feet, 4 inches; from Neely and Peters's position down the road when the shot was fired to the shooter's position as 165 feet; and from Neely and Peters's position down the road to the victim's position as 249 feet.

While taking these measurements, Cree came across another piece of evidence that had been previously missed. Lying in the middle of the road was the thin wafer-type paper wad that had come out of the shooter's fired shot shell. This paper wad was easily missed, as it was only about the size of a quarter and had a dark tan color. It had probably been covered with sand by foot traffic.

By luck or providence, it had rained since Cree had been back to the scene; the rain had washed the sand away, exposing the small piece of paper. Cree took photographs of the wad and its location. He then measured from the shooter's position to the paper wad in the two-path road as 31 feet, 5 inches. He placed the wad in an evidence bag to be added to evidence previously collected.

On April 23, the state crime lab completed its examination of the Remington Model 870 12-gauge pump-action shotgun and test firing of the Winchester Supreme three-inch magnum 12-gauge shot shells. Test firing and patterning the shotgun using the Winchester shot shell rounds revealed a pellet pattern diameter of approximately twenty-five inches from muzzle to target at a distance of twenty-eight yards. Cree concluded that he had enough information based on the evidence to proceed.

The report determined that Carl Fowler had seen the white papers in Warden Lender's hand and the dark form of the warden walking towards the decoy. Concluding that he was seeing a tom turkey responding to his calls, Carl then fired the round that almost took the warden's life. As a hunter, Carl knew the identifying features of the game he was hunting; but in this case, he saw the white notebook paper in Warden Lender's right hand and assumed it was the white on a turkey gobbler's head.

Carl's view was blocked by brush. If he had just been patient, his target would have been in full view as Lender neared the decoy. This is a classic and deadly type of hunting incident, where the victim is mistaken for game.

On April 27, a grand jury convened in the Moore County courthouse, where Warden Cree gave testimony of the events that had taken place on March 24.

After he was finished testifying, he waited to see if the grand jury was going to "true bill or no bill," the charge filed against Carl Fowler: "Misuse of a Firearm while Hunting," a felony. After about an hour, Assistant District Attorney (ADA) Thad Beasley came out to report that the grand jury had "true billed" the charge against Carl Fowler and that his office would be moving forward in prosecuting the case. Cree was pleased with the decision but could not have expected the troubles that were to come.

Not long after the hunting incident, Wardens Neely and Peters started a personal campaign to change policy. The wildlife law enforcement agency that employed them had the following policy, giving guidance to their wardens about when they needed to wear a florescent orange vest:

The intent of this policy is to establish a procedure to use of/ and wearing of daylight fluorescent orange material by all law enforcement personnel during the firearms deer season.
A) Daylight Fluorescent Orange Vest
To be worn as an outer garment by all law enforcement personnel while on routine foot or ATV patrol during fire- arms deer season.

After the incident with Lender, Neely and Peters were deter- mined to change that policy to include checking all hunters, especially turkey hunters. In addition, they wanted to have the law changed to require turkey hunters to wear fluorescent orange while in the act of hunting turkeys. They expressed their concern for their safety as wardens. The two wardens met with agency heads and state lawmakers, voicing their concern over their safety while doing their job. Before too long, Peters contacted Cree, try- ing to get his support in this cause.

Cree, a game warden at heart and an avid turkey hunter, would have none of it and refused to jump on their bandwagon. He knew from years of experience that a wildlife officer's best tool was stealth. Good cases could not be made if the violator saw you before you could observe them. Wearing an orange vest would simply not be feasible in all situations.

As for turkey hunters, wearing orange would work against their efforts to get a bird. A turkey sees colors similar to a human, unlike a deer, which is color-blind. If a turkey hunter wore orange, turkeys, with their exceptional eyesight, would spot the hunter a mile away. While Neely and Peters had good intentions, it just would not work.

Unfortunately, Neely and Peters spread their ideas to any- one who would listen. In response, the agency pulled up the turkey-hunting incident statistics for the previous few years to justify to state lawmakers why there was no need for a law requiring turkey hunters to wear orange clothing. The agency supervisor, Dick Header, was finally forced to state that the policy would not change. However, he added, if individual wardens felt that the situation warranted it, an orange vest should be worn.

After the hunting incident, Warden Lender could not remember exactly what had happened. His memory loss may have been caused either by the stroke or by the traumatic shock from the injury. However, word began to leak out within the agency that his section supervisor, Bart Harris, was attempting to influence his memory. This influence had reached a point where Lender was now saying he had loudly called out "Hey" to the hunter just before Carl shot him.

Cree got wind of the rumors and reviewed all the interviews again. As he already knew, no one had heard this "Hey." He contacted Neely and Peters and asked them if they had heard anything before the shot was fired.

Each man said, "No," he had only heard a yell *after* the shot.

They were only 249 feet away when Warden Lender was shot, and in the quiet of the morning, they definitely would have heard a loud "Hey" if Lender had called out. They had heard his yell even with the shotgun blast still ringing out through the woods, so a "Hey" before the shot would have been easy to hear.

As all the interviews concurred, Cree concluded that Lender had never shouted a warning. He contacted a headquarters supervisor and reported that the purported actions or shouts by Lender just before the shot could not be verified and therefore would not be put into his case file.

As the investigation was winding its way through the offices, Lender was trying to work his way home. He had suffered

multiple setbacks after surgery and required several blood trans-
fusions and medications to correct the problems as they arose.
After surgery, he had been placed in the ICU, where he remained
for several days.

Shortly after he was moved out of the ICU, medical personnel began getting him up and walking using his right leg in order
to keep the blood circulating. For approximately six weeks, the
large incisions along his right leg had to be packed with gauze
and cleaned with a saline solution twice a day.

By early April, Lender was making slow but steady progress
while his doctor dealt with conflicts between treating the stroke
caused by his blood loss and treating the leg. One lingering problem was Lender's struggle with words.

In mid-April, he was transferred to in-patient therapy. He
still had the open wound the length of his right leg and was in
a lot of pain; however, he was improving and beginning to smile
again. But his wife, Tonya, was not happy with the way in-patient
therapy was going. After three days, she asked the doctors to
release him and have home health nurses come to their home to
change the dressings. They also arranged for a therapist to come
by several times a week for the rest of April.

On May 2, Warden Lender was readmitted to the hospital
to have the open wounds on his right leg closed up and also to
get some skin grafts. He was released from the medical center
on May 10. His mind was a lot sharper, and he was getting restless. In the weeks ahead, he would face many weeks of intensive
therapy. By May 21, most of his pain came from the skin graft
location on his good leg.

The wounds on his right leg were healing, and he looked forward to getting the bandages off for good. He was now walking without any assistance and could navigate steps slowly. He

had even driven a vehicle a little over the past few days, but he still had a lot of intensive therapy ahead of him. By the time the trial came around in November, Warden Lender had progressed immensely. He could walk on his own, and his speech was back to normal.

Lender's healing was moving forward; so was the push for the trial. Warden Cree received his subpoena to appear at the Moore County courthouse on Monday, November 5. He immediately contacted ADA Beasley to find out what he needed to do and what he was expected to bring with him to court. ADA Beasley needed another copy of the incident scene photographs and another copy of the reenactment videotape. He also asked Cree to get there early on November 5 to assist him in selecting a jury.

Over the weeks leading to the trial, Cree had heard that Carl Fowler had once again changed attorneys, but he had not expected someone so eccentric. The first time Cree saw attorney Andrew Hill, he was wearing a derby hat, button-down shirt with bow tie, and dark pants with suspenders. Cree had also heard that the Sheffields, owners of the property where the incident had occurred, had hired and paid for this attorney.

Attorney Hill strolled into the courtroom, took off his derby, and approached ADA Beasley. Cree was standing beside the ADA, and in a display of arrogance that seemed to be pulled from a classic courtroom drama, Hill snubbed the warden, not even acknowledging he was there. When Hill strolled away, Cree couldn't help but think, *What a snob.*

What Hill did not know was that Cree was a force to be reckoned with on the witness stand. And Hill would have to face him eventually. While many law enforcement officers dreaded testifying in court, Cree loved it. His love for seeking justice in all cases led Cree to seek guidance on testifying early on in his career.

He also had taken courses at the state police academy about testifying and presenting evidence at trial.

Cree couldn't wait to get on the stand. Jury selection began, and it was soon obvious what Hill was trying to do. His first question to each potential juror was "Do you hunt or have you ever hunted?" Any potential juror who answered "Yes" was "struck." There had not been many hunters in the jury pool to begin with, and when selection was all over, Hill had gotten exactly what he wanted—a jury consisting completely of nonhunters.

Before the trial began, Cree had put a brown camouflage bug-tamer jacket and an MVD into a small box with a top on it, brought it into the courtroom, and set it down next to his seat at the prosecution table. The warden had learned long ago that if you brought in something you might want to present to the court and let it be seen by a defense attorney, the defense would have time to formulate a plan to rebuke your presentations. Cree found it best to use surprise whenever possible.

After the opening statements, Warden Cree was the first to take the witness stand. He stated his name and credentials and was qualified by the court as a hunting incident reconstruction expert. ADA Beasley asked him to go through his investigation and reconstruction and inform the jury what the evidence had revealed.

Cree explained to the jury what had caused Carl Fowler to pull the trigger on his shotgun and why it was important to identify your target before you shoot. He explained that Carl Fowler did not identify his target and that, as shown by the MVD, he had limited visibility looking through the brush.

The ADA then shifted gears and began to ask Cree general questions about turkey hunting. The warden stated that he had been hunting turkeys for approximately fifteen years, that he had bagged eighty-eight gobblers, and that he regularly wrote turkey-hunting articles for hunting magazines. The court then qualified him as an expert in turkey hunting. Warden Cree looked over at attorney Hill just in time to see him roll his eyes.

The ADA then asked what tactics are used in turkey hunting, how many species there are, what species we have in this state, and what the colors of a hen and a gobbler are. When the ADA finished, it was time for Hill to question the warden.

Hill attempted to pick apart the reconstruction techniques used, but Cree did not give him the satisfaction. Hill began telling the jury how Warden Lender had been dressed and how the brown bug-tamer jacket he had been wearing looked much like the color of a turkey; in fact . . . if he had one here he would show the jury.

Warden Cree took this moment to interrupt him. "I have one of them over in that box under the prosecution's table."

The ADA took his cue, reached into the box, and brought the jacket out to show the court and the jury. This had just the effect Warden Cree wanted. It was clear that the jacket was a surprise and threw Hill off a little.

Again, Cree had his own thoughts: *He just got sucker punched.*

Attorney Hill strolled over to the ADA, took the bug-tamer jacket, and went back to the jury box, sort of stammering through how it looked like the color of a turkey. He then directed his attention back to Warden Cree and went through another series of questions about the evidence and reconstruction. Hill then talked about the visibility his client had at the time the shot was fired and questioned how Warden Cree had come up with 65 percent visibility.

Cree explained how he used the MVD and how it worked. Hill then questioned its accuracy by asking the warden if it wasn't just a guess. Cree stated that it was an estimate. The attorney then strolled over in front of the jury box and stated, "If I had one of those measurement of visibility devices, I would show . . ." Again the warden cut the attorney off in midsentence: "I've got one of those devices over in the box at the prosecution table."

And again, as if on cue, the ADA reached into the box and brought the device out for the court to see. Cree could tell that this had surprised Hill again and that the attorney's train of thought had been interrupted.

When Hill regained his composure, he strolled over to ADA Beasley and took the MVD from him, announcing to the courtroom, "So this is a measurement of visibility device."

He asked Cree to show him and the court how the device worked. Hill went around the courtroom, hiding parts of the MVD behind chairs, poles, and tables and asking the warden to determine the visibility.

Cree kept his cool, and with each answer he told the court this was estimation and not a guess. After Cree had been on the witness stand for over two hours, attorney Hill finally finished questioning the warden and he was allowed to step down.

The next witness called was Warden Dave Peters. Peters did not help the case against Carl Fowler at all. When questioned by ADA Beasley, he kept his answers short and to the point. However, when questioned by Hill, he volunteered more information than necessary.

The first question Hill asked was "What did you think when you heard the gunshot?"

Peters replied, "I hope that was not Tom."

Attorney Hill began to insinuate that Warden Lender was overbearing and gung-ho. Peters did nothing to deny these innuendos or defend Warden Lender. After Peters stepped down, Warden Leo Neely was called to testify. Just as with Peters, Neely did nothing to help the case against Carl Fowler, and his testimony was very similar to Peters's. He too did not defend Lender when Hill insinuated that Lender was a little too zealous in his work.

After Neely stepped down from the witness stand, ADA Beasley turned to Warden Cree and said, "You know what has happened, don't you?"

Cree replied, "Those two have been talking with the defense." This frustrated the ADA, and Cree was furious.

All was quiet in the courtroom when Warden Lender was called to the stand. ADA Beasley began his questions, and Lender answered as best he could. He testified that he had spoken to the hunter and said "Hey" just before he was shot but also stated that he did not remember much after he was shot.

He then described his injuries. When the ADA finished his line of questions, it was time for attorney Hill to cross-examine the warden.

From the first question, Lender's responses were not beneficial to the case. He got angry, and that anger showed. He answered every question angrily, and the jurors watched his demeanor change. This played into what Hill had set up with Wardens Peters and Neely about Lender being overbearing. After Hill asked the last question, Lender looked at the jury and barked out, "He shot me!"

Both the ADA and Warden Cree knew that Lender's testimony and demeanor on the stand had not helped the case.

The defense then called their own turkey-hunting expert, who claimed to have bagged over 150 turkey gobblers. This expert testified how brown a turkey gobbler looked out in the woods. It was time for Cree to shake his head. Every turkey hunter knows a gobbler's feathers are black and a hen's feathers are brown.

After the defense expert testified, Pam Fowler took the stand and testified that she had seen the turkey coming toward the decoy and watched it fan out and strut. The rest of her testimony was in line with the statement she had given SBI Agent Ronnie George in her interview.

Finally Hill called Carl Fowler to the stand. His testimony was identical to the statement he had given Agent Comer. He too testified that he had seen a turkey coming toward the decoy and watched it fan out and strut. Carl Fowler was the last witness; when he stepped down, the trial was about over.

Cree listened as ADA Beasley and attorney Hill gave their closing arguments. He thought the ADA did an outstanding job trying to prosecute this case and believed it could not have been presented any better. However, he did not know if this was enough to get a conviction.

After closing statements, the judge charged the jury with their duties and sent them to the jury room to deliberate. The judge then called for a recess. Warden Cree left the courthouse, purchased a sub sandwich for a late lunch, brought it back to the courthouse, and sat on a bench on the courthouse lawn to eat it.

He had just taken one bite when a court official came up to him and said, "The jury is back; you are needed in the courtroom."

He knew from experience that this was too soon to be good. The jury had deliberated for less than an hour. Inside the courtroom, the bailiff called the courtroom to order, the judge took the bench, and the verdict was read: "As to the charge of Misuse of a Firearm. We the jury find the defendant, Carl Fowler, not guilty."

Carl Fowler and his family rejoiced as Warden Lender and his wife left the courtroom. Cree could tell that Lender was not happy, and he had every right not to be. Hill came up to Cree while he was gathering his documents and stuck out his hand.

Cree locked eyes with the attorney and shook his hand, but the two never spoke a word to each other. The three-day trial was over.

But no conviction or acquittal is the last word for any trial, and this one is no different. Carl Fowler still hunted after the trial. He was caught illegally hunting on a baited dove field later in the year and charged. He still resides in Moore County.

Regarding this specific case, Cree was never completely convinced that Carl Fowler had been the shooter. Even though he took the blame, the evidence at the incident scene suggested that an inexperienced hunter had operated the firearm. He always believed there was a good possibility that Pam Fowler had been the actual shooter.

Neely and Peters would be given meritorious service and life-saving awards for the actions they took to save Tom Lender's life.

And the victim? Warden Lender continued to heal from his physical wounds. However, his right leg will always give him trouble, and he still walks with a slight limp. After the trial, Lender became increasingly angry and frustrated. He was angry with Carl Fowler, he was angry with attorney Andrew Hill, he was angry with the members of the jury, he was angry with Wardens Neely and Peters for their testimony, and he was angry about the situation as a whole.

Warden Lender was knowledgeable enough to seek counseling and learned to work through these issues. And when he was able, he retained an attorney to represent his and his family's interest.

During the criminal trial, unknown to everyone, Carl Fowler's homeowner's insurance policy adjuster had sat in and listened to the entire trial. Immediately after the trial, he wrote Warden Lender a check for the maximum allowance for the policy.

About a week after the trial was over, Lender's attorney contacted Warden Cree. The hunting club where the incident occurred had its own liability insurance policy. The attorney had given a copy of the case file to the adjuster of the company that wrote the policy. The reenactment video Warden Cree had made was not included but was listed in a supplemental report. The attorney asked Warden Cree for a copy of the video, and Cree hand-carried one to him. About a week after this, the insurance adjuster wrote Warden Lender a check for the maximum amount.

Warden Lender was forced to retire from the state wildlife law enforcement agency on disability because of his injuries, but he made it known that he did not want to retire. When Warden Cree ran into him a couple of years after the incident, he seemed to be his old self again. The twinkle was back in his eyes and he was still somewhat of a jokester.

Lessons Learned

- The shooter violated one of the most important rules of firearm safety: "Be sure of your target and what is in front of and beyond it."
- The shooter never attended a Hunter Education course. In that state, he was exempted because of his age, but the course would have refreshed his memory about ensuring that all his hunts were both ethical and safe.
- Having well-trained, expert investigators is vital to any incident. The detailed re-creation, including videotape of this incident, did not have an impact at the criminal trial but played an important role in the victim's financial compensation.

14

Just Foolin' Around . . .

Any man can make mistakes, but only an idiot persists in his error.

—Cicero

ROBERT AND JASON WERE BEST FRIENDS AND NEIGHBORS, LIVING just down the road from each other. They had grown up together and loved to hike and explore in the woods behind their houses.

When they were old enough, they took the state-mandated Hunter Education class together, and the competition was fierce. Jason got the bragging rights; he got a perfect 100, while Robert only got a 98! Now they were finally old enough to hunt small game by themselves, and they went out as often as they could.

It was early fall, and squirrels were in season. They had been slowly walking the ridge behind the houses with their .22 rifles with no luck; now it was time to get home for supper. They arrived at Robert's house first and stood on the back deck as they unloaded their rifles. Robert had a magazine-fed semiautomatic; Jason had a tubular-fed bolt action.

Finished with the work, Robert went into the house then turned and waved at Jason through the large plate-glass window that looked out onto the back deck. Jason smiled back and, just joking around, raised and pointed his "unloaded" rifle at his closest friend. Finishing off the joke, he squeezed the trigger; the gun went off and *bam!* the window shattered.

Jason dropped his gun, terrified to see what had happened. He was relieved to see that his friend was still alive. Cut by the flying glass shards, Robert was horrified at the thought that he had almost died because his best friend was "just screwing around." Fortunately for both boys, the heavy plate glass had stopped the bullet.

The reaction from the families was as strong as you would expect. There were threats of lawsuits, demands, and declarations: "You are never going over to his house ever again" and "How can you be sure it was just an accident?" Eventually they all got over it—both the boys and their parents—and life went back to almost normal. But everyone would also say it was never quite the same.

Lessons Learned

- Always treat every gun as though it is loaded. Even if you just unloaded it or someone else did, treat every gun as though it is loaded all the time.
- Always keep the muzzle pointed in a safe direction. Never point at anything you do not want to shoot.
- Know your firearm thoroughly, including how to check to ensure it is unloaded. Tube-fed rifles, .22s in particular, can get a round stuck in the bottom of the tube. Work the action several times with the muzzle pointed in a safe direction to be sure all rounds have indeed been removed.

15

A Boar-ing Fourth of July

If you prick us do we not bleed? If you tickle us do we not laugh?
If you poison us do we not die? And if you wrong us shall we not revenge?

—WILLIAM SHAKESPEARE

IT HAD HAPPENED IN AN INSTANT. THERE WAS A SOUND OF crunching leaves in the thicket. Blood was already beginning to pool around Bobby Smith. The wound on his wrist was spurting blood, and it crossed Bobby's mind that he might bleed to death. He couldn't think about that now. A bigger problem was staring at him—literally. Bobby knew that if he didn't act quickly and make the right decisions, he might not make it out alive.

Bobby Smith and his hunting buddy, Mike Pool, had decided to go hunting on the Fourth of July. They met up at their hunting club in Duvall County, and the morning actually started off nicely for the two hunters. The weather was great, a perfect morning to be out in the woods. Not long after sunrise, Bobby and Mike spotted a big black wild hog in a large field on their club property. The hog looked to be about 350 yards away. With no way to stalk any closer, Bobby decided to take the shot. He propped up, steadied himself and his firearm, took aim through the scope, and settled the crosshairs right behind the hog's shoulder. Bobby squeezed the trigger on his Remington bolt-action .243 caliber rifle and sent the bullet toward his target. The hog flinched at the report of the muzzle blast, and Bobby heard the bullet make a smacking sound as it hit its target. The hog did not go down; instead it ran along the tree line and out of sight. Bobby didn't know it then, but he had missed the hog's heart by about an inch.

Knowing the hog was hit, Mike went to get their truck while Bobby took off through the field on foot. Bobby went to the place he had last seen the hog and found blood. He followed the blood a short distance and could see that it led into a thicket about the size of a small car.

The boar hog felt the force of the impact from the bullet behind his shoulder. His two-hundred-pound frame withstood the blow, and he did not go down. He flinched and instinctively ran for the first cover he saw, a small thicket in the field.

About this time he saw a predator walking in the field toward the thicket where he had taken cover. The boar's instincts told him this was the predator that had hurt him. The predator was stalking him.

Bobby neared the thicket where the blood trail led, fully expecting any second to see a hog lying dead. Meanwhile, the boar watched as Bobby approached the thicket. As Bobby neared, the boar took the offensive and charged the predator that was stalking him.

All Bobby heard was the crunching of leaves in the thicket before the two-hundred-pound boar was on him in a flash, taking his feet from under him. He had just enough time to fire his rifle from the hip, with the bullet missing the boar by just a few inches. Bobby fell on his back, and the boar was instantly on top of him.

Using his tusks, the boar worked his head back and forth to cut the predator that had been stalking him. It backed off, only to charge again, burying a tusk in Bobby's arm. Bobby tried using his rifle as a club to hold back the boar's head as it charged into him again and again. Each time the boar charged, his tusks sliced into Bobby's flesh.

On one of its bone-jarring charges, the boar drove his head hard into Bobby's abdomen. Luckily, Bobby's binoculars blocked the blow as the boar's tusks tried to cut into his body just above the lenses; the binoculars kept Bobby's gut from being ripped open.

Bobby never felt any pain, and he did not have time to be afraid; he was just fighting for his life. The Remington bolt-action rifle was getting its own bite marks and gouges along the barrel. Exhausted, Bobby could see the blood pooling on the ground around him.

As the boar backed off to charge again, Bobby knew he was hurt badly and that this might be his last chance. He worked the action on his Remington to chamber his last round and locked eyes with the boar.

As the boar lowered his head to charge again, Bobby squeezed the trigger at point-blank range, sending his last bullet into the chest of the boar. This time the boar went down, and Bobby felt his first bit of relief since the attack had begun. While the boar's attack had lasted only minutes, it seemed like a lifetime to Bobby. He could see blood spurting out of a gash on his wrist. Using his good hand, he kept direct pressure on the gash to slow the bleeding.

Mike had heard the shots but did not suspect anything was wrong. But when he drove up in the truck and saw both Bobby and the hog on the ground, he knew something was not right. Mike immediately helped Bobby into the truck and rushed him to the Duvall County Hospital emergency room.

That is where Bobby found out just how badly he was hurt. One of the boar's tusks had severed the artery in his wrist and sliced through three tendons. The tusks had also sliced through his boot and severed his calf muscle. It looked like a small explosion had gone off inside his lower leg.

It took orthopedic and vascular surgeons nearly four hours to repair the damage the boar's tusks had inflicted on Bobby. He had lost three pints of blood during the attack, and if he had not killed the boar when he did, he might not have survived.

Being a true hunter, Bobby told Mike to retrieve the boar and have it processed at the butcher's. Bobby even had the boar's skull cleaned and a place picked out on the wall to hang the skull, with its four-inch tusks . . . the trophy that came very close to costing him his life.

Warden Tom Skipper got the call on this hunting incident on the afternoon of July 4. Skipper is a member of his agency's Critical Incident Reconstruction Team (CIRT), which is tasked to investigate and reconstruct the state's most serious hunting incidents and boating accidents. When he first got the information on this hunting incident, he could not believe what he was hearing. When the victim was released from the hospital, Skipper interviewed him at home to take down all the pertinent information and fill out the required hunting incident forms. After verifying the events, the warden would later comment to his CIRT supervisor, Warden Brian Cree, "You are not going to believe this."

Lessons Learned

- First aid and survival are important parts of all Hunter Education courses. Being prepared to take care of yourself or your fellow hunters can literally be a life-or-death situation. Most injuries while hunting are not firearm related, but cuts with knives or broad heads or trip-and-fall injuries.
- Always have at least basic first aid supplies handy and have a way to call for help if you get injured.

16

One Step Back, Two Steps Forward

If you don't like the way the world is, you change it. You have
an obligation to change it. You just do it one step at a time.
—MARIAN WRIGHT EDELMAN

THE FALL AFTER THE FROG HUNTER SHOT ME, I WAS WORKING
with a state trooper friend when we got a call to go see a local
judge at his house. When we arrived, the judge explained that a
hunter had just shot at his sons, both in their twenties, and almost
killed them.

As we questioned the young men, they explained they were
walking across an open field back toward their truck when a doe
ran out of the woods, across the field, between them and the road.
They could clearly see a house right across the road, so they didn't
consider taking a shot at the deer.

Suddenly a car skidded to a stop in front of the house and a
guy stepped out into the middle of the road. They watched as he
put his shotgun on the top of his car and started shooting at the
doe and, as a result of their position, at them! They hit the ground
as they heard the slugs hit the dirt all around them. They had both
been wearing blaze orange from head to toe. How could this guy
possibly not see them?

They took us to the scene of the incident, and we took pictures that clearly showed their imprints like snow angels; we could see the skid marks from the slugs that had barely missed them. We talked to the lady who lived in the house across the road, and she verified their story. She explained that she had been standing at the roadside waiting for the school bus with her daughter when this "crazy guy" stopped right in front of them and started shooting from the middle of the road!

We had a great case here. Nobody was hurt, but there were several witnesses and plenty of charges to be filed. We took statements from the two hunters and the neighbor and sat down to collaborate on the case file for the district attorney. The charges would include "Reckless Endangerment," "Possessing a Loaded Firearm in a Motor Vehicle," "Discharging a Firearm within Five Hundred Feet of a Residence," "Attempting to Take Wildlife from or across a Roadway," and "Attempting to Take Wildlife with the Aid of a Motor Vehicle."

My trooper friend and I put together a thorough and impressive file and made an appointment to see the DA to ask him to prosecute these crimes. We were stunned by his response.

Although it seemed he was listening to our story, he took a quick look at the file and then, literally, just tossed it back to us across his desk.

"Anyone who is damn fool enough to go into the woods during deer season deserves to be shot at! Get out of here!" he said curtly.

Through this incident and others, I knew there was something more that could, and should, be done in regard to documenting these incidents. Too many times, if a hunting-related shooting even managed to make it into a newspaper, it was several days after the fact, with vague details.

Any investigation would be limited to having a wildlife officer stop by the local sheriff's office to get a copy of a very basic report. The overall mind-set at most agencies was that these were "just accidents." They were not seen as a high priority, and officers received no training as to how to handle them.

Eight years later, when I was a lieutenant in the Investigations Bureau, another lieutenant became more interested in how we investigated these hunting accidents as well. In our area we had several fatal cases that were only being documented with such seemingly innocuous phrases as "Hunter A shot at a running deer and killed Hunter B. It was just an accident."

There were no real police investigations, and no background checks were ever run on the hunters. There might be a ticket here and there for not having the right licenses or maybe some other violations of the wildlife laws, but there was no accountability for shooting people. The general attitude, from hunters and law enforcement alike, seemed to be that if you went hunting you might get shot. It was nobody's fault; it just happened.

My coworker came up with the idea to review all accidents in the state for the past five years; I was very happy to help on this project. We would collect our own data, including a criminal history on all shooters, and see what we could find out. Soon, several patterns emerged.

The first result we saw was that many of the shooters involved in these "accidents" should never have been carrying firearms to begin with, as they had criminal records. In fact, these shooters were two and a half times more likely to have a criminal record compared with the general population! The convictions covered the spectrum, from DWI to assaults to sex crimes. These convictions made it another crime for them to even touch a firearm, let alone take one hunting and end up shooting someone. Finally, much to our surprise, in a few cases the computer check revealed that the shooter did not exist! A number of the hunters involved in shooting incidents had obtained their hunting licenses under false names. The officers at the incident scene had never thought to ask to see any other identification.

By good coincidence, we were just pulling a report of this study together when the new fall deer season rolled around. Perhaps we would get a chance to put our new knowledge to work in the field. I never thought I would become a statistic in the report—a victim of the people we were studying. But my personal experience gave me even more reason to help motivate the agencies to change their methods.

Lessons Learned

- Safety must always be the first thing on every hunter's mind. It is far more important to be safe than to get a full game bag. No trophy is worth hurting another hunter . . . or worse. This shooter was willing to violate a long list of laws—in the middle of the road, right in front of witnesses—and almost hit two other hunters.
- Be sure that there is a safe backstop every time you shoot. Two hunters in blaze orange walking across a snow-covered field are pretty hard to miss, if you are paying attention.
- Justice can be fleeting. It is the job of the investigator to put together the best possible case file. After that, it is up to the prosecutor, the judge, and the jury to do their parts; but justice is best served when first responders do their very best.

17

Left Behind

*We never fail when we try to do our duty; we always fail
when we neglect to do it.*

—ROBERT BADEN-POWELL

PAUL SMITS WAS YOUR TYPICAL FIFTEEN-YEAR-OLD BOY. HE
liked movies, girls, guns, and hunting, not necessarily in that
order. Bottom line: He loved life. Paul had been born in another
country along with an older brother, and his mother, Tammy,
had moved them to the United States. She had divorced their
father and come across the Big Pond to make a new and better
life for them. Paul loved America and the freedoms that came
from living here. As a boy just on the verge of becoming a man, he
was enjoying the transition and doing things young men do. He
looked forward to going to the shooting range for target practice.
Along with shooting, he enjoyed hunting. Paul's love for guns and
shooting had influenced him so thoroughly that he already had a
career plan in mind after he graduated high school. He was going
to join the US Air Force.

Paul's mother had met George Thompson shortly after they
arrived in America. He took a "likin" to Tammy right off, and the
courtship began. George was an avid outdoorsman and loved to

be out in the woods; he hunted all types of game, but his favorites were wild hogs, wild turkeys, and deer. One of his favorite places to hunt was a state wildlife management area (WMA) near where he lived.

Tammy liked this outdoorsman side of George and eventually accepted his proposal of marriage. George not only got a new bride but also became stepfather to two young boys. Like many newlyweds, Tammy discovered something about her groom she had not known during their courtship: George had a temper.

On March 7, Paul got up with two things on his mind. Loving the outdoors, he was excited to go hunting with his stepfather. Also loving movies, he was anxious to watch the Academy Awards telecast that night because *The Hurt Locker*, a movie he liked very much, had been nominated for several awards.

The morning had started out cold; Paul had gotten up to thirty-degree weather, but it was gradually warming. By the time his stepfather decided it was time to go hunting that afternoon, it had warmed up into the low sixties. The weather was great for hunting—a sunny, almost-clear sky with just a cloud here and there. He and his stepfather got their hunting equipment ready, meaning they put their guns in the truck and George put his GPS unit in his pocket. The area George planned for them to hunt was his favorite, the WMA; located right off a major river system, it had a special two-week wild hog season going on.

To George and all the locals, the area was known as the Tupelo Swamp. It was somewhat rugged terrain, with swampy sections along with dry hammocks crisscrossed with river sloughs. He knew the area very well, but he still carried the GPS unit, mostly for marking future hunting locations.

George and Paul drove out of their yard and headed toward the WMA. Paul was excited to be going hunting and hoped he would get a shot at something that afternoon. George pulled the truck off the paved road onto a dirt road and drove a short distance. He parked near a property adjacent to the WMA the locals called the Oaky Community.

George and Paul got out of the truck and loaded all three of their guns—a Remington .22 caliber rim-fire rifle with a scope, a Mossberg Model 835 12-gauge pump shotgun, and a Stoeger semiautomatic 12-gauge shotgun. They got their hunting equipment in order, including a ThermaCELL to keep the mosquitoes at bay, but decided to leave their cell phones in the truck. This was a hunting trip, and they did not want anyone giving them a call that might spook the game they were after. Furthermore, this was a river swamp; they knew that wading water was just part of the hunt and that a cell phone and water don't mix.

Paul pulled on his waders and a jacket while George applied hunter's camouflage paint to his face. Paul slipped his camouflage mask over his head. Together, George and Paul left the truck and began walking through the Tupelo Swamp in search of game.

George and Paul hunted through the WMA for the rest of afternoon into the evening. They ended up several miles from their parked vehicle without seeing any game. It was getting late and the temperature was dropping, so George decided it was time to call it a day. Paul was glad; he had had about all the fun he could stand for one day. Walking in those hip waders and wading through water for hours had been tough; he was tired.

Before too long, two problems became evident to both the hunters. One, they were a long way from their vehicle; two, it was getting late. Without any choice, they began the long hike back to their truck. George took lead and, try as he might, it was hard for Paul to keep up.

Paul constantly fell behind, which angered George. And with the temperature dropping as night fell upon them, they were going to be in a serious situation if they did not get out of the Tupelo Swamp soon. Still miles from their vehicle, Paul constantly had to stop and rest. He was exhausted.

George was furious! They were going to be caught in the swamp after dark just because his stepson could not keep up. He was already carrying all three guns; now he was going to have to physically help Paul through the swamp. He did not like it, not one bit.

As darkness fell on the Tupelo Swamp, closing in around the two hunters, the temperature began to plunge almost to freezing. George knew they were in very serious trouble. He had been using the GPS unit to mark locations along their route, and the batteries were getting weak. It would not be long before the unit lost power completely.

Still moving forward in the direction of the truck and trying to get his stepson to pick up his pace, George's agitation grew. Several hours after dark, and still more than two miles from the truck, Paul gave out. Totally exhausted, he could not go any farther.

Paul's strength failed while he was wading through a particularly wet area in the swamp. He came to rest on his knees in twelve to eighteen inches of water. George tried to get him to get up, but Paul, cold from the dropping temperature and exhausted from all the walking, could not get his feet and legs to move. He just sat there in the water. George, carrying all the guns with him, turned and walked away in the dark, leaving his stepson behind, exhausted and on his knees in the cold water.

Tammy Thompson began to worry when her husband and son did not come back from their hunting trip. It was after dark, and they were way overdue. By 8:30 p.m., she was really concerned; she knew Paul really wanted to watch the Academy Awards. With the broadcast about to come on and still no sign of her husband and son, she decided it was time to give them a call. After numerous calls to their cell phones went unanswered, her worry began to edge into panic. She began to telephone members of George's family and discussed calling the police, but her husband's family told her she was overreacting.

They assured her that George and Paul were fine. George knew the woods and swamps like the back of his hand because he had hunted the area most of his life. This did not ease Tammy's mind. She decided to drive over to the area where her husband usually parked his truck and see for herself.

She could drive in only so far once she left the paved road, so she parked and walked the rest of the way on foot. As she walked, Tammy could feel the cold, frosty air against her face and body; it was freezing. Luckily, it wasn't long before she found her husband's parked truck. Looking around, she saw no sign of either her son or husband. There in the dark, she dialed her son's cell phone again. Immediately she noticed a cell phone light up on the console inside her husband's truck. Realizing it was her son's, she really began to panic.

George walked approximately thirty yards from his stepson before he found dry ground. Instead of going back to help his stepson out of the water, he left him behind.

Standing there in the dark, George heard what he thought might be his stepson talking. He would later state that it had been his stepson making a gurgling sound. George did not check on his stepson's condition. In fact, he really did not care what happened to him. If he could not keep up, could not carry his load; if he could not make it out on his own, George sure wasn't going to help him. Paul could stay there all night as far as George was concerned. Who knows, it might teach Paul a lesson and make him more of a man.

In the cold water of the swamp, Paul's core body temperature slowly dropped to a dangerous level. He had been shivering uncontrollably, but now his shivering was beginning to subside. He actually had a somewhat warming feeling on the outside of his skin. What Paul did not realize was that he was developing a deadly case of hypothermia. It was not long before Paul's thinking was not clear and he began to feel very sleepy. Still on his knees in the twelve to eighteen inches of water where he had first fallen, Paul succumbed to the hypothermia that sapped his body. His core temperature plunging to a deadly degree, Paul lost consciousness and fell forward, face down in the cold water. The sound George heard had not been talking at all. With his stepfather listening just yards away, Paul was drowning. When the gurgling stopped, he was dead.

At fifteen years of age, Paul died cold and alone in the Tupelo Swamp as his stepfather listened to his last breaths. He had played many roles that day, first and foremost as a son, then as a hunter while pursuing game with his stepfather. As the darkness and hypothermia set in, alone and scared in the Tupelo Swamp, the life left his young body and he became a victim.

At some point, George walked approximately one hundred yards from his stepson's body, laid the .22 caliber rifle down at the base of a big oak tree, and leaned the Mossberg 12-gauge shotgun against it. He also put down his ThermaCELL and canteen. George gathered up tree limbs and placed them in a pile as though to make a fire. He took a buckshot shot shell and cut it open to expose the gunpowder inside and shot four times with turkey-hunting loads. He would later state that he did this to try to start a fire because his Bic lighter had gotten wet and would not work. He also ejected one live shell round onto the ground. After all this was done, he picked up the most expensive gun of the three he carried, the Stoeger shotgun, and began to make his way out of the swamp.

It was after midnight before Tammy and family members decided to notify the Moore County sheriff's office. The sheriff's office contacted other rescue personnel and the state's wildlife law enforcement agency to assist in the search. After all personnel were briefed on the situation, the search for the two hunters began; it was 3:15 a.m. on March 8.

The WMA covered nearly thirty thousand acres of river swamp, hammocks, and sloughs, and the wildlife officers familiar with the area knew it was rough terrain. At night, in the dark, it would be nearly impossible to search. About the only thing that could be done was to ride the access roads and trails and hope for the best until morning. All rescue personnel split up into teams to try their best.

George made it out of the woods around 6:15 a.m. on March 8. He had left two guns and all his hunting equipment at the big oak tree, one hundred yards from his stepson's body. He did bring out the Stoeger 12-gauge shotgun and the GPS unit. Once out of the swamp, he walked past several houses without stopping or knocking or trying to get help and finally ended up at a friend's house. Once there, the sheriff and others were finally called.

He was cold and appeared to be somewhat disoriented. He told his story of what had happened during the hunt—how they had become lost and as they wandered through the swamp, trying to find their way out, his GPS unit had malfunctioned . . . how Paul had become too tired to walk any farther and he had carried him as far as he could. He later stated he could not carry

Paul anymore and made the decision to leave him and go for help. George claimed his decision was necessitated by the weather and circumstances. After talking with investigators and changing his clothes, George was now ready to help in the search for his stepson.

With the coming of dawn, the search efforts from all agencies involved intensified. The state wildlife law enforcement agency took the lead in the search and was joined by the state police; they immediately dispatched their helicopter to the search area. State corrections officials brought in their bloodhounds for tracking. By midmorning, the search for Paul had grown into a multiagency effort involving not only the Moore County Sheriff's Department and state agencies but also county firefighters, local city police, county rescue personnel, and many volunteers. By noon, despite all these searchers and assets, Paul still could not be located.

About this time, one of the game wardens decided to take a look at the GPS unit George was using in the swamp and said had malfunctioned. The warden went to the Thompsons' residence and retrieved the GPS unit. A quick examination determined that the unit's batteries were dead and it just needed recharging. The warden recharged the unit.

Using the information found on the GPS unit, the searchers split up into three teams. One team would take the GPS information and try to backtrack off those locations, another team would take George back to the swamp and see if he could retrace his steps to Paul's location, while the third team would use assets such as the helicopter and bloodhounds to continue to try to pick up a trail.

Warden Ryan Croft ended up on the team with George. Warden Croft had worked for the state wildlife law enforcement agency for many years and was a member of their Critical Incident

Reconstruction Team (CIRT). This team was tasked with investigating and reconstructing some of the state's most serious hunting incidents and boating accidents. He was no stranger to these types of situations.

The warden and several other searchers took George back to the Tupelo Swamp and began their search. It was rugged terrain and slow going, especially following George's lead. Before long, Croft noticed that George seemed to know the swamp a lot better than Croft realized. As George made his way through the swamp, he pointed out places where he had killed a deer, a particular ridge where he had killed several turkeys.

As George continued to make these comments all along the search route, Croft wondered why George could remember the places he had killed game animals so well but could not remember where he had left his stepson. The warden also began to realize that at times George was leading them in circles. Croft began to get very concerned about George's behavior.

In another area of the Tupelo Swamp, Warden Jerry Wade, WMA manager Steve Tubbs, and other county officers were backtracking the coordinates found on George's GPS unit, doing a line search through the area along the route the coordinates indicated. Approximately three miles from the nearest paved road, one of the searchers found the big oak tree where George had left the guns and hunting gear.

Wade, Tubbs, and the other county officers immediately began to do a spiral search out from the area. Slowly extending their search from the center of the big oak tree area, they were approximately one hundred yards from the big oak tree when they discovered Paul's body.

It was 3:00 p.m. and the search was in its twelfth hour. The men found the victim lying face down in the water and fully clothed. Wade immediately radioed in, advising everyone they had found the boy. Wade gave them the location's GPS coordinates, which were then given to the state police helicopter. The helicopter flew to the location to act as a hovering reference point so that other searchers and law enforcement could find the scene. The search was over, but the case was just beginning.

It took Warden Croft more than an hour to get to the scene. Once there, Wade took him through the scene and pointed out what they had found at the tree. He then took him to the body. After viewing the evidence at the scene, Croft thought the scene at the tree looked staged.

It seemed to his experienced eye that everything had been put in place after the fact to give the appearance that something had taken place when it actually hadn't. At this point, the Moore County sheriff decided to bring in the state Bureau of Investigation to assist on the case. This was definitely a suspicious death of a young person, and the sheriff wanted to make sure he covered all the bases to find out what had actually taken place in the swamp the night before.

At 4:45 p.m., the victim's body was still at the scene in the swamp. The state Bureau of Investigation was beginning to process the scene with assistance from the state wildlife law enforcement agency. The agencies would be doing parallel investigations—the state Bureau of Investigation because it was a suspicious death of a young person and the state wildlife agency because it fit the definition of a "hunting incident." In the meantime, workers and searchers were trying to cut a half-mile passageway from a dirt WMA access road to the scene in order to retrieve the victim's body. The scene was processed at 6:30 p.m., when the victim's body was finally brought out of the swamp and transported to the state crime lab for examination.

The autopsy report was made available a few weeks later. This report revealed that Paul had died from drowning due to developing hypothermia. George's account of what had happened in the swamp began to change.

At first he said he had left his stepson on high ground. Later he said he had left Paul standing in shallow water and had walked a short distance alone, found dry ground, and tried unsuccessfully to start a fire. Family members and other persons questioned during the investigation all said George knew that area of the swamp like the back of his hand. This led investigators to believe that George was hiding something.

On June 17, the state Bureau of Investigation secured warrants for George Thompson. He was charged with Felony Murder and Cruelty to Children. The warrants stated that Paul Smits (victim) had died as a result of George Thompson's (stepfather) actions. Tim Dugan was the agent in charge of the state Bureau of Investigation's office that covered the Moore County area. Agent Dugan explained that Felony Murder is sometimes charged when someone dies as a result of another crime, in this case, Cruelty to a Child. Dugan stated that Thompson had left the teen unattended at night in a swamp without a light, sufficient clothing, and the materials necessary to maintain a sufficient body temperature to survive. The investigators involved with the case believed Thompson could have done more. Officers arrested Thompson on the same day the warrants were secured.

George Thompson appeared before the superior court judge in Moore County the next morning. The judge ordered him released on his own recognizance. Everyone involved with the case thought this to be odd considering the severity of the charges.

The case took on another strange twist when it was scheduled to be presented to the Moore County grand jury during the month of December. By a strange coincidence, Thompson was called to serve on the very grand jury that was going to be tasked with deciding whether to indict him!

The district attorney was informed of this turn of events and was as surprised as everyone else. The prosecutor immediately withdrew the case and made plans to present it before the next grand jury.

On May 16, District Attorney Harvey Wilds presented the case to the grand jury and George Thompson was indicted on two counts of Malice Murder and a single count each of Felony Murder, Involuntary Manslaughter, Second-Degree Cruelty to Children, and Contributing to the Deprivation of a Minor.

On May 18, the superior court judge received the indictment. Based on evidence uncovered during the investigation, the indictment was clear about Thompson's role in his stepson's death. The charges included "malice aforethought" by causing him to drown, "reckless disregard" for his stepson's life by leaving him alone in the swamp at night when the young boy, who was weak and fatigued, wasn't wearing adequate clothing to survive in the cold, wet environment. His conduct was "extremely negligent" and created an unjustified and very high degree of risk of death or serious injury to the victim.

The Felony Murder count was clear as well. George Thompson had killed Paul Smits according to the laws pertaining to the felony crime of Second-Degree Cruelty to Children by intentionally leaving the young boy alone and unprepared in the cold, dark swamp. His actions caused "cruel and excessive mental pain" to the victim. The indictment charged George with Involuntary Manslaughter via reckless conduct in disregarding the danger to the safety of his stepson. Finally, the deprivation charge stated that

George had failed to provide proper parental care and control necessary for Paul Smits's "physical, mental, and emotional health."

More than a year passed before George entered a Moore County courtroom to be tried before a jury of his peers on those charges. His trial began in early October. By this time, Tammy, Paul's mother, had divorced him. The trial lasted five days, and jurors deliberated nearly six hours before reaching a guilty verdict on the charges of Involuntary Manslaughter and Contributing to the Deprivation of a Minor.

The superior court judge presiding over the case sentenced George Thompson to five years in prison plus five years probation. Everyone thought the case was finally over.

George had served approximately two months of his sentence when the case took on another twist. George's attorneys learned that one of the jurors who heard the case, and voted on the two guilty verdicts, had contacted a family member during the trial.

During a hearing before a superior court judge, the juror testified that he had talked to Paul's older brother in the courthouse during the trial. The juror had also sent text messages to Paul's brother during the trial. George's attorneys asked the judge to grant a new trial based on juror misconduct.

The judge ruled that the juror's texting and talking with the brother was intentional and therefore warranted a new trial. George's attorneys immediately asked for a bond hearing, and he was released from jail on a six-thousand-dollar bond.

In April of the next year, now a little more than three years after the hunt, George Thompson accepted a plea bargain offered by the district attorney. He pleaded guilty to Deprivation of a Minor that resulted in the death of a minor and was sentenced to five years' probation.

Lessons Learned

- There are no real lessons an investigator can learn from this case that cannot be learned from real life. People are capable of extraordinary kindness and extraordinary cruelty. You will be surprised on both counts at who chooses which path.
- A thorough investigation of every case is the first step to true justice; every victim, and his or her family, deserves that.
- Always be prepared for the worst when you enter the woods to hunt. Carrying some basic survival gear and cell phones in waterproof sandwich bags could have saved a boy's life.
- Planning your hunt and sticking to that plan is always important. Keeping track of time and how far you have wandered from your vehicle helps you know when it is time to head back.

18

Hunting "Accident" or Murder?

Justice delayed is justice denied.
—William E. Gladstone

As we read reports submitted for our review, we sometimes shudder at the paths some investigations have taken. As a course of business, we make ourselves available for both civil and criminal cases as they connect with hunting-related shootings. We do not accept every case that is presented to us; we review the particulars of each case and evaluate the situation based on numerous criteria.

As with most opportunities in life, sometimes you only get one chance to "get it right the first time." In our business, when a case falls apart, it could be due to lack of attention, lack of administrative support, being led in a wrong direction, or just not having an investigative team with the knowledge and skill sets to collect all the facts in a "timely and correct manner." Every criminal case guarantees the defendant's right to due process. And in each case, you must follow the evidence.

This was a twenty-year-old cold case, and accepting it required hour after hour of reading case files, depositions, autopsy reports, and court records. The newly elected prosecutor had requested that the facts of this old case be studied as a lesson in how a group of people went on a hunt and one of the hunters didn't come home alive.

When evaluating such a hunt you must ask, "Does it make sense, and what is the evidence telling us?" We look at how each person participated. Did everyone follow the standards of firearm safety? Is what allegedly happened even physically possible? It's always important to evaluate the location of the wound and what positions a body must take to position a long gun. Is the shooter able to reach the trigger somehow and discharge the firearm in a way that resulted in contact with certain places on the body? Other factors come into play as well, such as the condition of the firearm.

This particular case took many twists and turns, and decades of time had passed. Its problems came not only because of the time delay but also because of the lack of immediate and continued actions by every person when the incident actually took place. Together these impacted the case's eventual outcome.

The hunting party involved in this particular deer hunt included Craig and Linda, a husband and wife; their daughter, Kelsey; and Linda's father, Nick. The four hunters had spread out on a property waiting to get a shot at a deer. After a little while, Craig shot at a deer with his .30-06 caliber rifle. Shortly after, he heard another shot that seemed to be rather close. Moments later he heard his daughter yelling, and it seemed to come from where Linda was hunting.

Craig headed toward the sound of the shot, thinking Linda may have shot a deer. As he headed toward the yelling, Craig saw Kelsey bent over her mother, who was lying on the ground. Linda's .243 caliber rifle was lying near her feet. Linda was lying there—not moving, not breathing. Linda's father, Nick, who had also heard the shots, ran to see what the commotion was. Craig and Nick began CPR with no success, and it became obvious that Linda had died from a gunshot wound. The group decided to transport Linda's body to town to report the incident to the sheriff's office.

Nick told the sheriff's officers that he had heard the two shots; the first one sounded like it was a larger caliber rifle. The officers seized both Craig's and Linda's rifles, as they were apparently the ones who had shot. It should be noted that no officers visited the scene that day; they waited until the next day to investigate the scene.

The next day, Craig, Kelsey, and Nick accompanied the sheriff's officers to the scene. At this time, Craig shared his version of the incident with the officers. One of the officers became doubtful that Craig was telling the truth, and these suspicions increased in the following days, weeks, and months.

Autopsy results revealed that Linda had been shot with a high-velocity projectile at close range.

In the days following the incident, facts continued to unfold that indicated possible motives involving Linda's husband, Craig. Very soon solid evidence was uncovered and Craig admitted he had been having an affair with a "Nancy Johnson." Only days after Linda's death, Craig announced he was going to marry Nancy, and they were married approximately a month later.

The investigation also uncovered that Craig had purchased a large life insurance policy on Linda, naming him as the beneficiary, although through court actions, his children with Linda ended up sharing in the insurance proceeds. Craig later admitted that he had forged Linda's signature on the policy.

Through the course of the investigation, it was alleged that Craig had actually shot and killed his wife and then made the second shot from a different location to cover his actions. This was based on the evidence collected by investigators, including the fact that Linda was using a .243 caliber rifle while Craig was using a larger .30-06 caliber rifle. Together with the extramarital relationship, subsequent marriage, and life insurance policy, the prosecutors felt there was a clear motive and finally charged Craig with the homicide of his wife, Linda.

As this case proceeded over many years, both the prosecution and the defense would argue many facts. The witness statements of the sounds of two different rifles being shot from two different locations became a major issue. Could Craig have shot Linda with her own rifle and then run over to another location and shot his rifle or vice versa? Was that even possible when Linda's father, Nick, said he knew where everyone was at all times?

Due to the long-drawn-out process of this case, key evidence was misplaced or lost by the legal custodians charged with maintaining the records and evidence. In addition, during this long period of too many judicial delays, Linda's father, Nick, passed away.

Over the years, Nick had become an important witness for the defense, as his statement documented that he knew where each member of the hunting party was and that the shots came from different rifles and from different locations.

Despite there being no statute of limitations in a homicide case, all of these factors worked toward Craig's advantage and defense. Throughout it all, Craig maintained his innocence and continued to hold onto the story that Linda's death was just "an accident."

Even though the physical evidence existed and many facts were presented, the court dismissed the case for delay of prosecution based on a motion filed by the defense. However, the court made it clear that if new evidence was presented or a confession was brought forth, Craig could once again be charged with the homicide of his wife. To date, this has not occurred.

Lessons Learned

- In any hunting-related fatal shooting, it's imperative that the incident be treated from the beginning as a possible homicide. This due diligence by all the agencies involved requires trained investigators to "drop everything" and focus on adjudicating, or resolving, each and every case.
- Each member of the investigative team as well as prosecutors must understand the seriousness of the mission and strive for cooperation.
- Everyone involved owes it to the victims and their families to keep the case moving forward. As a society, we must not allow the death of an individual while hunting to be treated as though nothing sinister could have occurred simply because the victim was hunting or wearing camouflage.
- "Do-overs" only happen in childhood games. Hunting-related shootings take place in real life and, sometimes, death. You only get one chance to "get it right the first time."

19

Death beside the Tracks

Drink moderately, for drunkenness neither keeps a secret nor observes a promise.

— MIGUEL DE CERVANTES

JED WALLACE WAS AN ENGINEER FOR THE RAILROAD. ON November 1, Wallace went to work just as he had many mornings before. He would be engineering a train hauling a major load, and Wallace thought it would be just another uneventful day on the tracks. His duties were to make sure his haul would make it to its destination on time and to blow the whistle at road crossings for public safety. Little did he know that this day on the tracks would be different, very different indeed.

On the night of October 31, Lenny Roberson went to a party. Lenny was a young man, just in the prime of his life at the age of twenty-one, but he was also an avid hunter who liked deer hunting in particular. His plans that night were to go to the party, stay a little while, have some fun, maybe meet up with a few girls, have a few drinks, and just hang out with his friends. Lenny also had plans to go deer hunting early the next morning and was looking forward to maybe getting a deer. Before he left his home for the party, he put all his hunting gear, including his rifle, in his Toyota truck, just in case he crashed somewhere else besides home after the party.

Lenny had a good time at the party. He did just what he wanted to do—met a few girls, hung out with friends, and drank several alcoholic beverages. He drank so much that he decided he was not going home when the party was over. Heck! He wasn't even going to crash at someone else's house. Lenny decided that he was going to get ready and go deer hunting. He went out to his truck, got all his gear ready, put on his fluorescent orange vest, then drove to the area he intended to hunt. It did not occur to Lenny that it was several hours before daylight and legal hunting hours; in other words, it was still dark outside.

Despite being in a somewhat drunken state, Lenny managed to drive to the area he intended to hunt without wrecking his truck. He parked his vehicle, loaded his Remington Model 742 rifle, and then made his way through the dark to his stand location. Lenny did not have a problem finding the area where he intended to hunt, even though it was dark, because he planned to hunt along the railroad tracks that morning. He knew where several deer crossings were along the tracks and had hunted in this area before. The railroad tracks made it easy to walk and find his way in the dark. After walking down the tracks for some distance, Lenny was satisfied that he had reached the area he wanted to be hunting when daylight broke in the next few hours. Lenny sat down alongside the tracks and realized he was tired. He had partied pretty hard that night and decided he might just take a nap before daylight. Lenny lay down on the railroad bed, parallel with and right beside the tracks, and went to sleep.

Around 7:00 a.m., Jed Wallace was operating the train on the same tracks Lenny had lain down next to and fallen asleep. The engineer happened to be looking out the window of his engine when he spotted Lenny lying on the railroad bed. Except Lenny wasn't asleep anymore; Lenny was dead. Wallace immediately radioed in his discovery and alerted the Hamburg County Sheriff's Office.

When the sheriff's deputies and their investigator arrived on the scene, they found a Toyota truck parked near the railroad tracks. They followed the tracks south, using the information given by the train engineer. They found Lenny's body a little more than three-quarters of a mile from where the railroad tracks crossed the main road. His body was lying parallel with the railroad tracks at a slight angle off the sloping shoulder of the gravel railroad bed. His right arm was outstretched toward the tracks, which put his fingers approximately twelve inches from the end of a railroad tie. His left arm was positioned parallel down the left side of his body, and his legs were positioned straight out from his body, with the legs crossed at the ankles.

Lenny's firearm was lying up against the steel rail of the track at the end of his outstretched right arm, the scope almost touching the rail. The barrel of the firearm was pointed in the direction of the victim's head. Approximately ten feet from his body, beyond his head, a gray stocking cap was found lying on top of the railroad bed.

Upon examining the victim's body, the sheriff's department investigator immediately noticed a large wound on the right side of the victim's head. The wound started at the victim's cheek right behind the eye and angled up and back approximately five and a half inches toward the top of the head. The width of the wound at its widest point was approximately two and a half inches. It appeared to have the characteristics of a gunshot wound. The investigator then concentrated his attention on the victim's firearm. He was hoping this was going to be a self-inflicted wound, either a suicide or an accidental discharge. If the incident wasn't one of these, it could end up being a long and hard investigation—one in the category of having a victim with no shooter, which meant that no one had come forward with information that he or she or somebody else had shot the victim either accidentally or on purpose. Upon examination of the firearm, it was found to have the safety in the safe position. The firearm's action was opened, and an unfired cartridge was found in the chamber. A search of the area did not turn up any fired cartridge cases.

The investigators' concerns had been met; they definitely had a victim and no shooter. Considering the victim was in the act of hunting when this happened, the investigator thought it might be a hunting-related incident. He decided to contact the state's wildlife law enforcement agency for assistance with the case.

The investigator contacted the local game warden, who in turn contacted his supervisor, Warden Vick Morgan. Realizing the severity of this case, Warden Morgan thought it best to contact his agency's Critical Incident Reconstruction Team (CIRT). This team was assigned the task of investigating and reconstructing the state's most serious injury and fatal boating accidents and hunting incidents. The warden put in a call to the CIRT supervisor, Warden Brian Cree. Warden Cree advised Morgan that he was "10-7/off-duty" and out of town, but he would contact the nearest CIRT member to the incident scene and get him en route.

Cree called Warden Jack Bozeman, who lived in the adjacent county to the north. Bozeman let Cree know that he would be en route as soon as he could get his equipment together. He would give Warden Morgan a call to get directions and more information about the incident.

The victim's body had already been removed and transported to the state crime lab for examination and autopsy when Warden

Bozeman arrived on scene. He met with Morgan and the sheriff's department investigator and was brought up to date on the situation at hand. Bozeman surveyed the scene, took measurements of evidence locations, and searched the area for any signs or evidence of the shooter. None was found.

On November 2, the case took on an unusual twist. The medical examiner, Dr. Dan Mills, examined and autopsied the victim's body. He agreed with the investigators that, at first look, the wound to the victim's head appeared to be a gunshot wound. However, further examination of the victim's body after removing his clothes revealed more injuries. The medical examiner discovered that the victim not only had a large head wound but also a laceration on his right forearm, a contusion near the elbow, and a fracture of the right humerus (the large bone in the upper arm) near the elbow. He also had abrasions on his left wrist and abrasions on his buttocks. X-rays of the victim's head revealed that there was no trace of metal bullet fragments in the head or around the large wound. Rather, the skull was fractured almost all the way around. Finally, Dr. Mills determined that the victim had been alive at the time the blow to the head was received. The medical examiner's conclusions were that the victim had died as a result of blunt force trauma to the right side of his head.

The examination revealed the facts. Sometime before daylight, and before engineer Jed Wallace's train came along, another train had traveled down the same tracks. This train was trying to keep on schedule. The engineer never blew a whistle, as he was not near a public crossing. But it was still dark and he didn't see Roberson. At some point, perhaps still drunk, Roberson woke up to discover the outside edge of the train cars gliding over him.

Confused and probably scared, Roberson made the bad decision to raise himself up instead of rolling to his left out from under the cars. This action caused him to make contact with a moving train car, inflicting the fatal wound to the right side of his head.

Lessons Learned

- The victim violated one of the important rules of firearm safety: "Avoid alcoholic beverages before and during shooting, and/or hunting." Even though a firearm did not cause this hunting incident death, if Lenny Roberson had followed this hunter education safety rule, he would have avoided death by having the clear mind needed to make proper decisions while planning his morning hunt. He also would not have been sleeping on the railroad tracks in the dark!

20

"He Moved from Where He Was Supposed to Be!"

Setting a goal is not the main thing. It is about deciding how you will go about achieving it and staying with that plan.
—Tom Landry

As always: Plan your hunt and hunt your plan. Hunter educators have used this phrase for many years in the classroom and with hunters in the field. What it means is that you, along with your hunting companions, agree at a pre-hunt meeting, in a very detailed and specific manner, how your hunt will be deployed. Everyone, no matter how many are in the hunting party, agrees to and reviews the rules of the hunt established before heading out. A comprehensive plan includes an aerial photograph or a map of the area to be reviewed. Each hunter is assigned a place and/or route to follow. Each member should then have a map to refer to during the hunt, along with the exact time to be where you are assigned to be. Once a plan has been agreed to, each member has the responsibility to follow it!

On an opening weekend of deer season, a group of family and friends who had hunted the same public forest area for many years headed out. The older hunters were assigned to the edge of the timber as "standers" where open meadows and rolling pastures begin. The younger members of the hunting party would "push," or "drive," the deer toward the standers waiting along the tree line at the other side of the section.

As the deer exited the forest area, the rule of the hunt was to let them proceed out into the meadow so there would be a proper backstop beyond the target, affording a clean and clear, safe shot.

On this particular drive, one of the hunters, Brian, apparently bored from standing at the fence post where he had always been assigned, decided to move about fifty yards out into the meadow. It was only fifty yards, but that simple move meant he was now out of sight of the other standers.

The standers were located about one hundred yards apart along the tree line. One of the standers reported that he saw nine deer run out of the forest area. They stopped and looked back into the timber long enough for one of the standers, Pete, to take a shot—it was a miss! He took aim again and shot two more times as the deer ran and disappeared into a small ditch then ran back into sight again about eighty yards from Pete.

Pete realized the deer had actually come out near the post that Brian was supposed to be standing by, but no shots were heard from Brian's gun. That was strange, because Brian should have been in the right place to make a safe shot to harvest that deer. After taking several more shots, Pete watched a deer go down but waited until the drivers began to come out of the edge of the tree line.

Suddenly Pete heard one of the drivers yell, "Brian's been shot!"

Pete worked his way toward the other hunters who had begun to gather around Brian's lifeless body. Brian, dressed in brown coveralls and an orange sandwich-board-style vest, had been shot in the neck. Pete began to shake and became physically sick and managed to stammer, "He moved from where he was supposed to be!"

That fact, together with the type of vest Brian was wearing, made it impossible for Pete to see the blaze orange Brian was wearing when he was standing sideways. Pete continued to repeat over and over, "He moved from where he was supposed to be!"

As this fatal hunting-related shooting incident was reconstructed, it became clear that from where Pete was standing when he made the shot, he could *not* see Brian. The type of vest Brian had on was not visible when he was standing sideways to Pete. He was also wearing a camouflage cap, which helped him blend into the environment instead of standing out. If Brian had stayed near the post he was assigned to, he might have had the opportunity to harvest a deer. More importantly, he most certainly would have had the opportunity to go home to his family and live to hunt again.

Lessons Learned

- Deviating from "the plan" is never a good idea. The hunting plan created at the pre-hunt meeting is an agreement between everyone involved in the hunt, for the safety of everyone involved in the hunt. Planning your hunt is always necessary, and not following the agreed-to plan can have long-term effects on every member of the hunting party.
- Choosing your safety gear is important, and choosing the wrong gear became a factor in this particular incident. You want to be *seen* by everyone from all directions when hunting with any group, large or small. Most states require blaze orange—an unnatural

color that sticks out and helps identify you as a hunter and has proven to save lives.

- The sandwich-style vest, which only covers the front and back, is not visible on the sides. The net material of these vests can reduce the visibility even more compared to a solid blaze orange vest or jacket, especially in different light conditions.
- Always wear a blaze orange cap. Even standing in the shadows can sometimes result in reduced visibility. You owe it to those you hunt with to be seen—and they owe it to you!

21

Pheasant Country

I do hunt, and I do fish, and I don't apologize to anybody for hunting and fishing.

—NORMAN SCHWARZKOPF

GROWING UP AS A YOUNG BOY IN PHEASANT COUNTRY CREATED lifelong lessons and a passion for the outdoors. The anticipation of "opening day," that special Saturday in the fall when pheasant season opened, meant having difficulty getting to sleep the night before because tomorrow you got to go hunting!

It was hard work helping to prepare the German shorthairs and English pointers for the hunt, but having well-trained bird dogs made the experience even more special. The memory of rising early on that Saturday morning and putting on a red-and-black plaid wool shirt that matched my dad's is etched clearly in my mind. We loaded the dogs into the dog box in the back of family's 1961 blue station wagon along with our shotguns and the snacks that Mom had fixed. Then we headed to the local Izaak Walton Club for a hunter's breakfast. I was feeling like I had finally made it; I was a *hunter!*

The club was where I had just taken the Hunter Safety class with my best friends, taught by "Mike the Game Warden." Now

I was sitting down for bacon and eggs across the table from real men, men dressed in brown drab clothing wearing their hunting boots with smiles on their faces and a cup of coffee in hand.

Everyone was talking about where they were headed to hunt. Hunters asked Mike, the game warden, questions about this year's bird numbers.

Yes, I knew these were my people. Growing up here and being accepted into manhood meant being a hunter. As shooting hours neared, I left the Ike's with a full belly; we headed out to our favorite spot, a spot Dad had hunted for years. I had managed to sneak a strip of bacon from my breakfast as a treat for the dogs.

As we pulled into the edge of the field, where the freshly picked cornfield met the acres of soil bank, you could hear the cackle of rooster pheasants off in the distance. That call brought an unforgettable smile to Dad's face. "Sounds like it's going to be a good day!"

By now the dogs were as excited as I was. They could hardly wait to begin their instinctive crisscrossing motion, stopping only at the sound of Dad's whistle and his occasional words of praise for his favorite dog. "Back, Sue, back."

It didn't take long for Sue to start to get "birdy." With her nose to the ground, she began to move in slow motion, tail straight out and then . . . front leg lifted.

Dad told me, "Get up here and get ready. Get your safety off; she's going to flush a bird!"

Then, as though a huge explosion had just taken place, a rooster came up out of the deep grass as I raised my 20 gauge. *Boom!*

The bird fell to the earth and was scooped up by Sue and returned to my dad's side. Both he and I were wearing big smiles! I had just bagged my first pheasant. Yes, now we had supper! I'm not sure who was more proud at that moment, Dad or I. By late morning we had nearly reached our limit when he said, "Come on, hurry up; you're like a cow's tail, always behind!"

As I think back on those days of hunting pheasants, the rules are still the same. Safe hunting required staying in a line, watching where the muzzle of the gun was pointed, keeping the safety on and *never* putting your finger in the trigger guard until you're ready to fire, and never swinging your gun toward another hunter when the bird flew!

Flash-forward twenty years!

I had just hung up from talking to Mike on my police radio. He was checking to see if we were all going to meet, as we always did, at the old American Legion Hall where the Methodist Church ladies made the best beef burgers, chili, and homemade pie for their annual hunter's lunch in Laurel.

Yes, I'm referring to the same Mike who was the local game warden back when I was a kid. We now got to work together once in a while. Opening day of pheasant season had become much different from when I was a kid. I now proudly wore the uniform of a conservation officer, a game warden just like Mike.

Instead of hunting pheasants on opening day, I was checking hunters for compliance with hunting laws, including checking licenses, making sure hunters were transporting their guns safely, and checking the number of birds for possession limits.

Just as some of the other guys in the district were about to take a break for lunch at Laurel, the sheriff's dispatcher called out over the police radio. She needed a conservation officer to cover a pheasant-hunting accident.

I was the district safety officer who responded to and assisted with investigating hunting-related shootings. Pheasant season opener was always a busy time. During those years we expected to have 250,000 hunters in the field statewide on opening weekend. Nonresidents made up a large number of those hunters. On one opening weekend we had eighteen people injured from "swinging on game" incidents. This call would be one of three on this day for the same type of incident.

As the dispatcher provided the details, I headed for the local hospital while another officer headed for the farm where the incident had happened. As I pulled into the emergency room parking lot, I noticed two pickups with nonresident plates. Men wearing blaze orange and sad expressions were standing there checking on their dogs. I grabbed my clipboard with my report forms, jumped out of my truck, and went over to them.

As I introduced myself, their heads hung low. I asked how their buddy was doing.

One of the guys began to speak, and his voice cracked as he said, "I didn't see him until it was too late."

I asked him and the others for both their driver's and hunting licenses. I told them just to hang tight and I would be back. Once I had their IDs, I went into the emergency room to check on the victim.

The first person I came in contact with was a nurse, who said, "I'll bet you're having a busy day!" Little did she or I know that the day was going to get much busier!

The victim was sitting upright on the gurney. He was a big guy in his fifties. His shirt was off and his face and arm on his right side were peppered with pockmarks. One very close to his right eye looked like it had nearly hit his eyeball. He asked, "How's it look?"

I said, "Lucky. You look pretty lucky to me."

He looked like a Saturday-morning cartoon character. I could easily picture him drinking a glass of water and having the water pour out of the holes now covering his skin. I asked him what had happened.

He said, "We were nearing the end of some standing corn and a bird got up to my right. Before I could get my gun up, the bird flew back behind me and *bang!* It felt like a bunch of bees had stung me all at once. It knocked me down and I thought, *I can't believe it; I think I just got shot!*

Just as I was about to begin filling out my report form, the doctor came in.

The doctor said, "His layers of clothes helped keep the wounds superficial. It looks like he took about twenty-eight pellets total. I'm not going to start digging around trying to remove them. That just seems to make things worse."

The doctor said he would give the victim some antibiotics and send him on his way. I filled out the report as the injured hunter muttered that his wife was not going to be happy.

When I returned to the parking lot, the mood had lightened a little. The friends gathered there had begun to talk about how it could have been much worse. The group had planned on staying one more night and hunting on Sunday, but they decided to head home two states away and buy their buddy a big steak, if he felt like having one.

I gave them back their licenses and finished filling in the necessary information on my report. Then I heard back from the officer at the farm. The farmer had helped find the area where the incident had occurred. The officer found the empty shotgun shell and the blood in the cornfield. He was putting a diagram together and taking some photos of the area—all very typical for such an incident.

The next report, however, was a little different. A group of four hunters and two dogs, they had three roosters get up, fly a short distance, and land ahead of them. They decided to hold the dogs and send two of the hunters to the end of a tallgrass waterway in a picked cornfield. The other two walked along the edge and "blocked" in deep prairie grass at the end of the draw. As the two hunters with the dogs got closer, a rooster got up and one of the guys in the deep grass took a few pellets to the head, once again just missing his eyes.

The third incident of the day came in just before the end of shooting hours. That group was making one more pass through some standing corn. One of the dogs ran ahead, and the owner ran up to try to catch him so he wouldn't scare up any pheasants ahead of the rest of the group. Due to the standing corn, not everyone in the group could see where he was. A pheasant came from the left, running down the cornrows. The hunter who saw the pheasant attempted to shoot the bird on the ground but instead shot his buddy who was chasing the dog. The victim was struck in the lower part of his buttocks and upper rear thighs.

When I got back to the hospital, a new shift had replaced the day shift. As I walked in, a different nurse said to me, "Boy, I bet you've had a busy day!" She had no idea!

This time the ride home for the nonresident hunter was going to be a long one. His buddies were going to make a bed for him in the back of their big SUV and let him ride facedown on the way home, three states away. The doctor was going to give him a shot to help reduce the pain for the ride. I am sure that between the guilty shooter, the tired dogs, the wounded pride, and injured hunter lying in the back, it was a long, quiet ride home.

Lessons Learned

- Growing up in pheasant country and working with hunters my entire career has generated many memories. These memories have inspired me, motivated me, and made me thankful for the resources I've been privileged to have and the people I have met.

- I've worked under very difficult situations, especially considering the events that brought many hunters and myself together, but I'm still a hunter. I share the hunt with those around me who want to learn the safe and ethical methods, people who know that every time you pick up a gun, you pick up a responsibility.

- Hunting with family and friends, and pheasant hunting in particular, requires everyone's attention at all times. Communication among hunters at all times is crucial. Knowing the "safe zone of fire" is very important, and not violating it is critical. If you stretch your arms out at forty-five degrees, looking straight ahead, the zone out in front of you is *your* safe zone of fire. Do not cross that line by swinging a firearm! If a bird gets up and flies beside or behind you, *never* attempt to take that bird.

- Safe hunting is the responsibility of everyone in the group. When in doubt, *don't!* No shot or no target is worth injuring someone. If someone is not following the rules of safe gun handling, don't be afraid to speak up. You could save someone's life, including your own. Some of the best and most memorable times I have had in my life have been in the hunting field. These are still my people—they are hunters, and I am too!

22

Something Horrible in the Woods

Where belief is painful, we are slow to believe.

OVID

ON THE OTHER END OF THE PHONE, WARDEN BRIAN CREE COULD hear the cracking in the voice of one of his most experienced and best investigators of the Critical Incident Reconstruction Team (CIRT). Warden Matt Hall said, "We . . . had a . . . a . . . hunting incident in . . . a . . . Tugaloo County this afternoon."

Cree could tell that what Hall had seen at the incident scene had shaken him. Cree had worked with this officer on numerous occasions, on some of the worst boating crashes and hunting incidents across the state. He knew Hall had witnessed many autopsies, which alone can unnerve even the most seasoned officer. What had the warden so shaken?

After a short pause, Hall continued to report to Cree what had transpired that afternoon in Tugaloo County. When Hall had finished, Cree was a bit unnerved himself.

On the afternoon of November 26, a father, son, uncle, and cousin decided to go deer hunting. At approximately 3:00 p.m., they all arrived at their hunting club. Everyone was anxious to get a shot at a deer that afternoon. They split up and went to their assigned deer stands, planning to meet back at their vehicle around dark. Everyone got settled into his or her stand. With the anticipation of seeing a deer, each hunter waited and watched. As the cool autumn afternoon began, they didn't realize that only three of them would be coming back to the truck. For one, this was their final hunt.

Not long after they had been in their stands, the cousin shot and killed a doe deer. This was an exciting moment for her. She watched the deer fall and decided to sit still until it was time for everyone to come down out of the stands. From their stands, the father and uncle had not seen the kill take place.

At approximately 4:00 p.m., the father heard two shots back to back. He thought those shots might have come from the direction of his son's stand. He picked up his cell phone and sent his son a text, asking if he was the one who had fired those two shots. The text went unanswered. After thinking about it for a minute, he decided those shots hadn't sounded like they came from his son's stand after all. He switched back into hunting mode and waited for a deer.

Sitting six hundred yards from his father, the son also heard those two shots. Shortly after the shots, his cell phone began to vibrate. He picked it up and saw that the message was from his father. The son opened the text: "Is that you who fired those shots?"

The son typed the single word "No" but decided not to send this answer to his father. He did not clear the text off his cell phone but just placed the cell phone back in his pocket. There the son sat for another hour. At approximately 5:00 p.m., the son pulled the trigger of his rifle.

The father heard a single shot at 5:00 p.m. Now he was absolutely positive it was his son who had shot. He just knew his son had killed a deer. Picking up his cell phone again, he sent his son another text asking, "That You?" That text also went unanswered.

At 6:09 p.m., a little after dark, the father climbed down out of his stand and went back to the truck. His son was not there, although by this time, he should have been. The father picked up his cell phone once again and this time dialed his son's number. His son did not answer the call. Concerned, the father drove the truck down to his son's deer stand. There he found his son, still in his ladder stand. He had not only found his son but also an apparent victim.

When Warden Matt Hall arrived at the hunting incident scene, sheriff's office personnel and EMT Rescue were already on-site. Hall met sheriff's department investigator Clint Duval at an area near the scene. Investigator Duval briefed the warden on the situation; then they both got into Hall's vehicle and the investigator directed him to the scene.

Arriving on scene, Hall could see people moving around a truck parked about forty yards from the victim's stand. Since those people were not law enforcement or rescue personnel, he inquired as to what they were doing there. The investigator told him they were field dressing a deer. Hall thought this to be odd, but he would later learn that it was the uncle and cousin cleaning the deer the cousin had killed.

The investigator then led Warden Hall to the scene. It was a field approximately an acre in size, with a wooden ladder stand on the left side of the field. The ladder stand was made of two-by-four lumber and fastened to the tree with a nylon strap. Hall shined his light up onto the seat of the stand and illuminated a horrible sight.

The victim was still in the stand, lying backward and slightly on his right side across the seat, with his feet hanging off the left side of the stand. Hanging off the right side of the stand was only part of his neck, as he had no head. The victim's head and face were gone.

The victim's left arm was lying across his chest, and his right arm was draped in a downward position. His right leg was braced against the foot of the seating platform, and his left leg was hanging off to the left of the platform. Blood was everywhere.

Above the stand, on the trunk of the tree it was attached to, the blood spatter pattern went upward for several feet. Hall could clearly see brain matter and flesh on the trunk and limbs above the stand. The victim's hat hung on a limb approximately four feet above the seat platform. The rifle was lying on the ground at the bottom of the ladder stand, with blood on its barrel and scope. It took Hall several minutes to take in and process all he was seeing and to regain his composure. This was the most horrific hunting incident scene Hall had ever had to work.

Hall then found the victim's father and began talking to him; he learned that the father had found his son. Hall then began to carefully question him about what had taken place before he had found his son.

The father informed Hall about the details of the hunt— what time they arrived at the hunting club, who was with them, the shots he had heard, and the text he had sent his son that went unanswered. Hall then questioned the father about the son's knowledge of the firearm. The father stated that his son was very familiar with the firearm he was using and had been through a Hunter Education course in another state. He said his son had been hunting for about four years and had just shot his first deer about two weeks prior to this incident. The father knew that his son was safety conscious and felt comfortable leaving him alone in a deer stand. He noted that his son would normally use a retractable device (pull cord) to raise and lower his firearm from the stand.

Once the interviews of the father and other witnesses were complete, it was time to work the incident scene. This facet of the investigation involved locating, documenting, and photographing all evidence in order to reconstruct the incident so as to be able to find out what happened to the victim. This detailed work helped answer the most important question: how the victim died. This aspect of the job is never easy, but Hall knew this case would be an especially difficult scene to work. There was blood spatter, brain matter, and body tissue everywhere—not to mention the fact that it might not be an accident after all.

Hall's first step was to photograph the victim and all the evidence found at the scene before the victim was removed from the scene. Hall inspected the firearm found on the ground at the base of the ladder stand. It was a .243 caliber Remington 700 bolt-action rifle. The firearm was found with the safety in the fire position, one spent/fired cartridge case in the chamber, and three live rounds in the magazine. Hall secured the firearm in his vehicle.

With assistance from the county's rescue personnel, a rope was placed around the victim's body and he was lowered out of the ladder stand onto the ground. Hall examined the body for evidence of what happened, and the only injuries he could find were to the region of the head. He could see what was left of the chin area and found what he believed to be the entrance wound midline, underneath the chin, where discolored skin and tissue appeared. Hall believed the discoloration to be gunpowder residue. He could also see there was no stippling on the victim's skin.

The wound appeared to have been caused by a close or hard contact with the barrel of the firearm when it was fired. Hall then searched the victim's clothing and found his cell phone. He scrolled through the phone and found the unsent text message to his father: "No." Hall also took measurements of the victim's arms, measuring from armpits to fingertips. These measurements would help determine whether the victim had sufficient reach to pull the trigger himself. Hall noted that the measurements were approximately twenty-five inches. The victim's body was then transported from the scene and turned over to the county coroner.

After seeing the victim loaded and removed, Hall continued to work the scene and collect additional evidence. He climbed up the ladder stand and onto the bloody seat platform to retrieve the victim's cap. The cap showed definite signs of being worn by the victim at the time of the shot. There was what appeared to be a bullet hole in the top of the hat, and the brim was almost detached, held on by just a few stitches of thread.

He also located a fanny pack in the stand that belonged to the victim. Inside he saw the deer-hunting paraphernalia and the pull cord for raising and lowering a rifle in and out of the ladder stand, just as the father had said. When finished with the scene, Hall went to talk to the father again. He also spoke with the uncle and cousin. They were all asked to provide written statements.

Hall then went to the father's vehicle to inspect the box of ammunition the victim had been using; it was Federal Premium Hydro-Shok, hundred-grain soft point. Returning to the father, Hall asked some general questions about his son's behavior.

The father stated there had been nothing wrong that he was aware of and spoke of his son working toward his Eagle project for the Boy Scouts. He also talked about his son's hunting experience and familiarity with the firearm he was hunting with that afternoon. He repeated that his son had been hunting for about four years and had shot his first deer only weeks prior. The father was insistent that his son sat with his firearm lying across his lap with the safety in the safe position. Hall closed out his interview, making sure the father had his contact information. He told the father he would be in touch with him soon.

After leaving the scene, Hall was contacted by Brian Holly of the state crime lab. He informed Hall that he had spoken with the county coroner and was aware of the fatality in Tugaloo County. The warden discussed the investigation and relayed his concerns that it had not been a hunting incident but actually a suicide. Due to the victim's age and manner of death, Holly said he would speak with one of the medical examiners and see if they could perform an assessment of injuries. Later that night, Holly contacted Hall and asked if he could be at the state crime lab the next morning to discuss the investigation with the medical examiner. Hall assured him he would be there.

The next day Hall not only discussed the investigation with the medical examiner but also attended the victim's autopsy. At the conclusion of the autopsy, the doctor advised Hall that he too felt that the wound under the victim's chin was intentional and self-inflicted. He would wait until the tissue samples were tested before putting that conclusion in his final report. The medical examiner confirmed that the entrance wound was under the chin and said he was able to locate the exit wound following a reapproximation and reconstruction of the victim's head. The examination and tools used for the autopsy showed that the path of the bullet was upward and did not divert to one side or the other.

In light of the father's concerns regarding the firearm's safety, and the fact that the firearm's functionability was of great importance to this investigation, the firearm was taken to another branch of the state crime lab for examination. Firearms technician Kate McCord would do a full examination of the firearm and put it through a series of rigorous tests.

On February 3, Hall spoke with McCord, who stated she had completed the assessment of the firearm. She had tested the firearm, including trying to make it discharge accidentally by slamming the bolt and dropping the firearm. She had also tested the firearm's safety mechanism thoroughly and taken it apart to examine it.

McCord tested the trigger, which was still set at the Remington factory setting of 3.5 pounds of pull force. Because there were no limbs or anything else in the vicinity or at the height of the deer stand to catch on the trigger, the victim had to have consciously pulled the trigger. The firearm performed without fault and passed every test and was determined to be in good working order. With the firearm report, autopsy report, and no evidence to suggest otherwise, this fatality was ruled a suicide.

As difficult as it was to process, all physical and forensic evidence suggested that the death of the victim, age sixteen, had been a suicide and not a hunting incident. Even though there was no note or other form of communication left behind to explain why he would do this, the evidence did not suggest that this had been an accidental discharge.

In the end, however, the Tugaloo County coroner was adamant that the incident be ruled an accidental shooting. The pressure was so great that the case went before the Child Fatality Review Board in the county in which the victim lived. Both Warden Hall and the medical examiner testified before the board with their findings. The board ruled that the evidence did indeed support the conclusion that the death had been a suicide, but despite this ruling, the county coroner never changed his report. The coroner's report still lists this tragedy as a hunting accident.

The victim's father contacted Hall several times throughout this investigation, asking him to change his report. The father informed Hall that his wife's father, the victim's grandfather, had also committed suicide, and he did not want another death certificate in his family stating suicide as cause of death. Hall refused these requests. During his last conversation with the father, Hall was asked to withhold the findings of the investigation until he and his wife got back from a cruise.

Even though Warden Hall was pressured by the victim's family and the county coroner to change his report, the warden knew he had made the right call on this case. Warden Hall followed the evidence and let it tell the story of what had taken place that tragic day in the woods. Sometimes these cases reveal things about the people involved that are not pretty or tell a story that is not for the faint of heart. Being the investigator that he is, Hall revealed the truth—and sometimes that is not just the truth as to what happened to the victim but also the underlying truth surrounding the persons involved.

Lessons Learned

- As an investigator you must be prepared to handle anything and everything that you encounter. Often the things you encounter are shocking and emotionally charged; sometimes they are horrible. Sometimes evidence found at a scene is hard to look at. Investigators have to gather their thoughts and keep their composure. A job has to be done, and it is up to you to find out what happened and the cause.

- Keeping your emotions in check and putting your mind in a place where you look at everything found on scene as evidence are vital. This evidence is going to tell the story of what took place and give you the clues you need to figure out the cause. No matter how horrible the scene, the investigator is the key to the outcome of the case.

- Integrity is the backbone of any good investigator. Outside pressures from other law enforcement agencies, prosecutors, or friends or family of the victim often try to sway an investigation. Good investigators always report the facts and the truths and never anything but.

23

Uncle Grouse

*Facts are stubborn things; and whatever may be our wishes,
our inclinations, or the dictates of our passions, they cannot
alter the state of facts and evidence.*

—JOHN ADAMS

A MAN IN HIS MID-THIRTIES WAS HUNTING RUFFED GROUSE ON
a steep, heavily wooded hillside with his uncle. The area had been
logged over twenty years ago and was shouldered by a steep ravine,
providing some patches of ideal, thick-growth grouse habitat. The
plan was for them to hunt uphill, with the uncle walking the edge
of the ravine.

The nephew was walking and stopping occasionally to listen
and look for grouse. He thought he had a good idea of where his
uncle was when a ruffed grouse flushed to his left, heading for the
ravine. Reacting quickly, with the hope of a hit, he swung fast and
fired his 12-gauge shotgun. In seemingly the very same instant,
he was stunned to hear his uncle yell out.

He immediately ran toward the sound of his uncle's shouts.
As he ran, he stepped in a hole, tripped, and almost fell. He continued on, desperate to reach his uncle.

He soon came upon his uncle sitting on a log at the edge of the ravine, wiping blood from his face. His uncle had been hit in numerous places by the birdshot, including his right arm, shoulder, upper chest, and face. The distraught nephew helped his uncle wipe away most of the blood before he began the long trip of leading his uncle off the hillside, to the car, and then to the hospital.

Although they arrived at the hospital just before noon, the police were not immediately notified. By the time the investigators got the call, it was too late in the day to head out for a full investigation. However, the lead investigator called the nephew and made an appointment to meet the next morning. The nephew readily agreed. He would take the investigators back to the scene of the accident, as the site was too remote for him to describe its exact location.

Clearly filled with remorse that he had hurt his beloved uncle, the nephew was ready to be as helpful as he could. He had been there after all, and he knew the facts the investigators needed to know. While his uncle's injuries were not life-threatening, some of the pellets had gone deep into his face and shoulder, and he would likely suffer from them for a long time.

First thing the next day, the nephew and two investigators hiked up the mountain and found the log where the uncle had sat down after being shot. No one was surprised to see the bloody handkerchief that had been used for cleaning up. There was blood on the log, and the vegetation was well trampled from the two hunters standing there the day before.

The nephew then took the investigators to where he *knew* he had been standing when he fired the shot. He had hoped to hit a ruffed grouse but had hit his uncle instead. He confidently indicated the location, just on the other side of a deeply rutted skid road and about forty-five yards from the uncle's location.

Arriving at the spot the nephew pointed out, the investigators began looking for the evidence that should have been there, including the spent shell and wads, along with any vegetation that had been clipped by the pellets. The leaves would still be green, and many of those would have tiny pellet holes in them from the shot.

The investigators carefully searched and evaluated the scene but did not find any physical evidence. There was not a single hole, or even one pellet that had hit a tree or the thick brush. Ready to believe the nephew's story, one of the investigators even climbed a dogwood tree that lay directly between where the uncle and nephew had allegedly been when the shot was fired. Despite looking at every leaf and branch, the investigator could not find a single pellet strike. Looking uphill, the investigator was a bit surprised to see a single red shotgun shell on the ground about thirty yards away. It was the same color as the ammunition the nephew said he was using.

Carefully approaching the shell so that he did not disturb any other possible evidence, the investigator began looking for the missing evidence he knew had to be there. From his vantage point, he looked toward the uncle's location and immediately saw the torn leaves and the little holes with sap trails in the trees and brush that he was expecting.

As the investigator began flagging those locations, the nephew became upset and kept asking, "Why are you bothering with this location? I was never there! I was farther downhill, on the other side of the skid road! Are you calling me a liar?"

The investigator stayed calm and explained to the nephew that while he had *thought* he was someplace else, the physical evidence clearly showed that the round that had hit his uncle had been fired from this location. The nephew was using a shotgun that ejects the shell directly down between his feet, and there was the shell. All the pellet holes, broken twigs, and torn leaves formed a cone that started from this point, going up and to the left toward the uncle.

When all the evidence was located and flagged, brightly colored string was pulled taught along the outer edges of all the pellet strikes. This visual display and outline of the evidence allowed the nephew to clearly see the pattern from the shot that started just in front of the red shell and continued up and over to the place where his uncle had been. The lower edge of the pattern was about the same height as his uncle's elbow and matched his injuries exactly.

Only then did the nephew see a small depression in the ground, right in front of where he had obviously been. It might have come from a tree stump that had rotted away over a hundred years ago. That was the depression where he had almost fallen when he ran to his uncle's side; it had not been the skid road after all.

The nephew sincerely thanked the investigators. The evidence was clear, while his memory was not. He was not a liar, and the investigators never thought that he was. But in the aftermath of the accident and shock of shooting a dear uncle, his recollections were not as reliable as he thought they were. Seeing the evidence for himself was key. He left the scene, saying again and again that he never would have believed it if he had not seen it for himself.

The investigators left the scene, reminded of important details. In many cases, the initial report may not be entirely correct. A witness's account may not be entirely accurate according to the evidence.

After completing the investigation, it was clear that the nephew had not been lying or trying to deceive the investigators.

He took full responsibility for his actions. He hadn't lied about where he was, but he still had been wrong.

In the panic and fear that usually follows these incidents, people often have false memories of where they were and what they did. It is the investigator's job to listen carefully to what the witnesses say but also to trust in the hard facts of the evidence. In this case, the evidence told the accurate story with all the details, some of which the nephew and his uncle couldn't remember or didn't even know. Their accounts, along with the evidence, told the whole story, the real story.

Lessons Learned

- Always be sure you know where all the members of your hunting party are before you shoulder your gun or fire.
- Your "safe zone of fire" moves and changes with every step you or your hunting partners take.
- Take the time necessary to be aware of this safe zone before each and every shot you take. Always be sure the area is safe, including behind and in front of, above and below, left and right of your target. This is most important, and more difficult to do when you are swinging on running game or a flying bird. It is better to lose a shot at game than to lose someone's life.
- There is no arguing with the facts of the evidence.

24

The Drive for Child Support

There are no rewards or punishments—only consequences.
—WILLIAM RALPH INGE

ON THE EVENING OF DECEMBER 31, WARDEN BRIAN CREE
had not been home long from a full day of patrolling when
he received a telephone call from headquarters that a hunting
incident had occurred in Marshall County. As a member of the
Critical Incident Reconstruction Team (CIRT) responsible for
the investigation and reconstruction of such events, he requested
the details surrounding the incident. The headquarters personnel
advised Warden Cree that this was just a notification and that he
and his team would not be needed. The Marshall County sheriff's
office, along with the local warden, would be handling the case.
Cree thought it was probably a mistake not to let the CIRT work
the incident, but he did not voice his opinion. The call ended, and
Cree wondered why he had gotten the call in the first place if his
department was not going to let the CIRT respond.

On January 4, Warden Cree received another call from headquarters. He was informed that CIRT assistance would now, in
fact, be needed in the Marshall County incident, and could they
make plans to be there the next day? Cree let them know he would

contact all CIRT members and make preparations to go to Marshall County the next day. He asked why CIRT's assistance was needed now, after five days had passed. He was told that the victim had a wife and three children, and the widow was causing an awful lot of disturbance among the local law enforcement about their handling of the investigation. Therefore, CIRT had been called in.

Cree hung up the telephone and began calling all CIRT members to coordinate a plan of action. All the team members were instructed to meet at the Marshall County sheriff's office on the morning of January 5. After this, Cree spent a couple of hours making sure all his CIRT equipment was in working order and packed up his vehicle.

Warden Cree left his home early on the morning of January 5 to make the four- to five-hour drive to Marshall County. During the drive, as always, he went over the checklist in his head on things that needed to be done and questions that needed to be asked when he reached his destination. The long drive to Marshall County was uneventful.

Needing a break and some food, he stopped at a McDonald's restaurant for breakfast when he entered Marshall County. He ordered and went to pay, but to his surprise the cashier would not take his money. Warden Cree asked, "Are you sure?"

"Yes," the cashier replied. "Thank you for your service."

This nice gesture stuck with him the rest of the day. When he finished his breakfast, it was time to go to the sheriff's office.

If anything in Warden Cree's career stands out, it is the fact that he has always been punctual. He is usually early for meetings and work details, and this day was no different. The first CIRT member to arrive at the sheriff's office, he went in and introduced himself. Marshall County Investigator Colby Hand filled him in on the details of the incident.

Investigator Hand made a strange statement as he handed Cree photographs of the incident scene: "I will help you in any way I can, but if you tell me to stay the hell out of the way, I will stay the hell out of the way."

Taken aback a bit, Cree replied, "We are here to assist you with this investigation, and working together is the only way we will be able to get to the bottom of what actually happened. I do not want you to stay out of the way. We will be needing your help."

By this time, other CIRT members had begun to arrive: Warden Hank Folly, Warden Joe Hunt, and Warden Ken Gillis. The case was discussed in length with Investigator Hand while arrangements were made for the shooter to be brought out to the incident scene later in the day so that CIRT members could question him again.

During the meeting, the CIRT learned there were seven people in the hunting party. The seven hunters were doing a deer drive when the incident took place. During a deer drive, several hunters in a hunting party move through the woods, usually in a line. The goal is to jump deer out of their bedding or hiding places and get them to move toward the watchers at the other side of the woods, where the hunters can get a shot at one.

They also learned that several members of the hunting party had hidden their guns and had hunting license violations. The local warden and the sheriff's office had sorted everything out and found all the firearms and hunters involved the evening of the incident. The CIRT members reviewed the case file and photographs, noting that the photographs showed the victim had been shot in the head, the bullet entering behind the right ear and exiting under the right eye. The victim had been wearing Mossy Oak Bottomland coveralls, a fluorescent orange vest, and a gray stocking cap with the bottom turned up. The turned-up fold was a light, white-gray color. The team discussed a plan of action, and then it was time to visit the incident scene.

The CIRT members followed Investigator Hand to the scene. Upon arrival, Hand walked the team members through the scene and showed them where the victim had been found. Blood pattern evidence on the ground indicated that it was, without a doubt, the location where the victim had been shot. The team members discussed what needed to be done first, and assignments were given.

Hand was asked if he knew where the shooter had been located when the shot was fired. He reported that they had not found the shooter's location. Cree said the shooter could probably give them an idea of where he was when he arrived at the incident site. A command post site was picked, and CIRT members began to unload equipment from their vehicles.

Since the faint blood patterns were the only verifiable evidence of the victim's location, they were marked first. After talking with the Marshall County investigator and examining the photographs, it was ascertained that the bullet had exited the body. Cree and Folly used the metal detector to try to locate the bullet.

They immediately encountered a problem they had never before run across. Minerals in the ground and rocks at the incident site caused the metal detector to continuously signal as though it had passed over something metal. This problem rendered the metal detector useless. A systematic search of the area also revealed nothing. It was time to bring the shooter to the area to see if he could fill in the missing pieces of the puzzle.

When Hand returned to the scene with the shooter, Cree was the first to question him. After a brief introduction and thanking him for his assistance, Cree asked the shooter if he would be willing to go back into the woods and show him where he was standing when he fired the shot. The shooter readily agreed.

Warden Cree followed the shooter back into the woods, and the shooter walked over to one location and indicated that it could have been the spot he fired from but he was not sure. Cree tied orange flagging to a bush at that location.

Cree advised the shooter to take his time, that there was no hurry, to look everything over. The shooter then went to another location and stated that it could have been here. Cree again tied orange flagging to a bush at the location. The shooter was confident it had to be one of those two locations. Cree thanked him for his help, and the shooter was escorted out of the area. Gillis was assigned to continue questioning the shooter back at the vehicles.

Cree and Folly decided to try the metal detector again. Hand had told them that the shooter must have ejected the shell casing from his bolt-action rifle after he had shot the victim—a live round of ammunition had been found in the shooter's firearm when sheriff's deputies seized it the evening of the incident.

Cree and Folly knew they had a spent shell casing somewhere at the incident scene; they just had to find it. Folly ran the metal detector over and around the first place the shooter had pointed out, but other than a few false signals because of the minerals in the area, nothing was found.

After a thorough search of the area, Folly and Cree moved onto the second location the shooter had pointed out. Folly ran the metal detector over the area and immediately got a strong signal at one spot. A closer search of the spot uncovered a spent .243 caliber shell casing. They had just found the shooter's location.

The casing's location was marked and left undisturbed for the time being. Cree stood at the spot and looked in the direction of the victim's location. He immediately noticed a large growth of briars and realized that the victim and shooter had been less than thirty yards apart when the shot was fired. Hunt was instructed to take photographs of all evidence that had been located and to document all evidence locations.

Once this was completed, Cree and Folly examined the growth of briars between the shooter's and victim's locations. These briars were thick, and the shooter had fired through them in order to hit the victim. They began to look for limb clips caused by the bullet striking the briars as it went through the patch but didn't find any. Somehow the .243 caliber bullet had passed through the briar patch without striking anything! It was decided at this point to get out the laser trajectory finder and tripod to see if the bullet's path could be determined.

Warden Cree examined the shooter's rifle, which had been brought to the scene by Investigator Hand. It was a Ruger .243 caliber Model M77 Mark II bolt-action rifle with a 3-by-9-by-40-millimeter Charles Daly scope. Cree picked up the spent cartridge case found at the shooter's position, placed the empty round back into the chamber of the rifle, and closed the bolt.

Shouldering the firearm, he ejected the spent cartridge. He did this numerous times, adjusting his position each time after ejecting the spent cartridge case. Finally the ejected cartridge landed in the exact location where the spent round had been found by the metal detector. Cree's position was marked, and the tripod with the laser trajectory finder was placed at this location. The laser was adjusted so that it was on the same level as the firearm when shouldered.

As Folly was the same approximate size as the victim, he stood at the victim's location, facing in the same direction the victim would have been. Then Cree activated the laser. The laser passed through the briar patch, unobstructed, and hit Folly behind the right ear—the exact location where the bullet had entered the victim.

This expensive piece of equipment had just paid for itself, during its first use by the CIRT, by helping determine the bullet's trajectory. It was time to pull strings and finish the reconstruction.

With the bullet's path determined, a string replaced the laser. String, or a shot line, was pulled from the shooter's position to the victim's position to show the bullet's path. Orange fluorescent flagging tape was tied at about two-foot intervals along the shot line. This flagging tape would help the line show up better in photographs. The scene was then photographed and documented by Hunt. Using the evidence found at the scene, interviews with the shooter, and witness statements, the CIRT was able to piece together what actually had happened during this hunting incident.

Going through all the evidence and photographs a few days later, Cree made a discovery that needed to be checked out. He contacted Folly, who concurred with Cree's observations. The photograph of interest was of the victim lying on his back. It showed the coveralls he was wearing, and on the upper legs/ thighs was a blood spatter pattern.

Cree and Folly both agreed this pattern indicated that at some point, the victim had to have been on his knees with his buttocks positioned back on or near his ankles. The pattern they saw was caused by an arterial-type spurt of blood projected out of the bullet's exit wound and onto the victim's upper thighs. This pattern could not have occurred while the victim was in a standing position. The victim had either been shot while on his knees or gone to the kneeling position after the shot was fired. All evidence at the scene seemed to indicate the victim had been shot in the standing position. However, this blood spatter pattern told another story. The blood spatter on the coveralls could help to clear this matter up; it had to be checked out.

Needing to examine the victim's coveralls, Cree and Folly made arrangements to meet at the state crime lab, where the victim's body and evidence had been sent. At the crime lab, technician Mosley retrieved the coveralls, and Cree and Folly were given a room to examine them. Cree took a series of photographs to document all sections of the coveralls, along with the blood spatter evidence located on each section.

Upon examination of the coveralls, the story began to unfold about what had taken place on that tragic day. Without a doubt, the victim had gone to his knees after the shot, with his buttocks back toward or on his ankles. This is when blood projected from the exit wound under his eye, in an arterial-type spurt, had landed on his thighs. He had fallen to his knees and then onto his left side. The victim had remained in this position until members of the hunting party moved him back up into a sitting position.

The blood pattern on the left side of the coveralls and the blood pattern on the front of the coveralls in the area of the upper chest revealed this. After members of the hunting party sat the victim up, he was then laid on his back until rescue services arrived. The blood flow pattern found inside the coveralls made this fact clear. After a thorough examination of the coveralls and a review of all witness statements, Cree and Folly determined that the blood pattern evidence corresponded with both the witness statements and the evidence found at the incident scene. The victim had indeed been in a standing position when the fatal shot was fired.

The deer drive planned for December 31 had not turned out as expected. The hunting party of seven hunters entered the woods with everyone in the party carrying a rifle. The hunters got in a line and proceeded to travel up a slight hill. The terrain was somewhat open in spots, with other areas of thick brush and briars. All the hunters said they were within sight of someone just about at all times. However, they also admitted that everyone would at times lose sight of the others as they traveled through the areas of thick brush and briars.

At approximately 3:47 p.m., the shooter lost sight of the victim, who was in line with him. The shooter stated that he heard something in front of him. He looked and saw movement. While this movement was actually the victim, the shooter saw and concentrated on the white-gray portion of the victim's stocking cap. The high briar patch hid the victim's fluorescent orange vest.

The shooter's bullet passed through the briar patch, traveled twenty-eight yards, and struck the victim. This impact caused the victim to fall to his knees, as shown by the blood spatter pattern found on the victim's coveralls in the area of the thighs. The victim then fell onto his left side, where he lay until other members of the hunting party sat him up. The witnesses at the scene corroborated this fact in their statements. The shooter was charged with Careless Use of a Firearm or Archery Tackle while Hunting Wildlife, a felony.

The district attorney for the judicial district did not want this shooter to serve time in jail. He had another sentence in mind. He wanted the shooter to pay child support for the victim's three children until they were all eighteen years of age. The DA explained that the shooter could not do this if he was in jail.

A year following the incident, the shooter pleaded guilty to felony Careless Use of a Firearm while Hunting Wildlife and was fined one thousand dollars and sentenced to two hundred hours of community service, ten years' probation, and $4,243.75 in restitution fees. In addition, he had to pay for the victim's burial and monument marker and child support to the victim's children until they were eighteen years of age.

Lessons Learned

- Without knowing exactly where the victim was, the shooter took aim through the scope of his Ruger .243 caliber rifle, violating one of the most important rules of hunter safety: He "failed to clearly identify his target" and still made the decision to pull the trigger.
- The shooter knew the victim was in the general area of the movement he saw. Even if it had been a deer, he should never have considered shooting in that direction; it was not within his "safe zone of fire."
- Deer drives harbor inherent risks. Losing sight of other hunters in your party is always possible, and a hunter's movement can easily be mistaken for the movement of the game being hunted.
- Before the hunt, consider carefully the value of your hunting plan. Then make that plan clear to every hunter involved—and follow it.

25

The Last Time I Got Shot . . .

But those who wait upon God get fresh strength.
They spread their wings and soar like eagles,
They run and don't get tired,
They walk and don't lag behind.

—ISAIAH 40:31

MY LOVE FOR ALL THINGS OUTDOORS, HUNTING AND ANYTHING that goes with it, my faith, and the importance of family all go a long way back—long before my career as a conservation officer began. I will happily and proudly credit my father with starting it all.

My dad was one of thirteen children whose parents had come to America from Belgium in 1911. His father had given him a love for hunting, which he passed on to all ten of his children, to my five brothers and me in particular.

When I was growing up, my dad's day job was running a big store in my hometown. It was not a department store in the modern sense of the word, but it wasn't an old-fashioned general store either. The Outdoor Store carried everything from clothes and shoes to paint, toys, and fabric. I began working there when I was eight years old, doing odd jobs until I could be hired legally, just as all my siblings did both before and after me.

But it was in the large sporting goods department, which eventually became its own store, that I found my heaven on earth. I spent hours carefully studying all the different rifles, shotguns, and handguns. I learned the specifics of every box of bullets. I anxiously awaited the new product catalogs that would arrive each year. I memorized all the makes, model numbers, and ballistics of every type of firearm and ammunition we sold. Before too long, I became a veritable encyclopedia of all things hunting.

As my brothers and I grew up, Dad would take one or two of us along whenever he went deer hunting. Our job there was simple: The first one to see a buck our dad later harvested would get a silver dollar. We all quickly gained eagle eyes, a skill we retained long after hunting season was over.

During long summer drives through the country, you would hear one of us yell "There's a deer!" every time we spotted a whitetail, even though deer season was a long way off. As we got older, the annual hunting party became "Nick and His Boys." Like his dad before him, Dad would take a stand at the end of the woods, and we boys would bust through the brush, stomp through the swamp, and hopefully push "the big one" to Dad.

My dad hunted with his boys for some twenty years before the owners closed the store. My parents thought they would like warmer climes, so they moved to Florida and then on to Virginia, where Dad helped run similar stores. But time eventually caught up with him, and he retired. My parents moved back home to be with their children and grandchildren, including my own three kids.

After living away for seven years, I was ready to head home and find my own piece of heaven. I was lucky enough to find thirty-two acres to buy just a mile or so outside my hometown. It was the first year my folks were home, and as my dad had not been deer hunting in many years, I made it my goal to get Dad a deer. Maybe it could be a small way to pay him back for all he had taught me and done for me over the years. Getting him his first deer in decades, on my own property, had deep, real significance.

The second Saturday of the season was unseasonably warm. Clear skies and sixty-five degrees were not what we wanted for tracking whitetails in the brush, but we headed out, hoping for the best. We both had tags for antlered and antlerless deer and were ready for either, but neither of us had any expectation of what was to come.

We sat in our stands for the first hour or so and then decided to do some small drives through the thick brush, since the deer did not seem to want to do any moving on their own. It was a good day for me to do the walking while Dad did the watching, and so we got started.

We had pushed through most of my property and then headed to the swampy area across the road, part of the land owned by my local sportsmen's club. Dad walked in across from the end of my driveway, and I went down the road a couple hundred yards to walk the overgrown area back in his direction. On a lane at the far end, near a radio tower, I came upon two familiar pickup trucks. I shook my head in frustration as I recognized them as belonging to a group of persistent knuckleheads I had been having trouble with since I had first bought my property.

My land had been neglected for many years before I purchased it. At one time, it had been a part of a farm; later it had been owned by an out-of-state construction company. They had used it as their headquarters when they built the interstate that now bordered the property, but they were long gone. After their departure, the property became the local place to party. People were free to ride dune buggies and dirt bikes without any visits from the local police or anyone else bothering them.

The property also was open to anyone who wanted to hunt there. The sportsmen's club that abutted the property had actually purchased it from the construction company but had never used it. I purchased the land, and just outside of town, at the end of a dead-end road, we built our dream home. Being able to hunt by just walking out my door was absolutely amazing. The hardest decision I faced each day was whether I go out the front door or the back to walk into wilderness.

My ownership of the property brought the first No Trespassing signs ever. Since my house was built from natural wood and hidden in the trees five hundred feet back from the road, I regularly encountered hikers and hunters. From the first year I lived there, I had to deal with people who were surprised to see the signs and the house. After a friendly greeting, I explained who I was. Many unsuspecting trespassers left with a quick apology and a handshake, but others weren't happy to know the partying, off-roading days were over.

One group in particular kept straying over the line, intentionally trespassing. This was especially true if they thought I had gone to work. The group was made up of a local father, who usually brought his son along with his brother-in-law and nephew from out of town. Since we both had permission to hunt the properties on the three sides of my place, we regularly bumped into one another. This particular year I had decided to try to be more neighborly, reminding them of the property lines if necessary but also talking to them about where they had been, what they had seen, and where we would each go next.

With a radio tower building close by and my neighbor's house just beyond, I was sure they must have walked the swamp, away from the trucks, to the south and toward the highway. I had left my shotgun home but was carrying my Smith and Wesson Model 681, .357 Magnum on my hip.

This revolver had been my first handgun issued on the job, and I had purchased it from the distributor when the state decided to trade them all in for Glock Model 17, 9 millimeters. The Smith and Wesson was a great shooter, and I had a real fondness for it. It had been with me for years. I had gone through Firearms Instructors School with it, and after shooting thousands and thousands of rounds with it in practice, I was very confident with it. If I did happen to see any deer today, it would be at very close range in the brushy swamp, so the handgun would be perfect. It was also much easier to carry through the brush.

I had only gone thirty or forty yards when my life changed forever.

Things happened very fast, but remembering it is like re-watching a familiar movie where you know all the details. I can remember this piece of my life story movie and watch it in slow motion, over and over again, getting all the details. I was wearing blue jeans, a flannel shirt, and a blaze orange vest and hat as I followed a deer trail into an opening in the brush. There were standing water and cattails to my right, real thick brush both in front of me and to the left, but I was standing in a small clearing of mixed grasses about ankle high.

Much to my surprise, I saw a deer jump up out of where it had been bedded down in front of me and run to the left. At the very same time, I saw a hunter dressed in full camouflage stepping out from behind a bush. He was about thirty-five yards away, and, with the deer directly between us, he started to raise his gun. He fired quickly, more from the hip than his shoulder.

Immediately I saw something big and white headed right at me. A lifetime of firearms knowledge, which began in my father's store, combined with all the years of hunting and being a police firearms instructor all led me to the same conclusion: A deer slug was headed for my throat. This same background, education, and experience told me that getting hit with a deer slug in the throat from very close range was a very bad thing. I needed to move—*now!*

I swung my left shoulder sharply away, trying to dodge the bullet, but found myself hit as if with a sledgehammer! I spun backward and fell to the ground, with the back of my head in the watery, cattail-filled ditch. Rolling a bit, I immediately began yelling, "Help, Help, I've been hit! I've been hit! *Help! Help!*"

Looking back, I remember hearing two more shots, one of which was really close and the other a long way off. In that moment, I took a quick assessment and realized my handgun was drawn and in my right hand, lying across my chest with my finger off the trigger. I certainly did not remember doing that, but my years of training had apparently kicked in to offer me some protection from my assailant.

Looking up from my awkward position on the ground, I saw a group of five hunters—the same troublesome trespassers whose trucks I had just passed—standing over me.

I immediately demanded, "Who shot me?"

I was not surprised as each one was quick to say, "Not me."

But my training was still at work, and despite the pain and shock of being shot, I noticed one of them did not have a gun.

Nodding toward the empty-handed young man, outfitted in full camo, I inquired, "Where is your gun?"

This question left the guy stammering, "Well . . . um . . . I . . . um . . . well, I uh, well . . ."

Pulling himself together, he tried again: "When I heard you yell, I dropped my gun so I could come here and help."

Not believing him for a minute, I replied, "Yeah, right. Let's find your gun."

Despite the horrible pain throbbing from my shoulder, I managed to holster my sidearm, get up, and head out with the jerk, all the while thinking, *What kind of idiot would hunt in this area with full camo?*

We did not go far and, as I suspected, there was his shotgun where he had thrown it. And as I suspected, and you probably have guessed, he was the one I had seen—the one who had shot me.

I quickly brought him back to the others. With the wound in my shoulder, my raging pain and anger on the rise, along with the discovery of the cast-off gun, I was pushed into full police mode.

I pulled together what I knew: I had just been shot in the upper left chest with a deer slug, and I was probably going to die. But before I did that, my plan was to get all the evidence I needed from these idiots and die on top of it all so that someone would be able to find the evidence, find these morons, and arrest all of them

Holding my left arm to my shoulder to try to control a bit of the pain, I ordered them to separate and sit down. I ordered them to put all their guns, knives, ammo, and hunting and drivers' licenses in nice neat piles in front of them. As I was doing this, I realized the bleeding had slowed down significantly and I was managing to get my breath back. With this realization, I changed my mind. I decided I was not going to die, I was not going to let them win, and no one else was going to handle this hunting accident. I was going to handle this. They would not get away; I would arrest them and happily fill out any forms I had to in order to make sure they were brought to justice.

I started looking through the assortment of evidence I had ordered them to produce and first picked up the pile from the kid who had shot me. He was a local nineteen-year-old and he only had a doe tag that was not even valid in my area. His first charge was an easy one. I told him he was under arrest for "Possessing Slugs Afield without a Valid Tag."

Next was his cousin from out of town. All he had was a back tag, no deer tags of any kind. When I asked him where his deer tags were, he mumbled that he had used them all. I told him he was under arrest for the same charge as his relative. Next came the father of the young man who had shot me; his tags, surprisingly, all turned out okay.

When I got to the uncle from out of town, it got a bit more interesting. I could clearly see all his tags were separated, bloody, and filled out, thus voiding them from future use. I told him he was under arrest too. He was indignant.

"For what?" he asked, and I repeated what I had for the other two, "Possessing Slugs Afield without a Valid Tag."

Imagine my surprise when he told me, the game warden, that "since I never filled the date in on my doe tag, I can use it again!"

I was almost giddy, probably from the pain, when I took an even closer look at the tag and saw that it was not only invalid for my area but was almost all filled out for another town to the north; in addition, it was covered with blood. It had obviously once been tied to a deer. He was right though . . . the date had not been filled in.

Not wanting to waste any of the breath I was trying to hold onto, I snapped back, "Shut up! No, you can't! You are under arrest!"

I did not recognize the fifth person in their group, but since his tags looked to be in order, he was not arrested. In fact, I was happy to see that he looked as though he was about to faint or throw up—maybe both. His obvious pain made my own a bit easier to handle.

I ordered them all to stay where they were, with absolutely no talking, and said I would be right back. A man on a mission, I walked to my neighbor's house, just over five hundred feet away, to call for help.

Bill, my neighbor, was clearly surprised to see me at his back door, but being a good neighbor, he asked, "Hey, Michael, what's up?"

Without wasting words, I told him I had just been shot and needed to use his phone. Ashen-faced and wide-eyed, he stumbled back into the wall and mumbled, "Yeah, sure," pointing me to the telephone.

This exchange was the first of many important lessons I learned from this shooting: I should not have blurted out to Bill that I had been shot. In the future I would be more careful in how I informed someone of an injury or death that I was investigating.

My first call was to 911; I identified myself as an environmental police lieutenant and said that I had been shot. I also informed them that I had arrested a large group of hunters and, as a result of all of this, needed some backup.

When the operator asked if I needed an ambulance, I had to pause and think, *Did I?*

I was really rolling now that I knew I was not going to die; I was going to be okay. Added to this wonderful fact was the reality that I had a bunch of prisoners and a crime scene to deal with, so, *No*, I did not have time to go to the hospital.

I also knew that if it had been anyone else and I was a first responder, I would do whatever I needed to do to make the victim get in an ambulance and get checked out at a hospital. I knew there was plenty of time and that other officers would soon arrive who could handle the scene. So I gave the answer I knew was correct but did not want to give: "Yes, please send an ambulance. Thank you."

My next call went to Don, the lieutenant, and good friend, with whom I was working on the Hunting Accident Research Project. Without meaning to or wanting to, I had once again become one of the statistics we were studying and, hopefully, preventing.

I wanted his expert eyes and experience on the scene, my investigation, to make sure it was handled the right way. I had no intention of my accident being mishandled like many others we had seen.

Finally I called my wife, Mary, who at the end became the real hero in this story. I told her I had been shot by one of those darn trespassers but that I would be fine. I also told her I had arrested them all and what I really needed was to get back to the scene. I reassured her with the fact that Don was on his way and would make sure the investigation was handled right.

Again I reassured her, "I will be fine."

As calm as could be, she rose to the occasion and reassured me that she would also be okay. She said she would see me soon, and then she wished me luck.

I hurried back to the scene to check on my prisoners. I was almost there when a "fly car," or rapid response vehicle, with an emergency medical technician (EMT) pulled into the lane behind me. The driver got out and said he had gotten the call that someone had been shot and asked me if I knew who or where.

He was a bit surprised to hear me say over my shoulder, "Yep, that's me. But I am in a hurry; you will have to follow me." I continued on to the scene.

With a startled look on his face, the EMT followed me down the lane and out into the swampy brush.

I was happy and proud of how well I was performing, and almost impressed to see that all five members of the group had obeyed me to the letter. They were all just where I had left them, with all the evidence still in neat piles in front of each of them.

Once we arrived, the EMT took over and had me sit down so that he could look at my wound. His first request was to ask me to move my arm away from my shoulder so that he could see the wound better. I was quick to say, "No!"

My left hand and arm had been resting on my chest since I had been hit, and I just knew my collarbone was broken. I had begun to think that since it didn't hurt nearly as much anymore, maybe I could just keep my arm folded against my chest—forever. That sounded like a perfect plan to me.

Meanwhile, other people started arriving in droves. The sheriff was the first in line, and I was certainly glad to see him. I needed to hand off the evidence and prisoners while I was distracted by the nuisance of being treated for my gunshot wound. I explained that these were my prisoners and all the piles were my evidence and asked him to guard them all for me.

Then the ambulance arrived, and it became clear that every ambulance attendant and police officer from the county and beyond were coming to see what was going on. Apparently the report that had gone out over the radio had given the impression that I was shot while trying to make an arrest. Everyone thought a manhunt for someone who had tried to kill a cop was being organized, and they wanted to help find the suspects!

In the midst of all of this chaos and noise, I heard Dad calling my name in the distance. In a flash I remembered the last shot I had heard. It had come from the direction where I knew my dad was.

I just knew he was calling me to let me know he had actually shot a deer and wanted me to come field dress it and drag it out for him. After all, isn't that what sons are for?

There were several people just standing around with nothing to do, so I called out to a guy wearing a volunteer ambulance jacket. I told him the man calling my name was my dad and that I had been hunting with him. I told him Dad was now looking for me and described how he was dressed and what he looked like.

I explained that my dad had some health problems and that I could tell from his voice, calling over the shouting and noise, that he was getting scared. I asked the volunteer if he would please go find my dad, tell him where I was, and, most importantly, tell him I would be okay.

The ambulance volunteer just stood there looking stupid until the sheriff told him to go find my dad. The volunteer headed off, leaving me thinking he had done as requested. I would find out later that he never did try to find my dad.

The EMT began insisting that I go to the hospital. Though I really wanted to stay, I knew it was the right thing to do; I agreed to go. I got in the ambulance, and the EMT radioed in that we were en route to the hospital, which was only about two miles away. I listened as the EMT told the hospital that they were transporting a patient with multiple pellet wounds to the upper left chest.

Still feeling the need to be in charge, I was quick to enlighten the ambulance crew: "No, it is not multiple pellets; it is a shotgun slug."

They were just as quick to ignore my expertise. "Stay calm, sir, it will be alright."

I was insulted by their condescension! I am a firearms expert and, as such, I certainly know what I got shot with! I tried again to explain, and they tried again to get me to lie back and remain calm.

On our way to the hospital, the EMTs finally convinced me to move my arm a little so they could look at the wound. Taking a look for myself, I could see a good many weeping bloody spots.

From what I could tell, it seemed that when I turned away from the rapidly approaching slug, it had traveled across my chest and made a striking blow across my shoulder before hitting the shoulder joint and bouncing off! The path the slug took across my body had left the top layers of skin peeled back and shoved together like a throw rug that had been kicked aside.

We arrived quickly at the hospital and I was admitted to the emergency room. I was lying in a bed when the doctor asked me, as had the EMT and ambulance crew before him, to straighten my arm so he could examine me. I repeated that I was real happy to leave it folded against my chest forever.

While not a medical expert, I remained convinced that my collarbone was not only broken but also that any movement could cause it to puncture my heart or lungs. But since they were the medical experts and I was not, they finally got me to straighten my arm out. My shirt was peeled back, and I could clearly see my wound for the first time.

It was now apparent that not only was I an expert in firearms, capable of surviving not one but two shootings, with the strength and stamina to arrest both of the shooters involved, but I had had a deer slug fired at me from less than thirty-five yards away and survived. In fact, this time the slug had bounced right off my shoulder!

It was now clear to me—I was Superman. I saw the bullet coming, decided to dodge it, and almost did. Even though the slug actually did hit me, it bounced off! The adrenaline was really flowing through my veins now, and except for a huge bruise and a lot of pain, it was plain to see—I was almost invincible!

Meanwhile, back at the crime scene, things were getting interesting. My dad was still wandering around, wondering where I was and who was going to help him with the deer he had just got, his first deer in over fifteen years!

Dad had been calling for me as he walked down the road. The road to my house is crooked, with several twists and turns. Coming around the last turn, he was surprised to see a vast variety of police cars and officers. He rightfully thought that it was "some kind of police thing and I was involved in it" but had no idea how much.

Dad asked the first officer he saw if he knew where I was. The officer did not know me and replied that he did not know where I was. Dad went to the next officer and got the same response. When he asked yet another officer if he knew where I was, he was told, "Yeah, somebody shot him; they just took him to the hospital."

My dad almost collapsed. Fortunately one of my own fellow officers, who also knew my father, saw him and told him I was going to be okay. My wife, Mary, arrived at the scene at that point, and she quickly drove Dad to the hospital.

I will never forget the sight of my dad in the hospital. He walked into my exam room at the hospital and, upon seeing me, let the tears flow. I felt the first huge wave of guilt as I watched him fall back against the wall and slump to the floor.

I couldn't help but think, *What have I done? I've made my dad so sad.*

Mary was right there, and she helped him to his feet. I assured him that I was going to be just fine, and he came to my bedside and gave me a big hug.

Dad was soon back to his old self, joking and letting me know that I needed to get up pretty quick so I could take care of his deer! One of the officers with me at the emergency room volunteered to go back with him and get his prized deer, fifteen years in the waiting, field dressed and back to my house.

After my father left, they took me in for X-rays, which revealed no broken bones. With this good news, I was in a hurry to get back to my prisoners, my evidence, and my crime scene. I was quickly bandaged and given a sling to advertise my injury; then I was on my way.

When I got back to the scene, I was amazed at what I saw. It seemed as though every police officer—local, county, and state— who was anywhere close to the scene had responded, and more were still arriving. As I stepped out of the car, a few of my friends stopped in their tracks and their jaws dropped. I was alive!

Coming to my side, they all said they were certain I was in the hospital, fighting for my life. Nobody just walks away from a shotgun slug at such close range. Their words proved, once again, my Superman status.

Seeing all the experts who came to help, I decided I would try hard not to be the investigator. I would take on the role of the professional expert witness and let the others handle the investigation.

The car radio was jammed as coworkers and friends called in, asking if more help was needed. They were quite surprised to hear my voice letting them know that everything was covered and they didn't need to come.

But in truth, they all wanted, and needed, to come and see my face and shake my hand. Before too long, my wife made her way back to the scene, accompanied by my youngest son, Jordan. They pushed their way through the crowd to reach me. When Jordan saw me, he ran up, hugged my leg, and said, "Daddy, I am so glad you are not dead."

The feelings overwhelmed me again for causing so much pain to my family, despite the fact that it was not my fault at all. First my dad and now my son was sad and worried, and I was happy, grateful, and excited about being alive. My wife, still stronger than I could have imagined, began thinking of all the friends and coworkers who had gathered to find out how I was and how they could help. Knowing they would be hungry, she said she would go home and make some sheet pizzas. She insisted that when we were done at the scene, I should invite them all back to the house for a party to celebrate.

I was grateful for her presence of mind, because all I could keep thinking was, *I got shot and the bullet bounced off!*

With all the investigators from several agencies and an evidence technician van from the sheriff's department there, I was confident that a great job was being done on the case. Various officers had the members of the hunting party in their cars getting statements. Everything looked good, so I just stood back and watched.

Later I found out it had not gone as well as it looked. As with the other botched shooting incidents I had been reviewing, mistakes were made. The sheriff's department insisted on taking the lead, and as too often happens, the members of my agency did not assert themselves and took a backseat.

Unfortunately the sheriff's deputies did not recognize the importance of all the deer tags, so they returned them to the hunters. They only kept the evidence from the young man who had shot me. This lapse in judgment over what constitutes important evidence would become an issue in many future cases as well.

When we finally cleared the scene, my fellow officers all came up to our house, where they showed me Dad's deer, dressed and hanging in my barn. We continued into the house to celebrate, laugh, and share pizza.

During the celebratory pizza meal, I got a call from my director at the state capital. He had heard about my shooting and wanted to know how I was. He assured me I was cleared to take off whatever time I needed to recover. I thanked him for the call but explained to him that I was going to be fine; after all, the bullet bounced right off me!

Soon one of my many nephews came by, excited to tell his own part of the story. He had just been at the video store and one of the guys in front of him was talking to another customer.

"Did you hear what happened? Somebody shot the game warden and the bullet bounced right off! He got up off the ground and arrested the whole lot of them!"

My nephew thought it might be me they were talking about and was ecstatic to discover it was. His uncle was famous! Hearing this side of the story made us all laugh again, and I completely agreed. But, I was quick to remind the friends and family surrounding me, that it was important for everyone to remember that I was, after all, "a skilled professional." I insisted that they "Do not try this at home." I got the laughs I expected.

The adrenaline, along with the medication I received at the hospital, was masking any pain, and I was on top of the world. I was Superman, the hero of the story. I was the guy that bullets bounced off, and I proudly showed off my injury, laughing and enjoying life completely.

Sunday morning, the next day, arrived. In those days I sang in the musical folk group at my church, and as I walked in with my family, heads throughout the church turned. Like a ripple in a pond, people poked the person next to them and pointed, and then poked the person in front of them.

Soon there were waves of congratulations and thumbs up from across the church. News travels fast in a small town, and my friends in the folk group were amazed that I was there. Their prayers had started the moment they were told I had been shot, and no one thought I would be up walking around.

Smiling at everyone, I repeated my new tagline: "Yep! I am a skilled professional. It bounced right off. Do not try this at home."

The laughter was contagious. It felt so great to be there, on the side of the altar, singing and praising God, so happy to be alive. Looking out into the congregation, as each person caught my eye, he or she would smile, wave, or give me a thumbs up. It was a wonderful time to be alive—until the last song.

A physiological and psychological series of events can happen when people are put in a life-threatening situation. I knew all about them. I am, after all, a professional. I even considered myself an expert.

Over the years, as part of my duties and training as a police firearms instructor, I had attended several "street survival" training sessions, where I learned about the stressors that happen to police when deadly physical force is necessitated. These stressors exist either when the force is used by the police officer toward someone or when someone uses it against the officer.

For years I had taught this exact topic to our recruit classes, as well as at in-service schools. One of the key lessons is the reality of the emotional and physical roller coaster that occurs when you get an adrenaline dump into your system.

While there is the immediate rush and a high that includes a sense of invincibility, this is often followed by a crash and a resulting adrenaline hangover as it finally leaves your system. This roller-coaster crash can be followed by feelings of remorse, anger, confusion, depression, and sleeplessness. The list of struggles goes on.

I knew all about this because I had taught it so many times. Obviously, though, I thought I would never get shot; and if I did, none of that would ever happen to me. I was a skilled professional. Teaching and knowing all about it should make me immune. Personally, I can tell you that my adrenaline high lasted exactly twenty-three hours and forty-five minutes.

I was shot just before noon on Saturday, and at 11:45 a.m. on Sunday, it all hit me like a ton of bricks. My roller-coaster high came to a rapid end while we were singing one of my favorite hymns, "On Eagle's Wings" by Michael Joncas. We just got to the part of the song that says God will lift you up when your world comes crashing down. You know in cartoons, when they want to show that their character is really scared? The illustrators drain the color from them, from their head to their toes, until they are just an empty white outline. That is exactly how I felt. I could feel every bit of my energy rapidly draining from me . . . it was as though I was losing my very soul.

I went from the best feeling in my life to the worst, in just a matter of seconds. I have endured loss before; my wife and I have struggled with grief and sadness. Years earlier we had been devastated to learn that our first child had died in the womb just weeks before he should have been born. This feeling, however, was even worse than that great grief.

Looking out into the church at my family in the front row, my fellow singers and musicians, and all the others who were smiling and singing, all I felt was fear! I have never been so scared! I did not want to be there, did not want any of these people looking at me, did not want to be the hero, and did not want to be

Superman! I wanted to find a way to disappear—to hide any-where, anyplace, alone and far away from everybody.

This unexpected fear was quickly joined by anger as I worked hard to hold back the panic. I needed to get out of there fast! As soon as the singing stopped, I grabbed my coat and told my family to follow me. "We are leaving!"

Of course my wife had no idea what had happened to me. She said, "Wait, all these people want to talk to you."

I told her to do what I said: "Get the kids and get in the damn car!"

My older son, Ben, could tell by my voice that something was wrong. "Dad, what's wrong?" he asked.

I had no time for his question. I told him to just shut up and get going. We were leaving! *Now!*

When we finally got out of church, my daughter, Jessica, looked scared when she asked if we were going out to brunch like we usually did. I had a good dose of anger ready for her as well. "Just get in the damn car! We are leaving!"

I became terrified at the thought that one of our friends would catch us before we could escape. They would want to shake my hand, to hear my story, to talk about it and wish me well. I had to get out of there before that happened.

As soon as we got home, I sat in my chair and fumed. I was raging uncontrollably. I was mad at the stupid kid who shot me. I was mad at his father and uncle, who had trespassed for all those years. I was mad at everything and everyone. I just wanted my life back; I just wanted it all to go away. I barely managed to hold back the tears, but inside I was a mess.

My family members were clearly confused by this change. They kept trying to get close to me and see what they could do to help. They asked more than once if I wanted anything, and I just snapped that I wanted them to shut up and go away! "Leave me alone!" It still hurts me today to think of how I treated them; they had done nothing but love me. But I had no control over my emotions and at the time had no idea what was going on.

My rage was for anyone and everyone. If an investigator had stopped by to get a statement from me that day, I would have thrown him off the property. The victim is usually very cooperative unless he or she has something to hide! In my mood, with my rage, it would have been easy for any investigator to jump to the conclusion that I was not cooperating because I had something to hide. In truth, I did want to hide myself from everything around me.

It snowed about six inches on Sunday, and as a result, the crime scene had changed completely. One of my friends assigned to work on the investigation called to see if I could go back and help take some measurements on Monday. My first thought was, *Hell, no! Why didn't you do all that yesterday? What the heck is wrong with you?*

But despite treating my family the way I had, I was able to bite my tongue and say, "Sure, call me tomorrow."

As the day went on, I was too tired to stay angry. I just went to bed, completely drained and exhausted. The next day was better. I told my family I was sorry for yesterday, that it was all the build-up from being shot and that I was better but still really tired. I could never take back what I had said; I could only apologize.

Monday morning came and with it the last week of deer season. I had tags in my pocket and snow on the ground. The only other hunters in the area had their guns seized as evidence, though I was sure they would never be back anyway. I had agreed to take a week off to recover, and still-hunting in new snow was one of my favorite things to do. Being alone with my thoughts in the winter woods is very soothing for both soul and mind, and just what I needed—or so I thought.

After breakfast I got bundled up and headed out the back door into my woods. I never got out of sight of the house. At the top of the ridge, one hundred yards out, I stopped. I knew there would be no one else around but me, yet I found myself feeling afraid. I knew there were lots of deer still out there, but I could not keep walking. I froze in my tracks, and the fear started to build inside me. With tears in my eyes, I turned around and headed home, filled with a profound sadness.

Next to my faith and my family, I love hunting the most. I love all kinds of hunting—with a bow or gun, small game or big game. It was an important part of who I was. Back home, I sat in my chair and fought back the tears. What if I never got better? What if the fear never left? What if I could never go hunting again? These questions haunted me.

The state Division of Law Enforcement has a Critical Incident Response Team (CIRT), which offers peer support for cases like this. A close friend of mine, Walt, was one of the responders. I thought about calling Walt but decided that, since I was a professional, I did not really need to bother him.

As with the ambulance incident, I knew that if it were anyone else, I would have insisted that the victim take the time to talk to one of the team, maybe just to have a cup of coffee or lunch. So I called Walt, who drove out the next day. After he said hello to my wife, we went to a diner for coffee.

I have no idea what we talked about that day and was amazed to realize that we had talked for over three hours. When we got back to the house, Walt asked to speak to Mary alone. They went in another room and talked for a while. Then he said his goodbyes and headed for home. Neither Mary nor I can remember what was said, only that we each felt much better and, more important, at peace after talking to him.

The next day I tried to go hunting again. I got a bit farther out but could not stay long. Each day I was able to venture out farther, and by the end of the week, I had worked through it and was enjoying the solitude of my walks in the woods. And while it had only taken me several days to feel brave enough to go out, a bit of nagging fear remained in the back of my mind for several years. I can remember wondering if it would ever go away, but I do not remember when it did.

While I was enduring my own struggles, I didn't realize it was much worse for my wife. For a long time, she did not let me know about her fears because she knew how much I enjoyed going out. However, when I went hunting again, she had to fight back panic attacks. Every time she heard a shot in the woods, she worried that it might be me. This fear worsened when the boys were old enough to go hunting with me. She suffered in silence every time, and although it did get better with time, it still bothers her today, almost twenty years later.

Over the next few days, weeks, and months while I worked on my home life, I kept up with the progress of the investigation. I took the measurements with my coworker, but without the missing deer tags, they had a long and detailed investigation to accomplish.

At the conclusion, the officers were able to determine that three of the party involved had killed several deer illegally and/ or failed to tag ones taken legally. It also turned out that four of the five had felony arrest records! While the two young men did not have felony convictions, perhaps due to their ages at the time of the arrests, both their dads had done serious time in prison for multiple felonies, including rape and violent assault.

They should never have had a firearm or even been in the woods that day.

I also found out why the fifth member of the group, the only one without an arrest record, looked so sick the day of the incident. It turns out he was a corrections officer who *knew* he was hunting with a group that included two felons, and a member of his party had just shot the game warden! He was sure he was going to lose his job, or worse.

My case caused quite a stir in the Division of Law Enforcement. We were not accustomed to doing in-depth police investigations and then filing charges in such cases. At one point, there was a meeting with everyone working on the case along with the director of the division, a captain from Albany, and the assistant district attorney (ADA) who was handling my case. The captain saw himself as some sort of legal expert, and at one point, he tried to lecture the ADA about the meaning of the different culpable mental states that might apply, such as *reckless*.

The ADA would have none of it. But then the captain said they did not want to start arresting hunters just because they shot somebody, because it would "give hunting a bad name"!

That was just too much! The ADA was as startled as I was, and he clearly stated, "Well, in this county when you shoot one of our police officers you get arrested, and that is all there is to it." Needless to say, this particular investigation did not make me popular with those same bosses in the future.

Another issue that complicated the investigation was caused by the very basic two-page report that New York and many other states were using at the time. As an example of the lack of value on this overly simplistic form, you were asked to describe the area where the shooting happened but were given only four choices to check and only allowed to check one: field, swamp, woods, or brush.

That form had seemed adequate until it came to my case. Because it was very brushy all around me, that box had been checked. Upon seeing the area was brushy, those in charge immediately concluded that since it was in a brushy area, it was not the shooter's fault. Brush would have prevented him from seeing me. He could not see me; therefore, it was just an accident.

However, in truth, all the boxes could have been checked and still would not have told the whole story. Yes, there was brush around me and the shooter was in the brush when he shot; but I was standing in a clearing with ankle-high grass more like a small field. In addition, I fell into standing water and cattails, so it was also a swamp. Just off to the left was a thick grove of white pines, so maybe we could say it was more of a woods. In spite of all the words on the form, none of the options on any standard form would have accurately described the situation that was unique to this investigation.

All that really mattered was could the shooter have, and should he have, seen me before he decided to fire that shot? I know that from the position where the shooter was and where I was, that I was 100 percent visible to the shooter.

But like the frog hunter incident eight years earlier, while I am sure the shooter did not see me before he fired, he certainly *could* have. Therefore, he *should* have seen me. In both cases, the shooters failed to follow the basic rule of being sure they had a safe backstop before firing.

In conclusion, multiple charges were filed against four of the men involved, and they all pleaded guilty as charged, including Possession of Slugs Afield without a Valid License, Assault in the Third Degree, and Criminal Possession of a Weapon in the Fourth Degree. Their fines totaled $3,500, all their shotguns were forfeited to the state, and the shooter was sentenced to six months of weekends in jail.

The case was starting to close, but there was one final detail. It was a revocation hearing for the guy who shot me. This is an administrative hearing to determine whether the shooter in an incident acted recklessly and should lose his or her ability to purchase a license in the future. For cases like mine, the penalty can be up to loss of license for five years, while in fatal incidents it can be up to ten years.

The hearing went as expected until the father of the shooter informed the officer in charge that he wanted to put in a personnel complaint against me. The hearing officer was another lieutenant I knew, and he followed procedure. "Of course," he asked, "what is your complaint?"

The father wanted to file a complaint based on the fact that after his son shot me, I yelled at them. I was so happy with the way the investigation was going at this point that I couldn't help but laugh out loud when the hearing officer replied, without a bit of sarcasm, "Do you think? You know, when you shoot somebody, it tends to really piss them off. I would have yelled at you, too!" That was the end of that.

In the words of the great Paul Harvey, we need the rest of the story. The white thing I saw heading toward me was actually the deer slug from my shooter's gun, with most of the fur from a deer's tail flying along with it. The shot was a glancing blow that nicked the right hip of the doe, took half the fur off its tail, and then continued toward me. They actually found that clump of deer tail fur, looking like a badminton birdie, about halfway between the shooter and me.

But in an even more incredible fluke, it turned out that the deer my dad shot was the same deer I had seen crossing my path—and the same deer nicked by the slug that went on to bounce off me!

I got hit by the deer slug, the same slug the doe was supposed to get, and my dad got the doe the slug was supposed to kill. Without knowing it, my own father collected a key piece of evidence used to prove that both the guy who shot me and his cousin had shot at an antlerless deer for which neither had a tag! My dad had continued to help me just as he always had; he just didn't know it! And just as I had thought, Dad was calling me to come and field dress this same deer and drag it home for him.

The investigators had collected the shuttlecock-shaped deer hair and placed it in an evidence bag. It was clear how the slug had pushed the hair toward me, with the white hair making it easy for me to see it coming.

Since this shooting, I have used my own story to illustrate and teach others important rules for hunter safety. And many times someone has questioned my story's details, in particular my claim that I could see the slug and move out of the way.

But as I have stated every time since, these are the facts. I was walking directly toward the guy who shot me on the same deer path he was on, but my wound and scar clearly came from right to left across my shoulder. This could only happen if I was turned ninety degrees away from the shooter when the slug hit the deer, and ninety degrees is a long way to turn when a slug is headed your way from just over one hundred feet away.

I have no doubt the good Lord had my guardian angel turn me away from the slug and certain death. Not that I want to complain, but more than once, I have thought it would have been great if my angel had turned me just a little bit harder. If he could have done that, the slug would have missed me completely, and I wouldn't have gone through all the stress or put my dad or my wife and my children through all the mess.

On the other side of the coin, my injury led to major changes in my life and also in the science of investigating hunting-related shootings. The issue of documenting visibility led me to invent the measurement of visibility device, which allows any investigator to accurately determine the visibility between the shooter and the victim. The investigator uses this tool to record a number, a percentage from 0 percent to 100 percent, which can be readily understood. Determining if a shooter had 100 percent visibility or only 10 percent makes sense to everyone involved in the investigation. It helps focus on the vital issue of what the shooter could have and/or should have seen.

The next year I heard about the Hunting Incident Investigation Academy that was held in Missouri and was able to get the state to send me. That is where I first learned about the science of hunting-related shooting investigations and where I met my two partners and coauthors of this book. The only bad thing about that week was that the captain from Albany also attended; not only that, he was my roommate—and he still didn't like me!

Lessons Learned

- Once again, the shooter failed to obey one of the most important rules of safe hunting: "Identify your target and what is beyond it." He saw what he was hunting, but he never took the time to look beyond that target to see if it was safe to fire in that direction. In this case, I was in plain view beyond the target, and the shot should never have been taken. There were also two trucks just behind me and a house just over five hundred feet away and directly in the line of fire, giving yet another reason not to shoot. The shooter was too caught up in the excitement of the shot to ensure the safety of the shot.

- Be aware of the emotions with everyone involved in a shooting incident. Knowing the victim will face anger, depression, and fear will make helping the person through those emotions a bit easier. Take full advantage of resources in the area, including public agencies and the private sector. Insisting on counseling and ongoing care will help both the victim and the investigation.

- Those involved in the investigation, from first responders to follow-up investigators, should remember the victim and his or her needs. Attending to the victim's requests as much as legally possible might seem inconvenient or unnecessary, but it is often essential. My dad would have been spared a lot of fear and suffering if the ambulance volunteer had done as I asked.

- Even if blaze orange clothing is not required, it is a good idea. It helps other hunters see you and know where you are, and helps you see the other hunters as well. When blaze orange is required and everyone in your hunting group is wearing blaze orange, it is important to remember that there may be hikers and other non-hunters in the area who may not be wearing orange.

26

They Were Unable to Save Him

To find fault is easy; to do better may be difficult.

—PLUTARCH

IT WAS LATE ON A SATURDAY AFTERNOON DURING THE DECEMBER shotgun deer season. My partner and I were working as one of the ground cars under the state patrol airplane, which was looking for groups of deer hunters to check. A call was broadcast on our police radio from state police radio dispatch, requesting wildlife officers to respond to a hunting-related shooting in a remote part of Houston County. They advised that first responders were already on the scene, preparing to transport the victim to the regional medical center.

My partner and I were about fifteen minutes from the medical center, so our supervisor instructed us to meet the ambulance at the emergency room (ER) to collect what information we could. Additional officers assigned as ground cars were sent to the scene to begin the field investigation.

We drove into the ER parking lot just as we heard the sound of the ambulance siren approaching. As the ambulance pulled into the ER garage, we ran up and joined the waiting medical team. The first responders quickly unloaded the victim and rolled him into the trauma room.

Suddenly the victim became very combative, but it was apparent he was fighting for his life! As soon as additional monitors were attached, he began to code. One of the ER doctors jumped up on the stretcher, yelling out orders to the expanding number of medical staff in the room as he began CPR on the victim. Another doctor inserted a chest tube into the victim. The chest tube was connected to a large glass container under the stretcher, which immediately began to fill with a bloody fluid. The level of intensity seemed to elevate with each passing second.

For the next twenty minutes, the medical staff attempted all types of lifesaving techniques to try to save this hunter. Finally the doctor who had taken the lead looked at the clock and solemnly declared, "Time of death, 16:41."

The room became very silent; looks of sadness were on every face in the room. They had been unable to save him. We just had to watch him die.

Upon their arrival at the ER, as they unloaded the victim from the ambulance, the first responders from this small rural volunteer fire department had described the wound on the upper left arm as a "grazing" wound. A gunshot wound is the type of call these volunteers rarely, if ever, are called to in this rural area. These hard workers are more likely to encounter farm-related injuries, heart attacks, or vehicle crashes. They advised the doctors that the victim had been conscious, talking, and calm all the way—right until the time they arrived at the medical center.

After the doctor pronounced the death, a portable X-ray machine was moved into the room. The doctor let us know that this was an entrance wound, not a grazing wound. He said, "Let's see what an X-ray will show us."

Everyone was asked to leave the room while the technician took the X-ray. Soon the technician brought the X-ray back to the trauma room. As light illuminated the X-ray, the outline of a slug up against the victim's heart was very clear. The doctor pointed out the slug, saying, "Even if he had been shot out in the hospital parking lot, we would not have been able to save him."

As the doctor had performed the CPR compressions attempting to save this man, he had unknowingly pressed the slug closer to the victim's heart with each push. The amount of blood that drained from the chest tube into the glass container told the story: The victim's chest cavity had been filled with blood. As nurses tended to the victim's body, we seized his clothing as evidence. The layers of clothing fibers also indicated that this was not a mere grazing wound.

My partner and I then proceeded to contact the officers out at the scene; we now had a fatal incident to work. Officers at the scene had already collected license information and taken statements from each of the eight members of the deer-hunting party. One hunter had shot at a running deer in thick brush, just moments before the discovery that their friend had been shot. The shooter told the officers he had shot three times at a running deer, apparently never hitting it. Because it was beginning to get dark, the officers marked the location of the victim before they left the scene. They had collected enough information, so they headed into town to share the information with us.

We decided to meet at the sheriff's office, where it was decided that three other officers and I would work the scene the first thing in the morning. We contacted the only hunter who had shot; he was going meet us at the scene to show us where he was when he had taken his shots.

The next morning we all met at a gate on the west side of the property. The suspected shooter and a friend of his who was part of the hunting party were included in the meeting. The landscape of the incident location was rolling hills covered in multiflora rose, cedar trees, hardwoods, and tall grasses. This natural environment was obviously going to make it difficult to see one another as we spread out to look for evidence, and, as always, we put on our orange jackets over our uniforms. It was still deer season, and the blaze orange made it safer and easier to see one another as we worked the scene.

We began our search for evidence where the victim had been found and discovered several wrapped hard candies that had fallen out of the victim's pocket. The grass had also been stomped down where he had stood, but no blood was found. The suspected shooter took us approximately eighty-five yards southeast of the victim's location. There we found three empty red 12-gauge shotgun hulls. The shooter pointed out where the deer had run from a northeast direction to the southwest. The direction in which the three slugs would have traveled was in the general direction of where the victim had been standing. The statement that the alleged shooter had written the evening before was reviewed with him by one of the officers on our team. They went line by line, making sure all our questions were covered before we released him from the scene. The suspect shooter told us he and his friend would be at his home if we needed to talk with him again.

We then began our search to determine the path of each of the three shotgun slugs by standing where our suspected shooter had indicated. Sure enough, each empty shell was still on the ground to the right of where he had been standing. This evidence made sense based on the ejection system of the pump-action Model 870 Remington, which was the gun used by the suspected shooter.

Using a pair of binoculars and standing in the approximate location of the shooter, we eliminated any peripheral vision distractions. That allowed us to focus on the height and direction of where the projectile (the slug) would have traveled.

As each slug passes through an incident scene's flora, the projectile causes marks and clips. Focusing through the binoculars, the well-trained eye looks for the evidence of each path. As these paths are discovered, team members mark the clips with orange survey ribbon. Corroborating each defined line of trajectory is always a slow and very methodical process.

In this case, our due diligence paid off. We were able to connect all the shots, including one that lined up perfectly with where the victim had been standing.

As our reconstruction of the incident continued, the reenactment of the sequence of events was next. As in this case, the alleged shooter will often say, "I knew he was there, but I didn't think he was right there." We placed an officer in the victim's location and one at the shooter's location to help us figure out the line of fire and how it had impacted the victim.

Based on the X-ray and our view of the wound at the medical center, the slug had entered the upper bicep of the left arm. The slug then passed laterally across the interior chest, resting up against the heart. It was not a "through and through" wound of the arm that then entered the chest.

As we turned the officer in the victim's position toward the direction the slug had come from, we had him move his arms into different positions to follow the path of the slug. Suddenly it became clear that we needed to place a shotgun in the officer's hands to complete the stance.

We grabbed one of our duty shotguns, also a Remington 870, out of a patrol vehicle. The officer reenacting the part of the victim mounted the shotgun to his shoulder as though he was preparing to shoot. This position allowed the line of trajectory to create the exact path of the slug, which had entered the victim's left arm and resulted in his death.

Our reenactment confirmed that the victim had heard the shots and was preparing to shoot at a deer himself if one came into sight. Meanwhile, the heavy brush prevented the officer who was standing in for the suspect shooter from seeing the officer standing in for the victim. Once again, the suspected shooter had known his hunting companion and friend was there—somewhere—but had not known his exact position. Yet he had taken three shots in that direction anyway.

After all the physical evidence was located, photographed, measured, diagrammed, tagged, collected, bagged, and recorded in the evidence log, a visit to the shooter's residence was the next step in the process.

It was only a short drive to the shooter's home, where we were invited to come in. We all sat down at the kitchen table, along with the hunting partner who had been at the scene with him. We explained all the physical evidence we had collected, as well as how we followed each of the slug paths on our diagram. He told us he already knew he was the shooter and was devastated to have it confirmed.

His friend provided words of support and assured us that he would stay with the shooter until his wife got home from work. His friend then called the others from the hunting party to come over and join them.

Events like this can be the most traumatic thing that ever happens in someone's life. It affects everyone involved. Being responsible for taking the life of a friend takes a heavy toll, not only on the person who pulled the trigger but also on all the hunting companions and their family members as well.

Lessons Learned

- Once again, plan your hunt and hunt your plan.
- Be aware of the location of every one of your hunting companions, no matter what game animals you are hunting or the type of cover you are hunting in. "Well . . . I knew he was there, but I didn't think he was right there" has become far too common a response.
- There is no excuse for shooting three times at a running deer in the direction where a hunting partner might be.
- Planning, communication, and patience are all part of being a safe and responsible hunter.
- When in doubt of a shot, *don't take the shot!*

27

A Death in the River Swamp

Be as smart as you can, but remember that it is always better to be wise than to be smart.

— ALAN ALDA

THE BLOOD SPATTER ON THE RIFLE HAD DRIED AND TURNED A dirty brown color. It did not want to give up its hold on the firearm. With gloved hands, Warden Brian Cree tried to scrub and wash all signs of the blood away. But it was as though the blood knew that when it was gone, it would take the true story it told along with it.

Little by little, the blood begrudgingly gave into the soap and water, until all that remained were the outlines of where the blood spatter patterns had been. With a heavy heart, Cree gave the rifle another look. He wanted to make sure he cleaned all the blood from the firearm; he did not want to leave any trace. This was the victim's firearm, and in a few days, he would be meeting with his widow to return it. Cree could not imagine returning it with the victim's dried blood still on it. The firearm alone would be enough of a reminder of what had happened to her husband. Seeing her husband's blood would only have made things harder.

As he washed the blood from the firearm, Cree began thinking back to when all this got started. He remembered where he
was when he got the call. He was with his wife and having a
great day—until he got the telephone call from Warden Allen
Johnson.

He remembered thinking after the call that some family was
getting the worst news of their lives.

As Cree and his wife exited the Bass Pro Shop after a long
day of Christmas shopping, they felt the first drops of rain as they
walked across the parking lot to their SUV. Putting their pack-
ages in the SUV in an orderly fashion, Cree was glad to be "10-7/
off duty" for the next nine days. They planned to visit his family,
who lived in the northern part of the state.

He started their vehicle, drove across the parking lot, and
pulled out onto the roadway. Cree turned onto the ramp that lead
to Interstate 101 and merged into the heavy evening traffic in the
northbound lane. It was about this time that the bottom fell out
of the sky and the heavy rain began to fall. He slowed along with
the heavy holiday traffic as his cell phone began to ring.

Warden Allen Johnson was on the other end of that ring.
Johnson worked in Cree's work section and was assigned to one
of the counties he supervised.

Johnson said, "I hate to bother you, but we had a hunting
incident down here in Stone County in the river swamp. I've got
everything under control."

Cree asked, "What happened?"

Johnson explained that two hunters had been dragging a
hog out of the woods that one of them had killed. Somehow,
one hunter stumbled and fell, and his gun fired when it hit the
ground. The bullet struck the other hunter and killed him. Cree
was in charge of his agency's Critical Incident Reconstruction

Team (CIRT), which is responsible for investigating the most serious of the state's hunting incidents.

Cree asked, "Are you sure you do not need a CIRT investigator to work this? I can call one and have him en route."

Johnson replied, "I think we can handle this; we are just about to wrap it up. I got Warden Brady to assist me, and it does not appear to be anything more than one hunter falling down and his gun firing accidentally when it hit the ground."

Cree told Johnson to be sure to get written statements from everyone involved and to collect, tag, and preserve all evidence. He reminded Johnson that he would not be back to work for nine days and would want to take a look at the case file when he got back. Finally Cree reminded Johnson to give him a call if he needed anything or had any questions or problems. Cree didn't talk to Johnson for the next nine days; his first call took place on November 12.

Back in Stone County, Wardens Johnson and Brady had been busy at the incident scene. They requested that blood be drawn on both the shooter and the victim and sent to be analyzed by the state crime lab. Together they questioned the shooter later that night:

Johnson: We're just basically trying to be clear and see exactly
  what took place. . . . We just need to make sure we get your
  side of the story so we can complete the accident investigation and because we really feel that . . . this is an accident. . . .
  First I need to read you something . . . I just need you to kind
  of listen to me and make sure that you understand me. Okay?
Shooter: Okay.
Johnson: You have the right to remain silent. Anything you say
  can and will be used against you in a court of law. You have

the right to talk to a lawyer and have him present with you while you are being questioned. If you cannot afford to hire a lawyer, one will be appointed to represent you at county expense before questioning if you wish. If you give up your right to remain silent and later wish to stop answering questions, no further questions will be asked. Do you understand each of these rights as I explained them to you?

Shooter: Yes, sir. I do.

Johnson: Okay. Having these rights in mind, do you wish to talk to us about the events or talk to us today?

Shooter: Yes, I will waive those for the time being, and let's get on with this paperwork.

The shooter gave his name and presented his ID and licenses, explaining that he had purchased his hunting license in the city the previous afternoon.

Johnson: All right. Chris, this is where you kind of . . . tell me about what took place today, basically . . . that way we can figure what happened. . . . I'll ask you some questions later . . . specific stuff.

Shooter: Let's see we all got up about 5:00 a.m. Scrambled up a little breakfast and a cup of coffee. A gentleman named Edwin showed up about 6:15 or 6:20, loaded us in his truck, put us out on the side of the road, and told us how to get to the stands. He put me in a tripod stand . . . so about 9:15 or 9:30 it started raining. He came back, picked me up and moved to another place with a box stand and I hung out there . . . watched it rain, watched a cardinal fly around. He came back and picked the other two guys up and came out and got me a little after 11:00. We went back to the cabin

... they hung out ... he hung out ... there was another guy there ... I don't think he came back this afternoon. They talked to us for a few minutes ... said we're going to run get some lunch. We ate a couple of sandwiches. The two guys I was with laid down. My gun's real bad about corroding. The cheap ammo I plink with at the range is corrosive. I already noticed that after a morning of rain it was picking up some rust in the barrel, so I scoured it out, cleaned it, set it aside. Bob, the deceased, and I guess Mr. White showed back up. They were standing there talking and ... the gentleman said, "I've been watching hogs all morning from the stand." Bob said I can take you out there right now and put you on it and you can get you a hog. I said great, threw on my orange vest and got my little toboggan, grabbed a handful of shells for that. We rode out there on a little Polaris thing. Got out, loaded up we walked in 100–150 yards, spotted a boar and sow, stalked up to them, and they looked away from us. We walked a little farther and turned, and he pointed out a little sow. I shot her and she went down. And it was kind of flopping around ... with open sights I really could only get it in a ten-inch circle and those sows are awfully small for that

Johnson: Uh hum.

Shooter: I shot a total of three times before he said, "Here just take mine and put the scope hairs on her head and drop her." So we swapped guns and I had to do that last shot, and then we swapped guns back and walked across the little slough, got our gloves out and grabbed her by the back hoof and started off toward that tree stand. And we stopped two or three times, you know, wiping the mud off and got a better grip and ... he was ... he was saying just as soon as we get to the stand, he said we can step over to the road and go get the Polaris and drag it out of here. As he was saying that . . . the butt of my gun I had it across my back . . .

Johnson: Uh hum.

Shooter: . . . The butt of the gun hit the tree and I tripped and went forward. I heard the bang, landed on my face, turned around. The gun was behind me at my feet. He was lying on his side holding his shoulder and he said, "You shot me. I think I'm going to die." I just stood up and he said, "Go get help, go get help!" I said, "Okay." . . . I said, "You've got to tell me where the road is, I am turned around." He said, "Tell my grandson I love him." And I said, "Well, I'll do that. You got to tell me where the road is." And he kind of leaned up a little bit, looked, and said, "That way." I said, "All right." And you know I just . . . he was lying on his back.

Johnson: Right.

Shooter: He had fallen to his side and rolled to his back. He was holding his shoulder. I looked at it real quick, and it just looked the way the shirts were torn that had gone up and I just kind of assumed that hopefully it had gone up into his shoulder and that he was able to be so clear headed to say the road was right over there . . . go get help. And I said, "All right. Sit tight. I'll be right back." I ran through there, hopped on that Polaris and drove out to the cabin. When I got there, Mr. White was the only person there and he was sitting in a truck, blind and unable to get out. So he had me back his truck over to the yellow house right across from the cabin. I went in, called 911 from there.

Johnson: Uh hum.

Shooter: Gave them directions. Told them we had to go back out into the woods and get him. We drove out there and we stopped at the big intersection and laid on the horn, waited for a second . . . he asked me, "Did I think we could get him out . . . that I could get him out," and I said, "Well he's still conscious; he ought to be able to help me get him out and shouldn't have a problem." We drove back and pulled off in there, and I went back and found him. He had rolled over onto his stomach and was cold. He was gone.

Johnson: Gone?

Shooter: He didn't have a carotid pulse. Then I just . . . you know I had that moment where I know bodies lie, but . . . I got a guy a hundred yards honking on the horn, yelling at me, "Bring him on, bring him on." I got him under the arms, made it . . . got a few feet . . . realized I wasn't getting anywhere and got him under the ankles and just started dragging as far as I could. When I got to where we left the body . . . Mr. White had yelled, "Leave him for now. Let's get Tony and get help." And so I laid him down and ran up and we got in the truck and we were headed out when the sheriff's officers were coming in. . . .

Johnson: Okay. Did you eject a round out of his rifle or anything?

Shooter: No, I did not. I just pulled the trigger once and handed it back to him.

Johnson: Okay. Was it on safety or off safety when you got it?

Shooter: It was on safety . . . his was on safety when he handed it to me. All right, because I squeezed at the off safety.

Johnson: All right. What about yours? Did you have yours on safety, or what did you do?

Shooter: Mine is a World War II rifle. It doesn't have a safety. Although, in theory, once it's cocked you are supposed to be able to beat on it without it going off.

Johnson: Okay. How long have you had that gun?

Shooter: I got it back in the spring. This is the first time I've hunted with it.

Johnson: Okay.

Shooter: I've been to the firing range a couple of three times.

Johnson: Okay. How familiar with that firearm are you?

Shooter: Fairly, because after I got it I got real interested and I bought a collector's book on it. Then I traded some computer work with a fellow I know and we went up in his attic and pulled out an even older model, an older model from a different country. . . . And so . . . yeah . . . I was.

Johnson: Okay. Have you had a lot of experience with firearms or anything?

Shooter: Well, I grew up with a .410 and a .22 hunting squirrel and rabbit.

Johnson: Okay. Have you completed a Hunter Education course?

Shooter: I have, and I think that card is in the rest of my stuff at the cabin. I did it about twelve years ago, went through the hunter's education course in my home state. . . .

Johnson: Right. Did you buy the rifle new, or did you buy that used or what?

Shooter: Oh, I bought it at a gun show. I handed the guy a hundred dollars, and he handed me the gun.

Johnson: Did you get any kind of paperwork or anything on it?

Shooter: No, I don't think he was the dealer. Just . . . you know . . . people at one of those big shows and everybody shows up with guns in pocket.

Johnson: Uh huh.

Shooter: I had seen several tables, saw his, looked at it.

Johnson: Where was the gun show?

Shooter: In Cityville. . . .

Johnson: Okay. Was anybody else with you other than just you and him?

Shooter: No.

Johnson: Okay. Nobody else other than you went to drag him?

Shooter: No. . . .

Johnson: The only thing I can point out is basically inexperience . . . Believe it or not, your firearm does have a safety on it.

Shooter: Okay. I found one book that says the US Army didn't like the weapon . . . it didn't have a safety. In the collector's edition book it talks about all the details. It says there is a particular way to pull and turn the bolt that locks it.

Johnson: Right.

Shooter: But I haven't been able to make that work . . . unloaded trying it and pulling the trigger. . . .

Johnson: Did you hear that close? In that position? (Warden Johnson shows the shooter his firearm; demonstrates the safety.)

Shooter: Right.

Johnson: Pull it back . . .

Shooter: There it is. . . . Okay.

Johnson: It won't go nowhere else. . . .

Johnson: I'm going to give you this little book thing here to write on. If you will . . . if it will work . . . all it says right here is basically like what I read you awhile ago . . . the Miranda warning. . . . I just need you to sign it right here stating that we done exactly what we read you.

Shooter: Right.

Johnson: And that you understand it, and this right here is where you actually agreed to talk to us and everything.

Shooter: Right.

Johnson: And then what we will do is we'll actually get you
    to sign it again after we get through with everything; and
    when we get everything done, we are going to get you a
    copy of this and everything.
Shooter: Okay.

Written statements were also obtained from all other hunters
and witnesses in the area. Johnson collected all evidence involved,
including the victim's clothes. He met with the county sheriff and
coroner, who had examined the victim and declared him dead.
The coroner also examined the gunshot wounds on the victim's
body and declared the wound in the middle of the back to be the
entrance wound and the wound on his upper arm to be the exit
wound. He would state as much in his coroner's report.

Johnson found himself caught up in this tragedy and was
very sympathetic to the shooter. So much so that he and Warden
Brady would get a card from the shooter and the shooter's family
at their district office.

Johnson discussed how the incident had happened with both
the sheriff and the district attorney. This conversation compelled
the DA to make a statement to the effect: "This is an accident, and
with everything that has been learned, there will be no charges
filed against anyone." All this also took place on November 12.

Upon his return to work on November 21, Cree gave the
incident his full attention. The first thing on his agenda was to
meet with Johnson and have him bring him up to date on the
case. He also wanted to review the case file to make sure everything was in order. Cree contacted Johnson and requested that
they meet at his office at the county sheriff's office at 1000 hours.

Johnson arrived on time, and they discussed the hunting incident case. Warden Cree began his review of the file and noticed

the shooter's firearm was a 7.62×54R caliber Mosin-Nagant. This was a Russian-made bolt-action rifle he was not familiar with. Cree continued reading through the file, and when he finished he looked up at Johnson and said, "We have a problem.

"First, the shooter states he tripped and fell after his gunstock hit a tree. He fell forward and heard his gun discharge. It indicates in the file that the victim was on the left side of the shooter and they were facing in the same direction. The coroner's report indicates that the bullet wound in the middle of the victim's back is the entrance wound and the wound on the right shoulder is the exit wound. How can this be if the victim is on the shooter's left and they are facing forward dragging the hog? This would mean the bullet trajectory path traveled back toward the shooter after passing through the victim.

"Also, if your diagram is right, the bullet entered the victim's body six inches below the neckline and traveled a straight path and exited the victim's shoulder. How can this be if the gun discharged after the shooter fell? At some point the shooter's gun had to be at a position that was level with six inches below the neckline on the victim's back in order to have a perfectly straight and level bullet path.

"Also, the shooter states he shot three times at the hog with his rifle and fired one time with the victim's rifle to kill the hog. Then there is the shot that killed the victim. This is five shots! All three witnesses hunting in the area gave statements indicating that they just heard two shots fired that evening. Where are the other three shots?

"These are major inconsistencies that need to be answered. This case is far from being over. We need to verify all shots; this means we need to find the spent cartridge cases at or near the scene. Also, I need you to bring me the evidence you have in your possession. We can secure it here at the sheriff's office evidence room until the case is over."

Cree asked Johnson to meet back here at his office on November 26.

A few days later, Cree received a telephone call from District Supervisor Doug Levy; the victim lived in the district Levy supervised. Levy informed Cree that the victim's wife had been in touch with him, and she did not like the way the investigation was being handled. She knew something was not right about her husband's death and was concerned it was not being looked into properly. Levy assured her it was being looked into and told her Cree was the best investigator their agency had in dealing with hunting incidents. If she would be patient and give Cree a little time, he would find out exactly what happened.

Levy told Cree this calmed her down a little, but it was evident that she was very upset and concerned about the handling of the case. Cree then brought Levy up to date on what he knew concerning the case so far and expressed his concern about the conflicting statements and problems with the victim's wounds. Cree thanked Levy for having confidence in his abilities as investigator and hung up the telephone. However, the very next day, he received a message from his district office to give the victim's wife a call.

Cree dialed the widow's telephone number, but he was not really sure of what to say or what state of mind she would be in. As he listened to the other phone ring, he tried to calm himself by taking a deep breath or two. A woman's voice on the other end of the line said, "Hello."

Cree introduced himself. "This is Warden Brian Cree with the state wildlife law enforcement agency. I was given your number by my office and am returning your call."

Following an awkward moment of silence, the woman said, "I am the victim's wife."

She went on to express her concerns about her husband's death and about how the case was being handled. She said she had contacted District Supervisor Levy and that he indicated to her that he, Warden Cree, was investigating the case.

Cree confirmed that he was the investigator looking into the case and explained that he could not discuss it with her at this time. However, he did tell her that he had several questions about her husband's death that needed to be answered. He assured her he would leave no stone unturned until he found out exactly what had happened and how. His professional assurances seemed to calm the victim's wife somewhat, and he told her he would let her know something as soon as he could.

Although he had not thought about it, Cree had already made a mistake. He had called the widow on his personal cell phone, with this number showing up on the widow's caller ID. As a result of this seemingly insignificant error, Cree would receive a call from the victim's wife every few days until the case was over. These frequent calls not only put tremendous pressure on Cree as an investigator but played havoc with his emotions as well.

As arranged, Cree met Johnson at his office on November 26. Johnson released custody of the victim's effects, which included a 7mm caliber Browning A-Bolt Stalker rifle, a detachable magazine still loaded with two live rounds of 7mm magnum ammunition, one fired cartridge case found in the chamber of the victim's firearm, and a open pack of Swisher Sweets cigars.

Cree took a series of photographs of the victim's firearm, still spattered with the victim's blood. He also numbered all live ammunition in the magazine and documented the order in which it was found. Photographs were taken of the fired cartridge case and the cigar pack.

Cree then secured these items in the sheriff's office evidence room. Cree advised Johnson everyone "10-8/working" tomorrow in the work section was to meet at the incident scene. He told Johnson they needed to find the location where the hog had been killed so that they could locate the fired/spent cartridge casings. Finding this evidence would help verify the number of rounds fired that evening. Cree also said they were going to search the area for the fatal bullet that had passed through the victim's body.

Everyone began to arrive at the river swamp where the incident occurred at approximately 10:00 a.m. Cree rode with Warden Tim Brady, and they were the first to arrive. It was not long before Wardens Allen Johnson and Robert Smarky arrived.

Johnson unloaded the all-terrain vehicle (ATV) used to transport equipment to incident locations. Following Johnson, all the officers walked through the woods of the river swamp to the location pointed out as the incident scene. Cree noticed that the scene was right beside a slough, which was currently dry. But he also knew there had been rains in the northern part of the state, so the river would begin rising. While water had not reached this slough, it probably would. Cree knew that if they did not find the evidence they needed today, the rising river could possibly interfere with future searches. It was time to go to work.

Cree got out the metal detector and began a spiral search of the area where the victim had been initially shot, carefully searching the area for the bullet that had passed through the victim's body. He was also looking for the fired cartridge cases of the Mosin-Nagant 7.62×54R caliber the shooter had used to shoot the hog. His search turned up nothing.

Using the directions provided by the shooter on the location of where he and the victim had shot the hog, the officers did a grid search of the area up the side of the slough for approximately 150 yards from the incident scene. They searched the area for four and a half hours but came up empty.

Cree believed that the shooter needed to be reinterviewed, even though he lived in another state. Cree decided to have Johnson contact the shooter to get more information regarding the location of where the hog had been killed. He thought it best if Johnson made contact, because he had already established a rapport with the shooter on the night of the incident.

On November 29, Cree went to his district office to meet with District Supervisor Ken Gillis and get his approval. He wanted to contact the wildlife law enforcement agency in the shooter's home state to see if they would be willing to have one of their investigators reinterview the shooter. Cree believed it would be better for a uniformed officer to do the interview in person instead of over the telephone. Gillis agreed. Cree contacted the wildlife law enforcement agency headquarters office in the shooter's home state and talked to Division Director Bob Newnan.

Newnan said, "I have just the man for the job, Officer James Vann. He is one of our best."

Newnan asked Cree to fax him the shooter's telephone number, address, and any other pertinent information that Officer Vann might need before conducting the interview. Cree thanked the director for his assistance and said he would be sending the fax later that day.

December 2 found Wardens Cree, Johnson, Smarky, and Brady back at the incident scene in the swamp. Cree had asked Warden Lloyd Smith to join them. Johnson had telephoned the shooter and gotten a more precise description of the location where the hog had been killed. As it turned out, the hog had been shot from the other side of the slough, approximately eighty-five yards up from the incident scene.

As Cree feared, the rising river waters had created a problem. The slough had completely filled with water. Using the ATV to transport equipment, the officers went up the slough until they reached the location described to Johnson by the shooter. Once there, Cree and Johnson waded the slough's now waist-deep water to do a search of the other side.

It was not long before Johnson found the first fired cartridge case. It was immediately marked, and a short systematic search of the area turned up two more fired cartridge cases. Cree now knew all of the shooter's shots could be accounted for—one question had been answered.

However, this left the questions about the victim's wounds. If the bullet had entered the center of the back, as the coroner indicated in his report, and the shooter's gun had discharged *after* he fell, why was the wound trajectory path six inches below the neckline and perfectly straight. These were all questions that needed to be answered before this case could be closed.

Cree instructed Johnson to transport the newly found fired cartridge cases to the state crime lab along with the shooter's firearm. They needed to be matched to the firearm to see if these cartridges had indeed been fired from the firearm in question. The lab also needed to completely check out the shooter's firearm to see if it functioned properly.

Cree had begun to develop a theory on how the victim's gunshot wounds had occurred. He had enlarged the photographs of both wounds, the one in the middle of the back and the one on the shoulder. After carefully studying these photos, he began to do research, relying on scientific materials that tackled the science and study of gunshot wounds.

Cree picked up a copy of *Gunshot Wounds: Practical Aspects of Firearms, Ballistics, and Forensic Techniques* by Vincent J. M. DiMaio, MD, which he found to be invaluable. Cree found a wound pattern in this book that was almost identical to the one on the victim's shoulder. The wound pattern was caused when the victim was in close contact with the muzzle of the firearm, with the firearm positioned at a slight angle when it discharged.

After his research, and based on the shooter's statement, Cree began to believe that the coroner had actually gotten the entrance and exit wounds reversed. Cree knew that disputing the coroner's findings was not going to make him popular. He also knew that until there was definite proof otherwise, the coroner's report would stand. There was only one solution—prove it was wrong.

Cree contacted Johnson and asked, "Did you collect the camouflage jacket the victim was wearing as an outer garment as evidence?"

Johnson replied affirmatively: "Yes, I got it in a bag with his other clothes."

Cree requested, "When you take the fired cartridges and gun to the state crime lab to be checked out, have them check the camouflage jacket for gunshot residue around the area where the shoulder wound was located."

Cree was looking for the specific residue that comes out of a gun barrel when it is fired. If this residue was found on the jacket in the area of the shoulder, it would prove that the entrance wound occurred in the shoulder and not in the middle of the back as the coroner's report stated.

On December 9, Cree telephoned Officer James Vann, who worked for the wildlife law enforcement agency in the shooter's home state and would be conducting the follow-up interview. He wanted to ensure that Officer Vann asked for some very specific information.

Cree wanted to know the title and copyright information for the book the shooter had specifically mentioned getting when he wanted to know more about his firearm, the Mosin-Nagant. The shooter had been adamant that he knew about his gun. Vann assured Cree that he would do his best and that he would be in contact after the interview. Cree thanked him for his assistance and hung up.

It was now December 12, and as he pulled on latex gloves to clean the victim's firearm, Cree reflected on how this whole case got started. He did not want to return the firearm to the victim's wife in the condition it was in; he wanted to remove the blood.

After he was finished, he mailed copies of the incident scene photos to Officer Vann to use in his reinterview of the shooter. That job done, Cree headed to the shooting range located on one of the state's wildlife management areas with the newly cleaned rifle. It was important to make sure it was in proper working order—a detail he could testify to if this case made it to court.

Once at the range, he loaded one 7mm magnum cartridge into the chamber, locked the bolt shut, took aim at a target left on the range, and squeezed the trigger. The Browning A-Bolt Stalker's recoil was absorbed by Cree's shoulder at the report of the muzzle blast. The firearm performed perfectly. It was now time to return it to the widow.

Warden Cree had never met the victim's widow face to face. Their many conversations—too many—had been by telephone. Now, sitting behind his desk, he waited for her to arrive. He was a little on edge. It's hard to plan what to say in these types of situations.

Cree had always found it best to be completely honest with victims' families. If he was asked a question he could not answer, he would always explain why. He knew the widow was looking for closure. This was something he could not yet provide, but he was getting close to having answers to most of the questions. He needed the state crime lab to finish their examination of the evidence. They just might supply him with the answers he needed to close this case.

There was a knock on his office door. The victim's widow, daughter, and a good friend entered and sat down. He introduced himself, but there was an awkward moment of not knowing what to say. The victim's wife began by thanking him for his work on her husband's case and asked if he had any more information. Cree bought them up to date on the investigation.

He told them he was waiting for the state crime lab to finish with the evidence before he would have any final answers as to what actually had taken place that day. They wanted to know if charges would be filed against the shooter, and Cree explained that decision would be left up to the district attorney. If the case kept proceeding in the direction it was headed, he was going to recommend that charges be filed; but he once again reminded them that all the evidence was not in yet—things could change.

The widow asked if it would help if she called the district attorney. Cree answered, "It could not hurt."

The three seemed to accept all his answers, so he finished the difficult meeting by signing over the newly cleaned gun to the victim's wife. It was December 18.

December 20 arrived as the long-awaited day for gaining some much needed knowledge. Johnson let Cree know that the state crime lab was through with the examination of the shooter's firearm and the three fired shell casings found in the swamp. He said he was on his way to pick the evidence up and would meet Cree at his office.

Johnson soon arrived with the evidence, which included the shooter's firearm and the shooter's broken gun sling. He also had some of the long-awaited state crime lab reports. The reports indicated the following:

1. Visual examination of the shooter's firearm revealed that it was in poor working condition. The sear and the bolt exhibit markings consistent with alteration and the firearm will discharge when dropped on the butt plate with the safety off. The firearm does not discharge when dropped on the butt plate with the safety on. It takes a force of approximately 2¾ pounds (+/- ¼ pound) to pull the trigger single action.
2. Blood alcohol test on the victim's blood. Alcohol result by gas chromatography: Negative.
3. Blood alcohol test on the shooter's blood. Alcohol result by gas chromatography: Negative.
4. Drug screen of the shooter's blood. Indicated negative for drugs.
5. The three fired cartridges found at the location where the hog was shot. Microscopic examination and comparison revealed the cartridge cases were fired in the shooter's firearm.

Cree finally had most of the answers he needed to close the case, but the report on the camouflage jacket was still out. This information would be crucial to solving what had taken place that day.

Johnson signed over the evidence to Cree and left. Cree took a series of photographs of the shooter's firearm and examined it. Looking at the gun sling, he found that the middle buckle on the sling was broken.

Recalling the case file, he remembered the shooter had been carrying the gun across his back and that after taking the fall, the gun had been behind him at his feet. This could be an important piece of evidence and another piece of the puzzle that could point to the cause of the incident. Cree then took a series of photographs of the sling and its broken buckle.

Needing a comparison, Cree headed out to Walmart and purchased the same kind of sling to get an idea of what an undamaged buckle would look like. He also photographed this gun sling. Not wanting to make any mistakes, Cree reviewed the case file again. The broken gun sling buckle meant there had been sufficient force applied to it at some point to cause it to break. Cree flipped through the file until he came to the statement he needed.

Shooter: I don't know if the gun hit the tree caused me to stumble and then I tripped over whatever was on the ground.

If the shooter had the gun slung across his back, only the butt of the stock and barrel would be sticking out beyond his body. The barrel would have been pointed upward and the butt of the stock sticking out at or just below his waist. The rest of the gun would be blocked by his body. If he had just walked close enough to the tree to hit it with the butt of the gun, it would not have been enough force to break the gun sling.

Cree realized the shooter must have tripped and fallen forward, and then the butt of the firearm hit the tree! The weight of the shooter's body, along with the sudden forward motion, would have applied enough pressure to the sling to break its buckle.

With the visibly poor condition of the gun mechanism, the butt striking the tree would have caused it to fire. This meant the gun had still been on the shooter's back when it discharged! The firearm had already discharged before it ever touched the ground. The broken buckle of the gun sling had now given Cree all the answers he needed to reconstruct the incident. Cree's satisfaction in having answered more questions in the investigation didn't last long. December 30 arrived, bringing both good news and bad.

Officer Vann's package arrived with all the information Cree had requested. It contained a letter stating that the interview with the shooter had gone well, and, as a result, Vann did not believe the shooter was a very experienced hunter. The package also contained a written statement by the shooter and a copy of the title and copyright page from the book the shooter said he had read about the history and operation of his firearm: *The Mosin-Nagant Rifle* by Terence W. Lapin.

Not long after, he received word from Johnson that the crime lab report on the victim's blood was in. The drug screen for drugs in the victim's blood had tested positive for both cocaine and marijuana. Cree shook his head, knowing that at some point he would have to give this hard news to the victim's wife. She had already hired a lawyer, and it was only a matter of time before he obtained the information.

Cree felt a strong obligation to give this information to the widow firsthand so she would not be blindsided. He telephoned her and, after identifying himself, said, "I just received the crime lab report on the blood that was drawn on both your husband and the shooter the night of the hunting incident. Both blood samples were run through the same tests, which were for alcohol use and drug screening. Your husband's blood tested positive for cocaine and marijuana."

There was silence on the other end of the telephone. The wife then said, "There must be some kind of mistake. Are you sure y'all did not get the blood samples mixed up?"

Cree could sense the shock and panic in her voice and attempted to calm her. "The way the samples were taken and labeled, there was no way they could have been mixed. The report is correct, and I just wanted to let you know before you heard this information somewhere else." She thanked him for that and hung up the telephone.

During the next couple of weeks, Cree worked with Johnson to make sure all information was included in the case file. They pulled together the photographs taken, all reports, officer statements, witness statements, and equipment information. Cree even made time to find the book the shooter had mentioned in both interviews.

When the book arrived on January 21, Cree read it cover to cover. He took special note of pages 59 and 60, which contained the information regarding the location of the firearm's safety mechanism and precise instructions on its operation. The book was detailed and clear on how to place the firearm on "safe." Cree now knew that if the shooter had read this book as he claimed, he knew his firearm had a safety and how to use it. It was obvious that the shooter had not been entirely honest during his interview.

It took another three weeks for the last crime lab report to come in, but it was worth the wait. When it arrived on February 10, Johnson notified Cree that the report on the victim's camouflage jacket revealed a press contact gunshot hole entry at the point of the shoulder. This significant detail confirmed Cree's suspicions—the coroner had made a mistake. The last piece of the puzzle slipped into place.

Cree telephoned the victim's wife and relayed his findings about how the incident had happened. When he was finished, she said, "That makes sense now. I knew something was not right, and now it makes sense." She thanked the warden and hung up the telephone. Cree hoped he had provided her some kind of closure. Cree wasn't there yet, but the Stone County Hunting Incident case was just about over.

The next day, Cree awoke with the feeling that usually came when he was close to wrapping up another complicated case. He went by the sheriff's office evidence room and signed out the shooter's firearm. Back at his car, he placed the firearm in the backseat of his patrol vehicle and began the forty-five-minute drive to Stone County.

Arriving at the incident scene, he met up with Wardens Allen Johnson, Lloyd Smith, and Jim McVee. Their mission for the day was clear: They were to create a reconstruction of the incident— put all the pieces of the puzzle/case together at the scene so it would make complete sense.

Cree even planned to do a reenactment of the incident; he cast McVee in the role of the shooter and Johnson in the role of the victim. He directed McVee to sling the shooter's rifle across his back with the barrel pointing up and left toward direction of the victim. He then filled a large bag with debris he found in the swamp. This was going to represent the hog the shooter and victim had been dragging. He put the two officers on the trail line the shooter had said he and the victim were on just before the incident occurred.

As the director of this film, Cree started it off with "Action!"

The two officers bent down, took hold of the bag, and began dragging it. Just as they reached the tree where the shooter claimed to have stumbled, he shouted, "Stop and freeze!"

The officers stopped and remained in their positions while Cree snapped a photograph. The reenactment had served its purpose well and made clear what actually had taken place that tragic day.

With the shooter bent down and forward while dragging the hog, his firearm lay perfectly level on his back and was pointing toward the victim's shoulder area. This was the position of the rifle when it discharged, causing the entrance wound in the victim's shoulder and creating a level bullet trajectory path before exiting the victim's back.

The day was well spent. Knowing now how the hunting incident had occurred, the case file could be finished and presented to the district attorney. Cree was relieved; the great weight of responsibility he had placed on himself was lifted. He could now relax a little.

Based on witnesses, witness statements, evidence, and crime lab reports, the reconstruction and investigation of the Stone County Hunting Incident case revealed the following facts:

On November 12, victim and shooter went feral hog hunting on the White lease hunting club property in Stone County. The victim was guiding the shooter on the hunt. The victim was carrying a 7mm caliber Browning A-Bolt Stalker rifle with a 3×9 Leopold scope. The shooter was carrying a 7.62×54R caliber Mosin-Nagant rifle with open or iron-type sights on the hunt. The shooter had stated that he did not know how to engage the safety on his firearm and stated that he had read a book about the operation of his firearm. A copy of the book the shooter spoke of was acquired; on pages 59 and 60, it gives explicit details on how to put the firearm on "safe." Therefore, when the victim and shooter entered the river swamp on the White lease to hunt feral hogs at approximately 1300 hours, the shooter knew he was carrying an unsafe firearm.

Once in the river swamp, the victim and shooter crossed a slough and began still-hunting up the side of the slough. At some point, a feral hog was spotted across the slough from them. The shooter took his firearm, aimed, and fired at the feral hog, ejected the spent cartridge from his firearm, and he and the victim went forward toward the feral hog approximately thirteen feet, ten inches. The shooter took aim with his firearm and fired at the feral hog again, ejecting this spent cartridge also. Again, he and the victim went forward toward the feral hog approximately twenty-five feet, four inches; the shooter took aim with his firearm and fired at the feral hog, ejecting the spent cartridge case. One of these three shots fired from the shooter's firearm severely wounded the feral hog where it was broken down and could not move or escape. At this point, the victim offered the shooter his scoped firearm to finish killing the feral hog. The shooter took the victim's firearm, aimed at the feral hog using the scope, and fired. This bullet finished killing the feral hog. Neither shooter nor victim ever ejected this spent cartridge from the firearm. The shooter was approximately 114 feet from the feral hog when he fired the last two shots.

After the feral hog expired, the victim and shooter crossed the slough to retrieve his kill. Using the sling on his 7mm caliber Browning Stalker rifle, the victim slung the firearm on his left shoulder. This rifle still had the spent cartridge case in the chamber from the shooter firing the killing shot at the feral hog. Using the sling on his 7.62x54R Mosin-Nagant rifle, the shooter slung the firearm across his back. The muzzle of the rifle was pointed at an angle toward his left shoulder, and the butt plate was down around his right hip. The sling on his rifle was across the front of his chest. Also, there was a live cartridge in the chamber of his firearm and the safety was still in the unsafe position. Both the victim and shooter grabbed one of the back legs of the feral hog and began dragging it back down the slough. The position the shooter took to drag the feral hog placed the barrel of his firearm pointed at an angled position in the direction of the victim.

They dragged the feral hog for approximately 253 feet down the side of the slough. When they neared a small oak tree, the shooter stumbled forward and began to fall. This put him slightly ahead of the victim. At this point, the butt end/rear stock of the shooter's firearm hit the small oak tree. The fall made his firearm pivot on his back, and the impact with the tree caused his gun to discharge/fire. The act of falling and impact with the tree placed the muzzle of the shooter's firearm in close or near contact with the victim's right upper arm/shoulder area. The bullet/projectile from the shooter's firearm entered the victim's right upper arm/shoulder area approximately six inches below the neckline.

The bullet/projectile traveled at a slight angle in a straight trajectory path and exited the victim's mid-back area six inches below the neckline. This injury caused massive tissue damage and blood loss. After the shooter's rifle had discharged, he continued to fall forward. At some point during the firearm's impact with the tree and the fall, enough pressure/force was applied to the gun sling to break the middle buckle of the sling.

This caused the firearm to fall from the shooter's back to the ground. Realizing the victim had been shot, the shooter went to get help. He located Mr. White and advised him of what had happened. An ambulance was called, and they went back to the area where the shooter had come out of the river swamp. As Mr. White is legally blind, the shooter went back by himself into the river swamp to the victim. When he got back to where the victim was lying, he began to drag the victim through the river swamp back toward the road and Mr. White. The shooter dragged the victim for approximately 247 feet until he gave out. It appears the victim was already deceased at this point.

The shooter left the hunting camp/lodge that morning with the victim knowing that he was carrying an unsafe firearm. He stated that he did not know how to put the firearm on safe but insisted he had read a book about his firearm's operation. In two interviews, he mentioned reading extensively about the gun.

In reinterviewing the shooter at his home, the wildlife officer specifically asked about the book. The out-of-state officer even sent the investigator a copy of the copyright and publisher page he received from the shooter, as requested. The investigator then acquired his own copy of the book, which on pages 59 and 60 gives explicit details on the location and operation of the firearm's safety.

Crime lab test reports indicate that if the shooter's firearm is in the "off" safe position, it will fire if impacted on the rear portion of the stock; however, if the firearm is in the "on" safe position, it will not fire if impacted. Despite being a graduate of a Hunter Education course in his home state, the shooter could have at any point during the hunt rendered his firearm safe by merely unloading it.

The act of not putting his firearm on safe or simply unloading it was the major cause of this hunting incident fatality.

After a couple weeks, Warden Cree met with the victim's family and the district attorney. He went through the case and expressed his opinion that the shooter should be prosecuted. The DA would not commit to bringing charges against the shooter; he preferred another avenue. The DA indicated that he would bring the case before the grand jury.

When the next grand jury convened, the DA presented the case. Warden Johnson was the only one asked to give testimony on the Stone County Hunting Incident case. After he testified, the DA talked to the grand jury members, but they "no billed" the case (refused to bring charges). It seems the widow's fears had been fulfilled.

Lessons Learned

- As an investigator, be sure not to use your personal phones, cell or otherwise, to contact any person involved in the investigation. This simple mistake can lead to needless interruptions and distractions in your off-duty life. Strive to keep your work and personal life as separate as possible.
- The shooter violated several of the accepted rules for firearm safety taught in every Hunter Education course across the United States, and the shooter's unsafe actions and decisions caused the victim's death.

1. Watch the muzzle, and control its direction at all times.
2. Treat every firearm with the respect due a loaded firearm. Unload firearms when not in use. Leave actions open. Firearms should be carried empty to and from shooting areas.
3. Never climb a fence or tree, or jump a ditch or log, with a loaded firearm
4. Never pull a firearm toward you by the muzzle.

28

The Lie between Hunters

An investment in knowledge pays the best interest.
—BENJAMIN FRANKLIN

THIS IS AN ACTUAL 911 CALL THAT CAME IN TO THE BRADY County Emergency Center at approximately 11:22 a.m. on January 8. Following the call transcript is an account of the investigation into the facts and circumstances that led to someone having to make a call such as this.

Operator: 911.
Moss: Ah . . . I got an emergency. I'm at the Big Buck Hunting Club. I just accidentally shot a member.
Operator: You shot a member?
Moss: I think he is dead.
Operator: You are at the Big Buck Hunting Club?
Moss: Yes, ma'am. I need an ambulance. He is lying on the ground with blood coming out of his mouth.
Operator: Where is the Big Buck Hunting Club at?
Moss: I don't know; I'm just a visitor. It's at ah . . .
Operator: Okay, hold on. How old is he and what did you shoot him with?

Moss: He is about fifty; I shot him with 12-gauge buckshot.
 He's got a shot in his chin; it looks like and blood is coming
 out of his mouth. Oh my God!
Operator: You shot him with a 12 gauge?
Moss: Yes, ma'am. Can you call an ambulance, please?
Operator: My partner is already taking care of that, okay. There
 is more than one of us in here, okay.
Moss: I think he is dead.
Operator: Did you not see him?
Moss: See? I'm right by him. I think he is dead.
Operator: Is he breathing?
Moss: No, ma'am.

At approximately 11:25 a.m., Brady County emergency medical services (EMS) and sheriff department deputies were dispatched to the Big Buck Hunting Club and directed to the incident scene. EMS personnel were the first to arrive.

Warden Matt Alman was notified by the Brady County Sheriff's Office at approximately 12:00 p.m. Warden Alman was "10-7/off duty" and immediately called in the next available warden in the area, Brad Taylor. Warden Taylor in turn notified his immediate supervisors, Wardens Mack Smith and Vick Wise. Wise, knowing this was likely to be a fatality, advised Taylor to put in a call to the nearest Critical Incident Reconstruction Team (CIRT) member. This team was tasked with investigating and reconstructing the state's most serious injury and fatal hunting incidents.

Warden Sam Pippin happened to be at his home when he received the call from Taylor. The warden gave Pippin all the information he had received so far about the incident, and Pippin told Taylor he would be en route. Taylor then asked Pippin for another CIRT member to assist him at the scene; Pippen told him to contact Warden Brian Cree.

Cree was out on routine patrol when he received the urgent call from Taylor in reference to a hunting incident that had occurred in Brady County. Cree looked at his watch; it was 12:45 p.m. He told Taylor it would take him about an hour and a half to get to the incident location but he would be en route. Cree reminded Taylor to make sure all witnesses were interviewed and to get blood drawn on both the victim and the shooter. Taylor assured Cree that he would be making arrangements to get that done.

Cree also asked Taylor what he knew about the incident thus far. Taylor explained that all he knew at this time was that the victim was dead and that he had been dogging deer at the time. Hearing the term "dogging deer" brought back memories of when Cree had first become a game warden.

Cree was a hunter and enjoyed still-hunting deer; he had never hunted deer with dogs or ever wanted to. Cree had worked illegal dogging deer complaints almost every day of every deer season for the first four years of his career; he was very familiar with how to do it from working these cases for many years.

The hunters usually stood alongside roads with shotguns loaded with buckshot. Some dog hunters did not care if it was a woods road or a public road. The dog hunters usually lined the roads while other hunters went to the other side of the stand of woods, often along another road. The dogs were then turned loose to run any deer toward the hunters with the shotguns. While a common practice and not illegal in this state, it was an acquired taste in hunting that Cree had no interest in developing.

Wardens Taylor, Smith, and Wise all arrived at the scene within minutes of one another. The sheriff's deputies on scene brought them up to date on the situation at hand. The victim's body had already been removed from the scene and transported to the local hospital, where he had been pronounced dead on arrival. The area where the victim's body had been was marked. The wardens were informed that the shooter was a juvenile, fifteen years of age, named Bobby Moss.

Smith took the lead and began interviewing the shooter with his father present. The shooter was read the Miranda warning and asked to write a statement about the events that had taken place that morning:

> *I was appointed to this stand by Tom Swain [victim]. As usual, he informed me/us that we would not be involved in this run. To my knowledge, the only person that I know about in the area other than Alan [sic] Edwards was Harry [a club member], who turned the dogs out. Me and Allen were where we were told to be for about ten to fifteen minutes when I heard the dogs in a distance start to go crazy, which told us they jumped a deer. Two–three minutes later I heard deer running through the woods, so I got ready. When they got close, I was waiting; then I saw a set of horns coming through the brush so I fired in front of it to lead it. Me and Allen quickly ran to see if I had hit it. Unfortunately, on the way to look we heard a disturbing noise. Farther in the woods, expecting to see a deer, we discovered Tom [victim] lying on the ground with a shot in his chin. Allen almost immediately ran for help. I called 911 and stayed on the phone with the lady following her instructions. Then when help arrived I gave the phone to a guy named Jerry. I never saw an orange vest, and Tom [victim] never yelped or yelled to inform us of him. After five minutes of doing everything, a pack of dogs came smelling their way through the same position the buck came in.*

Smith also questioned the only witness to the incident, Allen Edwards, seventeen years old. He was a member of the hunting club and had invited Bobby to the hunt. This is Edwards's written statement:

We got out of Tom's truck, got our guns, two (2) 12-gauges and one (1) .30-30 rifle. I put the .30-30 on my back, and he walked with me down across the ditch where the scene was. And we didn't hear anything. Then after a while we heard dogs, so we split up and about ten minutes later I was turned the other way and he said something like, "I saw one." Or tried to get my attention and I heard something in the woods, so then he shot. I looked, and at the time he was putting his gun down. He said before we saw what it was, he yelled, "Yea, I got a buck." So I went to see what it was and I saw him, so I told him [Moss] to stay with him and I went to call it in. And so I did and then I ran back and started CPR until paramedics arrived. Then I sat with Bobby and prayed.

The victim was on the other side of the block turning out dogs and started to walk straight through. When we turned out we yelled to let people know where we are, but he never yelled, and I guess he was just walking out woods and ended up where the accident happened.

When Cree arrived at the scene, Pippin, Smith, and Wise were already there. Pippin brought Cree up to date on the investigation and informed him that both the shooter and his father were at the scene waiting to be questioned again. He also told Cree that the father of the shooter worked for a law enforcement department in a neighboring county.

Cree and Pippin discussed the best way to proceed with the investigation and decided to talk to the shooter and his father first. Pippin took the lead on the interview and asked the father if it would be all right to talk to his son again about what had happened. Both father and son agreed to be interviewed.

The shooter told the wardens the same story he had written down for Smith; however, this time he injected both his thoughts and blame. Cree and Pippin took note of the fact that the shooter did not show or reflect any remorse.

Additional information not written down in the shooter's verbal statement was collected by the wardens as follows:

I don't want to be disrespectful to him, but I feel like he should have yelled or something. I had no understanding anybody was there. I never saw an orange vest. His vest ah . . . when we went up . . . really wasn't . . . it was dark colored. I mean I never saw it and I . . . ah . . . and one of my pellets hit him so, unfortunately. So we went up and immediately, when we got to him Allen kind of panicked and he ran, said, "I'm going to get help." I called 911 and she gave me instructions.

After providing this additional information, the father and son were asked to leave the scene.

The area where the incident occurred could best be described as a long straight woods road with shallow ditches on both sides that ran between a cut-over area. One side of the road had small pines planted in rows, thick with undergrowth on one side. The other side of the road had large timber with thick growth along the edge of the woods road and thick patches of undergrowth in spots throughout the big timber. A drainage ditch came up to the woods road on the big timber side, and a firebreak ran out of the big timber and came up to the road ditch.

A search of the area revealed a spent Winchester Super-X three-inch magnum buckshot. This spent shell placed the shooter in the middle of the woods road when he fired the fatal shot. An extensive search of the area between the shooter's and victim's locations for any sign of where a deer tore through the brush or had been shot, as indicated by the shooter, revealed nothing. There was no evidence of a deer sign.

A search of the area where the victim had been shot found marks where he had walked down the firebreak toward the road. The area where the shot had taken place revealed limb clips and pellet strikes on the tree just beyond his position. This evidence indicated that the victim had been caught up in most of the shot shell pattern. This particular shell held fifteen shot pellets; the investigators could account for thirteen, and six of those were in the victim's body.

After a thorough search of the scene, it was time to recon-struct the incident. The CIRT investigators ran a shot line from the shooter's location to the victim's. This line gives the investiga-tors the line of sight taken by the shooter at the time of the shot. With the shooter in the middle of the woods road and the victim just stepping out to the edge of the ditch at the road where the firebreak ended, there was no doubt as to what the shooter had been shooting at. There was no deer in between the shooter and the victim. The shooter had taken aim at the victim, which he had mistaken for a deer. When someone stood at the victim's loca-tion with an orange vest on, you could see parts of the vest. The shooter had either lied about what had happened or convinced himself otherwise.

ON JANUARY 8 IN BRADY COUNTY ON THE BIG BUCK HUNTING Club, a party of dog hunters were dogging deer. Allen Edwards, age seventeen, was a member of the hunting club and had invited his friend Bobby Moss (shooter), age fifteen, to join the hunt. Tom Swain (victim), age fifty-eight, had driven Edwards and Moss to an area along a straight woods road with large timber on one side of the road and small pines with thick undergrowth on the other. He dropped them off and left.

Moss was hunting with a Remington Model 1100 12-gauge three-inch magnum shotgun. Edwards was hunting with two guns, a Remington Model 1100 12-gauge three-inch magnum shotgun and a Marlin lever-action .30-30 rifle. Swain was supposed to drive to the other side of the block of woods, where the dogs were going to be turned out. After Swain left, Moss positioned himself near a drainage ditch that came out of the big timber and ran up to the road, taking a stand in the middle of the woods road. Edwards positioned himself approximately eighty yards down the road from Moss, in the direct line of sight. This is a typical unsafe situation in dogging deer–type hunting. Some of these hunters had a warped sense of hunter safety. Their justification for putting standers in such positions is that it is perfectly safe to shoot buckshot in the direction of another stander, just as long as you shoot to the left or right of the other hunter's stand position.

Not long after Moss and Edwards took their stand positions, they heard the dogs in the distance start to yelp. The yelping of the dogs increased, which usually signals that they have just jumped a deer or come across a really hot trail. The dog hunters' term for this is "they [the dogs] have got one going."

As the dogs' yelping increased, so did the excitement of the two young hunters. It was not long after this that Moss heard something coming through the woods toward the woods road. As that sound grew louder, so did Moss's anticipation for taking a shot.

For some unknown reason, Swain had left his vehicle and the road on the other side of the block of woods from Moss and Edwards's position. Swain was wearing the required florescent orange vest and carrying a Mossberg Model 930 12-gauge semi-automatic shotgun loaded with five rounds of three-inch magnum 00 buckshot. He came through the woods and ended up following a firebreak that led out to the woods road where the young men had taken stand positions.

As Swain reached the end of the firebreak that ended at the ditch on the edge of the woods road, Moss saw this movement coming from the same place where he had been hearing the walking/running in the woods. Moss then made a snap decision, a fatal decision, to shoot at the movement without clearly identifying his target.

Moss raised his shotgun and prepared to fire. Swain had just stepped to the edge of the woods road ditch when he looked to his right and saw Moss raise his shotgun to fire at him.

The fifteen buckshot pellets traveled 134 feet, 10 inches out of Moss's shotgun barrel, striking brush, trees, and the victim. It was clear from the wound pattern that Swain had not only seen Moss take aim at him but also had sought to protect himself. Six of the fifteen pellets struck the victim. Four pellets entered his body on the right side from the top of the hip to the middle of the knee; one pellet entered the underside of his right arm when he tried to shield his face.

The fatal pellet entered the center of Swain's chin, which clearly indicated that he was looking directly at Moss when Moss fired the shot. What is not clear is if the shooter intentionally lied or merely convinced himself of his lack of responsibility in the victim's death.

Lessons Learned

- "Be sure of your target before you pull the trigger." This is a tragic case in which the shooter violated one of the most important hunter education safety rules.
- Hunter education not only teaches you the basics and importance of hunter safety but also is required in all states. And while some may see it as an inconvenience or unnecessary, the fact remains that neither Moss nor Edwards had ever been through a Hunter Education course, which may have made a difference in the outcome of this tragedy.
- "Premature closure" is a factor in many hunting incidents. This phrase refers to a psychological process in which a person's thinking jumps to a conclusion, skipping important steps. In this case the shooter was hunting deer. He wanted to see a deer; he wanted to shoot a deer. He heard the dogs "get one going." The dogs were getting closer; that meant a deer was getting closer. He heard the sound of something coming through the woods; he saw something coming through the woods—and then "premature closure" took place. He skipped the final and most important step: identifying his target. He assumed that the thing he heard and saw was a deer and fired at it. Skipping that one critical step proved a fatal mistake.

29

I Am Still Struggling More Than Twenty Years Later

The bravest sight in the world is to see a great man struggling against adversity.

—SENECA, ROMAN PHILOSOPHER,
MID-FIRST CENTURY AD

AS I'VE SAT HERE AT MY COMPUTER FOR MANY HOURS, I HAVE struggled reaching back into my mind to recall the stories I am sharing. It's not that I am unable to remember them; it's that this process has taken me back to some dark places I am reliving. Many are as clear as though they happened yesterday.

One of the stories I have attempted to put into words is one I have decided I am unable to share. It's one that has haunted me for more than twenty years. I have used it as an example when teaching wildlife officers about critical incident stress and how important it is, as professionals, to work hard to not become part of the story. You must separate yourself from the work that you are there to do. There is no doubt that I suffer from some form of posttraumatic stress disorder (PTSD) due to this case. I continue to think about the two fourteen-year-old boys involved in this incident. I still have occasional nightmares about the impact this case had on the parents of these two boys, on the young boy who accidently shot his best friend, and on me. I still worry about how they are coping with the loss and guilt of this tragedy. This event has motivated me to work harder, to be more compassionate, to dedicate my life to the prevention of hunting-related incidents.

This case was the first child autopsy I attended. The story is so much like my own childhood. While I stood close by, observing every detail, I saw myself lying on the steel table that day as the medical examiner began his part of the investigation. This story involves two best friends on an early fall morning squirrel hunt. This is one of my memories at that age, growing up with one of my best friends.

Being "picked" to do this, being an investigator, has had many rewards, but it also at times has weighed heavy on my heart. It has had an impact on my personal life, yet many of those around me may not have seen the impact due to the hard, strong facade I have always presented. Still, when I look around at others and their careers, I know this life mission has been the right one, know that I have in some way made a difference. I have not been building widgets you can count, and there is truly no way to measure the difference I have made in preventing hunting-related shootings. I know I have seen the light of understanding come on in many wildlife professionals I have trained and have impacted their skills to find all the facts—that my due diligence has made a difference, even if it's in my mind. I take comfort in that. I know that when I told someone during an interview, "You may not think anything good will ever come of this, but I can assure you that the information we have collected will be used to keep this from happening again," that this has been my pledge to them. My signature line has always been: "The incident scene will speak to you; you must listen for the sake of prevention."

The exact details of the two fourteen-year-olds will not be in this book out of respect for those involved. May those involved understand that I still feel their pain!

Lessons Learned

- The typical hunting incident does not involve premeditation or intent to inflict personal injury or death on a family member or friend. Thus, the typical law enforcement officer working cases where one person intends to hurt someone else will take a much different approach. In these types of cases, it is imperative to build a rapport with those involved in the initial moment of contact—first to secure medical needs, but also to show compassion and sensitivity, all while taking control of the scene. We must make sure everyone at the scene is safe while we secure firearms and evidence. Every incident is traumatic to many other people, not just the victim and the shooter; witnesses, family members, and responders are all affected as well. Responders and investigators of these shooting incidents are sometimes exposed to overwhelmingly tragic sites and stories filled with emotion, and they need to protect themselves. The threat to the psyche is not obvious, and the impact cannot be prejudged in any incident.
- The interaction with those involved can have a long-lasting effect on investigators. The visual effect and stress of this emotional event do not disappear as soon as you pull in the driveway at home and climb out of the truck. Now, how do you *not* carry this into your house when you sit down at the supper table or when you finally lay your head on the pillow? These pictures will play over and over like a movie in your mind. As this timeline ticks on, it can affect your family life, your personal health, and how you respond to any-

one you interact with. This is where balance comes in to maintain your health and well-being as a professional—and as a human being. Most agencies will require a critical incident debriefing, where a trained professional sits down with responders and has them tell their individual stories in a controlled and confidential setting.

30

Blood on the Leaves

The ideal man bears the accidents of life with dignity and grace, making the best of circumstances.

—ARISTOTLE

IT WAS THE FRIDAY AFTER THANKSGIVING, AND THE GROUP headed out before daylight to hunt in a neighbor's woodlot. These six were not only friends but also family. Brothers and a brother-in-law, they looked forward to this holiday adventure all year long. There was a real bonus this year, as the state had moved the dates of deer season to align with Thanksgiving week. All the more reason to take the whole week off, return home to celebrate the holiday, and spend time in the woods with close friends and family.

This group had hunted together for many years, and they set up their lines. Four of the group, the "drivers," headed off to the far end of the property, while the other two, the "watchers," took up their usual standing or sitting locations at the other end. The drivers would move slowly through the woods, hoping to sneak up on any deer in the area. The spooked deer should then just run in the direction of the two watchers at the far end.

Since the drivers were spread out pretty far apart, it was important to try to stay in line for two reasons. First of all for safety: If one of the drivers got too far ahead, he might end up in the line of fire of one of the other drivers. Second, deer can be smart. Given the chance, the deer would either lay low or just sneak between the drivers and get away. As the drivers walked, some hunters occasionally whistled, called out, or banged a stick against a tree to signal their location to the others in the group.

Everyone in the group knew that Terry was not a real serious hunter. He was there for companionship and to enjoy the chance to be in the woods. He always volunteered to be a driver and loved the chance to explore new areas. Just point him in the right direction and tell him to keep walking until he came out the other side.

Today was no different; his buddies indicated the direction they wanted him to go, and he headed off for a nice walk in the woods. He never saw any of the other group until he came to the far side and saw his brother-in-law, Stewart, sitting on a stump near an ATV trail in the woods.

Seeing Terry come through so soon frustrated Stewart. It was only 7:30 in the morning! It should have taken him much longer to get there. The other drivers would now be far behind him, and all the deer probably had run the other way.

Seeing Stewart, Terry gave him a wave and continued to the edge of the woods, stopping to lean on a tree about eighty yards to the left of Stewart. Terry now realized he had come through too fast and would have to wait for the rest of the group. Since Terry was the second in the line of drivers, he knew Jim should eventually come right up to where Stewart was sitting and waiting. If Stewart leaned forward, he would see the blaze orange of Terry's hat and vest directly on his left.

Much to Stewart's surprise and pleasure, it wasn't too long before a group of five deer came trotting in their direction. Terry had goofed up, but it was now working out perfectly. At first the group was heading directly toward Terry, but at the bottom of the swale, the deer paused briefly before turning and walking directly at Stewart.

The largest doe in the group stopped only about fifty feet from Stewart, giving him a perfect shot. He slowly raised his bolt-action .30-30 rifle and realized he had the variable power scope set too high. With a magnification power of seven, the entire scope was filled with the deer. Stewart could not tell what part of the deer he was aiming at—it was all just brown fur. But when he thought he was aiming at the heart, he squeezed the trigger; the deer immediately dropped in her tracks.

Off to his left, Stewart was surprised to hear Terry yell, "You shot me!"

Impossible, Stewart thought; Terry was just goofing around. The shot was as perfect and as safe as it could be. Terry was about ninety degrees off to his left and almost one hundred yards away. The woods were pretty open, but there were still a good number of trees between them. The shot had been aimed down into the swale, well away from anybody and with a good backstop beyond the deer.

When Terry yelled again, Stewart looked over and saw him holding his right arm, his gun on the ground. What was going on? This was impossible! Stewart ran over and saw blood dripping from Terry's right hand onto his boot.

Terry bent over and picked up a mangled bullet lying at his feet. Although it was inconceivable, there was no doubt he had been hit in the hand and was bleeding. Terry walked out to his truck and drove to the closest hospital. Stewart stayed behind to tell the others in the group what had happened and to call 911 to report the shooting. This call was relayed to the state police, the county sheriff's department, and the state environmental conservation police; they all responded.

This investigation was pretty straightforward. Both hunters agreed on every aspect and fact of the story. The shot had been fired at a deer directly in front of Stewart, and Terry had been standing ninety degrees off to the left and almost one hundred yards away. Only one shot had been fired, and immediately after it had been fired, a bullet struck Terry. He gave the bullet to the state police investigator.

Back at the scene, the conservation officers met up with the rest of the hunting group. By this time the friends had found the dead doe and field dressed it but left it where it fell. They had also located some blood on the leaves where Terry had been standing.

Conservation Officer Thomas immediately noticed a fresh cut on a red maple tree that was just over waist high and only about six feet from the blood. Closer examination revealed it was the size and shape of a bullet strike. He marked the tree with flagging tape and went to examine the deer carcass.

With no blood or fur anyplace except on and around the deer, it was clear the deer had in fact dropped where it was shot. Officer Thomas located two bullet holes in the right side of the deer's neck. The entrance wound was toward the front; the exit wound was slightly lower and about six inches to the rear.

Thomas couldn't help but think, *Could the bullet have ricocheted once off the deer's spine, then again off the maple tree before striking Terry?* As impossible as it seemed, this scenario was the only one that made sense.

Terry was treated and released from the hospital. The bullet had broken the fourth and fifth bones in his right hand just above his wrist. It took one stitch to close the laceration and a cast to hold the bones and wrist in alignment while they healed. Once

Terry was released, he returned to the scene to show everyone where he had been and what had happened.

Terry took up his position, while Stewart went back and sat on the stump. The investigators took a large tape measure to get all the distances, and compass bearings were taken of the various directions the bullet had taken. Photographs were taken to document the whole scene.

As often happens, the actual measurements of an incident scene and the estimations of distance from those involved varied greatly. While Stewart thought the deer was ten to fifteen feet away when he shot, the distance was actually 52 feet, 6 inches. He also thought Terry had been about fifty yards off to his left, while it measured at 246 feet, 6 inches . . . just over eighty-two yards.

With all the measurements and photos taken, it was documented that Stewart had shot at and killed a doe that was 52 feet, 6 inches in front of him. The bullet had entered the front of the deer's neck, been deflected off the spine, and exited the side of the neck. From there the bullet traveled 183 feet, 8 inches off to Stewart's left before striking the maple tree. There the bullet was again deflected and had to travel only 5 feet, 6 inches before striking Terry's right hand. Stewart had been sure that Terry was ninety degrees off to the left of his line of fire, and the investigation showed it was close to that—a safe shot with all the other factors involved.

Checking out other details, it was discovered that while Stewart did have a valid big game hunting license, he did not have a valid antlerless tag for that area, so he was charged with illegally taking an antlerless deer. Stewart pleaded guilty and was fined in the local court. Terry did not have a hunting license at all and so was also charged.

Whenever there is a question about the reckless discharge of a firearm while hunting, a revocation hearing is held. In this case, the big question was: Did Stewart act recklessly when he fired his rifle, causing the injury to Terry?

There was no doubt in anyone's mind that the bullet Stewart fired was the same one that struck Terry. At the hearing, all the officers involved in the investigation agreed it had been a safe shot. In fact, they all would have taken that same shot themselves.

The question of hunting without a valid tag was also discussed, as it had rendered the shot illegal. Was it then reckless to have fired the shot because it was also illegal? In the end, the hearing officer ruled that while the shot was unlawful, it was not reckless. Stewart had not violated any basic rules of firearms safety. However, he would be subject to losing his hunting license as a result of the tag violation.

Lessons Learned

- Despite what people think or feel, read in the newspaper or hear in the news, our experience shows that firearm accidents are very rare. An accident, by definition, is an unfortunate incident that happens unexpectedly and unintentionally, typically resulting in damage or injury.
- In this case, the hunter followed all the rules of safe hunting and firearms use. He positively identified his target. He could see well beyond the target to see that he had a safe backstop. He knew where all the other hunters were and knew none of them were anywhere near his line of fire.
- In all our combined years of responding to these incidents, there was only one other case that could actually be called a "hunting

accident," and there is a great deal of commonality between the two cases.

- Both incidents involved a downhill shot, taken at a safe distance, and a ricocheting bullet. In the other case, a bullet ricocheted off a rock hidden under some leaves. That bullet traveled over six hundred feet before striking a man in his thigh, leaving a very slight bruise. Charges were filed in this other case as well, but for illegally baiting deer rather than not having a hunting license or the proper tag as in this case.

- Our experience tells us that true firearms accidents are rare, but they can happen; and as with any shooting incident, those involved can be forever affected. It is vital to follow up with necessary medical care and a thorough investigation. Getting expert answers from firearms investigators helps those involved realize the lack of fault and move toward healing, both physically and emotionally.

Conclusion

As authors, the landscapes in which we live differ, but our mission is the same. Our focus and life's work has been to concentrate on prevention through good investigations. We receive updates from around the world on a daily basis to stay current with everything from changes in the firearms industry to court cases and hunting-related issues. We hope the stories we have shared have educated, inspired conversations and thoughts, but most importantly reminded many people how important it is to be a safe hunter. The excitement of a brief instant—a misjudgment, an error—has caused many a lifetime of regrets.

Three lifetimes of acquiring a specific set of skills and an innate attention to detail have allowed us to uncover the facts. As you reflect on these stories, please understand that incidents like these are, gratefully, rare! Very few hunters have ever been involved in cases like these. But each incident is tragic to those forced by circumstances to become part of the story.

The media does not report hunting accidents because there are so many but because there are so few. Baseball and skateboarding are far more dangerous activities, but those incident stories rarely make the news.

Whether you hunt or not, hunting has been a major part of many lives for not only generations but centuries. It was once said, "Anyone that ever made a major difference in our country's history was a hunter!"

From the Minutemen who went from providing for their families to liberating our country to the hunters who became the first conservationists because of their love for wildlife and the outdoors—these are the true conservationists. Hunters are a major part of the North American Wildlife Conservation Model.

Our thanks especially go out to the over fifty-seven thousand hunter education volunteers for giving their most valuable commodity—their time. Volunteers guided by professional natural resources staffs have helped reduce the hunting-related incident numbers since 1949, when mandatory state Hunter Education programs were born.

A common question is: How many hunting accidents are there each year? According to the International Hunter Education Association–USA, in 2013, the most recent year the reports have tallied, there were 559 hunting-related shooting incidents nationwide; only 53 of those were fatal.

With 14.6 million licensed hunters, this translates to fewer than four injuries per hundred thousand hunters—a rate indicating that hunting is far safer than baseball, bicycle riding, or skateboarding. Injuries for these sports in 2011 were reported as 1,261, 1,382, and 1,644 per hundred thousand participants, respectively. The most common causes of hunting incidents, listed in order of occurrence, are:

1. Falls from elevated stands; failure to use haul line/safety harness
2. Failure to point muzzle in safe direction; careless handling of firearms; failure to control muzzle
3. Failure to observe safe zone of fire; shooter swinging on game outside of a safe zone of fire

4. Victim beyond target; victim out of sight of shooter; failure to check background; unsafe backstop
5. Victim mistaken for game; failure to properly identify target
6. Stumbling/dropping firearm; shooter stumbled and fell/ dropped firearm
7. Trigger caught on object
8. Victim in front of target; victim in line of fire
9. Loading/unloading firearm improperly
10. Loaded firearm in or around vehicle; removing/placing firearm in vehicle/discharge in vehicle

All these incidents, caused by lack of good judgment, are repeatedly covered in every Hunter Education course taught. Each incident represents a violation of the most basic rules of safe hunting and safe firearms handling. Following the rules makes all these incidents easily preventable—and the probability of an incident affecting you, your family, or your friends much less likely to occur.

HUNT SAFE!

Appendix A

What Does It Take to Be a Professional Hunting Incident Investigator, and Why Would You Want One?

I want, as game protectors, men of courage, resolution and hardihood who can handle the rifle, axe and paddle; who can camp out in summer or winter; who can go on snowshoes, if necessary; who can go through the woods by day or by night without regard to trails.

—Theodore Roosevelt,
governor of New York, 1899

Law enforcement has become a very specialized profession. Specific officers with special training and equipment will be called to respond to hazardous waste dumping, crowd control, automobile crashes, or crimes involving child abuse. The experts in the areas are the people you want on the scene of any accident or incident, as they are the best at what they do. When there is a problem, you call the best person for the job.

We would never think of calling a speed enforcement officer to investigate a train derailment. Would you want someone who never drove a car to investigate an automobile crash involving your family? If you do not know how to fly a plane, you have no business investigating why one crashed. This makes perfect sense, doesn't it?

Unfortunately, all too often the lead officers called to investigate a hunting-related shooting have no hunting experience and no specific training investigating these unique incidents. This approach is a disservice to the individuals involved and to hunting as a whole.

In today's society, we have high expectations that when something happens to you or a loved one, the facts will be accurately located, collected, documented, and preserved. For each tragedy that life throws at us, we need resolution. We want answers! No matter which side of the event you are on, the truth matters. You want and need the facts!

There is only one opportunity to do it right the first time. To make the most of this opportunity, experienced, competent, and well-trained investigators must collect the facts. The investigator must possess all the skills required to identify and gather each fact, to evaluate and analyze each component, to capture and understand the timeline of events. These are necessary for a quality investigation, but the ultimate use of these facts—outside of finding out who should take responsibility—is prevention!

Very importantly, the officers first responding to an incident have no way of knowing if the investigation will result in criminal or civil actions at a later date. Their skills, or lack thereof, may at some point be put to test in a courtroom. Proper justice, for both the victim and the shooter, will depend on their abilities.

With all that said: Who is the best qualified to be in charge when a hunter is shot? If we were to build an investigator from the ground up, what criteria would we incorporate? Let's look:

- **Be an active hunter.** The experience, knowledge, and understanding of how a hunter thinks can only be understood by another hunter. That experience provides insight into what makes sense out in the field. For example, while hunting a particular game species, certain techniques, equipment, and methods are utilized; knowing those sometimes slight differences is key to understanding the incident. Someone who may have done some hunting as a pastime at some point in the past is not the same as someone who has extensive hunting experience. An investigator who is also a hunter can better understand those involved in a hunting incident.

- **Be a wildlife officer.** Wildlife officers investigate outdoor-related crimes and issues on a daily basis. Their role as teacher in the Hunter Education classroom enables them to understand the preferred standards of hunter safety. They are familiar with laws that protect wildlife, hunters, and nonhunters within their jurisdictions. These officers understand the vast array of landscapes, have the experience from working poaching scenes, and will utilize the same techniques when it comes to a hunting incident. Wildlife officers are familiar with firearms and the implements used in the hunt. They handle hundreds of firearms of all types every year. They understand the firearms' capabilities and the ammunition used in particular types of hunts. Tiny details of an incident will jump out to a seasoned wildlife officer but never be noticed by many other officers.

- **Be trained.** The Hunting Incident Investigation Academy provides training to active, commissioned wildlife officers. The academy is taught *by* wildlife officers, both active and retired, *for* wildlife officers. The academy offers the opportunity to study, reflect on, apply, and improve professional practices based on the most recent investigative techniques and research related to hunting incident investigation strategies. Wildlife officers attending get hands-on, in-the-field training working side by side with the most skilled and experience experts.

- **Be properly equipped.** As with any other specialized job, there are tools of the trade that the investigator needs to possess and know how to use to complete a proper case file, documenting what really happened and why. Learn what those tools are and how to use them—and then use them!

- **Be willing to learn.** There are ample classes at both the state and national levels to help increase your knowledge, from newest techniques to latest developments. A willingness to learn from others with more experience is vital.

- **Have a passion for the truth.** As these stories have illustrated, the investigating officer often has to sort through misinformation; uncooperative victims, shooters, and witnesses; and incorrect reports from unqualified investigators. These cases are sometimes unpopular, but determining the truth is the best path to prevention. In many cases, the obvious first conclusion is incorrect. Many painstaking hours crawling across the ground in the cold and wind and mud and then more hours in the office poring over reports, interviews, and photos are needed to find the evidence that eventually solves the case.

Upon completing the academy, wildlife officers return to their respective jurisdictions equipped with the knowledge, skills, and confidence to further aid in the mission of reducing hunting-related shooting incidents. The outcome of good investigations by well-trained and experienced investigators is accurate fact collection. Every report must document what we "know" happened, not what we "think" happened. With this as a standard, the information collected can be utilized in the mission of prevention.

However, it is paramount that academy graduates receive continuing support from their agencies. The backing from all necessary agencies to bring justice, perhaps as the result of a trial, may seem an unnecessary burden to families who have already been through so much; but everyone deserves to know the truth—the victim, the shooter, others hunters, and society in general. Incomplete or inaccurate reports, or declaring that it was "just a hunting accident," does no justice to anyone.

Professional hunting incident investigators are the people who can get the facts everyone wants and needs when an incident occurs. And as there is only one opportunity to do it right the first time, seeking the most qualified investigator is important to everyone. In the end, all these efforts, from the education and safe practices of the hunter to the professionalism and skills of well-trained investigators, keep hunting a safe (and fun) activity.

Appendix B

Should We Prosecute, or Have They Suffered Enough?

I always thought that one of the single most important things a prosecutor could do is to seek justice for the families of victims.

—Nancy Grace

As the sciences of hunting incident investigations and reconstructions have evolved, so has the way state wildlife law enforcement agencies handle these cases and the public's perception.

In the past, persons involved in a hunting incident were not typically held accountable for their actions. Over the years, this approach revealed several ongoing problems that arise when there is no accountability. First, hunters become lax about being safe and responsible; second, it creates the perfect environment for those willing to break the law to get away with it.

In many states, there was a running joke among both hunters and wildlife officers: If you want to kill someone and get away with it, just take them hunting.

When states began to do thorough investigations and reconstructions of hunting-related incidents, it was realized that hunters should be held accountable for the tremendous responsibility they take upon themselves whenever they take up a firearm.

Hunters who pick up a firearm have the power of life and death in their hands. Every time you shoulder a firearm and take aim at a target, you must identify that target *before* you make the conscious decision to pull that trigger.

You have failed at being a responsible hunter if you fail to identify the target and still decide to pull the trigger, sending a bullet traveling hundreds or thousands of feet per second, only to discover that unidentified target was another hunter.

Most states now realize the need to hold hunters accountable and responsible for their actions and have enacted appropriate laws. This has been a major transition from the old philosophy of letting such incidents pass, the mind-set being, "It was just another tragic hunting accident, and those involved have suffered enough."

Most state agencies now realize there is both a social and ethical responsibility to all involved, and many have created specially trained teams of wildlife officers to investigate and reconstruct hunting-related incidents.

Prosecuting hunters has become more acceptable when the investigation clearly shows that hunter safety standards have been violated, or when grossly bad judgment reaches the level of reckless or criminal negligence. By prosecuting these types of cases, state wildlife agencies let both the nonhunting public and the hunting world know that hunter responsibility is a serious issue.

However, the most thorough investigation does not guarantee a successful prosecution, or any prosecution at all. In most jurisdictions, the chief prosecutors are elected officials and as such are subject to the pressures of public opinion. In more than one case, prosecutors have flat out told the investigators involved that they were up for reelection and there was no way they were going to indict and prosecute a hunter in a county where most of the voters hunt.

In other cases, the problem has been that the prosecutor does not hunt, does not own firearms, and may not socialize with anyone who does and thus is unwilling to push for a painful and complicated case on a topic that is completely foreign to him or her.

Hunting is often a social activity. In most of these stories, the injured person is a family member or friend. While the shooter did pull the trigger on purpose, he or she "never meant to hurt anyone." This mentality easily gives way to "Everyone has suffered enough." As a result, there are still too many times when no charges are filed, but the work continues.

Great strides have been made to prevent these incidents from happening in the first place. This approach has also helped emphasize the importance of hunter education in preventing these types of incidents. Facts gained from each detailed investigation and from reconstructing hunting-related incidents provide much-needed lessons.

These lessons learned go back into the curriculum focus of the next states' Hunter Education program for the next class of new hunters. This procedure ensures that the skills and knowledge of both present and future hunters on how to be safe and responsible hunters continually get better. Most important, it helps hunting remain a safe activity.

Driving while intoxicated was tolerated up until twenty-five years ago. Unless someone was injured or killed, DWI was considered a victimless crime and there was rarely an arrest or prosecution. However, as society realized it was an important issue and too many lives were being lost, driving while intoxicated was no longer acceptable. Zero tolerance is the norm today in regard to drunk driving.

Prosecuting criminal actions associated with hunting-related shootings is now moving in that same direction. Unfortunately, there is a long way to go. All too often, the simple investigation, and the news report, ends with "It was just a hunting accident." Our efforts, our experience, and our stories are an effort to reduce the times anyone has to hear that or endure its lingering pain.

Appendix C

The History of Hunter Education

A Pittman-Robertson Success Story

By Steve Hall, Executive Director IHEA–USA
(International Hunter Education Association–USA)

The passage of the Dingell-Hart Amendment (pistol and revolver excise taxes) in 1970 and the Dingell-Goodling Amendment (archery excise taxes) in 1972 bolstered Federal Aid in Wildlife Restoration (Pittman-Robertson) Act of 1937 funds, giving states the opportunity to further develop one of the greatest volunteer-led programs in the history of conservation: Hunter Safety Education. The program's main success has been the reduction of hunting accidents by over two-thirds since the 1950s and 1960s, but hunter education also has improved compliance with wildlife regulations and enhanced the overall image of hunters and hunting. Federal aid and state hunter education personnel have administered hunter education, developed safe target ranges for public access, and initiated or provided key assistance to programs such as shooting sports, bow hunter education, youth hunting, archery, and outdoor programs and expositions.

A North American "Conservation Education" Model

A voluntary hunter safety program began in 1946 in Kentucky's school and statewide camp programs, using firearm and hunting safety materials produced by the National Rifle Association (NRA), such as the *Ten Commandments of Hunting Safety*. Based on high numbers of hunting accidents at that time, as found in the *Uniform Hunter Casualty Report*, New York State kicked off the first mandatory program in 1949 and hired the NRA to conduct training and issue certifications. As more states followed suit, the International Association of Fish and Wildlife Agencies (IAFWA) appointed a Hunter Safety Committee in 1957, and the NRA hosted the first national Hunter Safety Coordinator's Workshop in 1966. This evolution led to the formation in 1972 of the North American Association of Hunter Safety Coordinators (NAAHSC), later called the International Hunter Education Association. In 1970 and 1972, respectively, key amendments to the 1937 Pittman-Robertson Act were passed, allowing states to fund Hunter Education programs and develop target ranges as part of their successful wildlife conservation programs. In 1974 NAAHSC affiliated with the IAFWA, and since then, all fifty states (as well as US territories, Canadian provinces, and other countries) have passed mandatory laws requiring hunters of varying age groups to complete hunter education prior to purchasing hunting licenses and/or going afield. Today, in the United States, IHEA–USA serves as a modern-day clearinghouse for information and caretaker of the hunting accident (incident) database—a role turned over to them in the late 1990s by the National Safety Council.

The success of hunter education has been one of the hallmark achievements of the Pittman-Robertson Act. The centerpiece of the effort is the volunteer instructor! Early on, with the many duties facing conservation officers (game wardens), fish and wildlife agencies realized they needed help delivering Hunter Education courses across each jurisdiction. From the ranks of a growing NRA rifle and pistol instructor program, as well as conservation and youth organizations, agencies recruited individuals as hunter safety instructors and trained them to instruct beginning hunters in the basics of safe firearm handling, hunting, and shooting practices. Along with the NRA and the National Shooting Sports Foundation, Inc. (NSSF), private companies, including the Conservation Department of Winchester (Olin Corporation) as early as the 1960s and Outdoor Empire Publishing and Madison Films in the 1970s and 1980s, fulfilled the call for student manuals, films, and other materials to assist instructors in providing higher-quality, standardized training across the United States. Sporting arms and ammunition industries also realized the marketing potential and worked with states to provide live firing and safety equipment, ensuring that students would be tested in safe handling and marksmanship skills.

Today, over 57,000 hunter education instructors, many of whom are volunteers or professional educators, teach more than 710,000 students annually throughout the United States. Another 15,000 instructors train 140,000 students in other countries. Hunter Education's mission has not changed over time: *to teach and promote safe, knowledgeable, responsible, and involved actions by shooters and hunters.* The objectives are comprehensive and include not only safe and legal firearm and hunting practices but also familiarization with all sporting arms, marksmanship, field activities, the role of today's hunter in wildlife conservation, outdoor preparedness and basic hunting responsibilities including good landowner relations, fair chase principles, taking care of game from "field to the freezer," and the development of good outdoor values. What has changed is the advancement in the use of technologies such as Internet study courses, registration processes, and social media to communicate with younger generations. However, evaluation of field, live firing, and hunting skills remains the same and is why hunter education will remain relevant in future years.

Providing Safe Ranges for Target Shooters, Hunters, and Hunter Education Students

A significant aspect of hunter education is the funding to enhance or build target ranges throughout the United States. The main goal is to provide accessible, convenient, and safe places where hunter education instructors can teach their students in the classroom and at the range—to provide ranges where citizens can enjoy the shooting sports, sight in their firearms for the hunting seasons, practice, enjoy friendly competition, and learn how to safely and competently shoot their sporting, tactical, military, historical, and other firearms. A secondary goal is to provide archery ranges where bow hunters and crossbow users can practice their sports.

Some states use the available funding to build and operate their own ranges open to the public; other states provide "third-party grants," where local communities, clubs, and range owners operate the ranges once they are built or enhanced. Either way, the development of target ranges, including assistance from the US Fish and Wildlife Service, NRA (range development, grants, operations and specifications expertise, and seminars), NSSF (range grants, listing, and information), Environmental Protection Agency, and other federal and state agencies, is an important tool in the Pittman-Robertson chest. Across America, if there isn't a safe place to shoot a rifle, shotgun, handgun, bow, or muzzleloader, many people would simply give up the shooting sports altogether. The formula for conservation success, the excise taxes collected from the sale of sporting arms, would also suffer as a result.

Appendix D

Glossary

Bait: To place feed, salts, minerals, or other substances in a location where they do not naturally occur in order to attract wildlife for the purpose of hunting.

Birdshot: Smaller pellets or shot designed to hunt birds or small animals. Pellet sizes range from 1 through 12 and also B through FF. Like shotgun gauge, the larger the number, the smaller the diameter; #12 shot is 0.05 inch and FF is 0.230 inch in diameter.

Breeched it open: In reference to firearms, means opened the action so the chamber is uncovered. This takes the firearm out of "battery," or disables it from firing ammunition.

Buckshot: Large pellets fired from shotgun shells and designed to kill large game such as deer. They range from 0.24 to 0.36 inch in diameter; labeled as 0 through 000 and referred to as "aught," "double aught," and "triple aught."

Bullet: The single projectile fired from a rifle or pistol. It is incorrect to refer to a complete loaded cartridge as a bullet.

Caliber: The diameter of the bore or bullets used in rifles and handguns; can be measured in inches or millimeters. The name of a given caliber may not accurately reflect the measurement, and the actual bullet fired will often vary from the measured bore diameter. For example, many rifles fire a bullet that is 0.308 inch in diameter through a barrel that measures 0.30 inch, including a .30-06, a .308, and a .300 Magnum.

Cartridge: A complete loaded round for a rifle or handgun that includes a case, primer, powder, and bullet.

Case: Often called "brass" and usually made of brass, the case holds the primer, powder, and bullet for use in a rifle or handgun.

Centerfire: Any cartridge that has a replaceable primer in the center of the shell or cartridge as a means of igniting the powder. Also used to describe rifles that fire that type of ammunition. Centerfire ammunition can be reloaded. Centerfire calibers range from .17 through .500.

Climbing stand (aka climber and climber stand): These are portable hunting stands that are attached to a tree and used as a climbing aid. Hunting from an elevated stand allows the hunter to see farther while avoiding being seen or smelled by the animals.

Covey: A number of quail grouped in a particular location. When "flushed," each quail flies in different directions and lands a short distance away.

Decoy: Created to represent a game bird or animal, decoys are most commonly used to hunt waterfowl and wild turkeys. Large "spreads" of decoys are used to attract waterfowl and single decoys are used to attract big game and predators.

Diaphragm call: A device that looks much like a cross between an orthodontic retainer and a small mouth guard. It is placed between the tongue and the roof of the mouth. The sounds are used to replicate various calls; most often used for turkey hunting but also for elk and predators.

Dogging deer: 1) In the southern United States, this means using dogs to chase deer toward other hunters. Once fresh deer tracks are located, the hunters will then release, cast, or turn loose one or several dogs to follow the tracks, much like bloodhounds. The dogs then will push/drive/run the deer toward others in the hunting party. 2) In other parts of the United States, this means a hunter locates tracks in fresh snow, dirt, or mud. The hunter then follows the tracks, hoping to get close enough to harvest the deer.

Drive: When one or more hunters walk in a particular direction to push or attempt to move the game toward other stationary hunters. The walkers are called "pushers" or "drivers," and the stationary hunters are called "standers," "blockers," or "watchers." This method is used most often to hunt deer but can also be used for other game, such as pheasants.

Flush: The time when an upland game bird takes flight out of its habitat. Sometimes the flush is anticipated, as when a pointer breed of dog has locked on the scent of a hidden bird or covey and is waiting for the command to flush. At other times it is very much unexpected. In all cases it has the element of surprise, which results in excitement for the hunters and results in birds flying off in any direction. Special care must be taken to avoid swinging on other hunters or the dogs as shots are taken.

Game warden: A police or peace officer whose primary responsibility is the enforcement of fish and wildlife laws. Game wardens are most often employed by a state agency but also may work for federal agencies, military police, or Native American tribal governments. They can also be called wildlife officer, game protector, conservation officer, environmental conservation officer, ranger, conservation warden, or conservation agent. Some enforce only wildlife laws; in other jurisdictions they may also enforce any number of environmental laws, including but not limited to air and water quality, hazardous waste, boating, ATV and snowmobile laws, and the patrol of state parks. In most states these officers have full and complete police powers to enforce all state laws. Most of these state officers also carry US deputy game warden credentials, which enable them to enforce US Fish and Wildlife rules.

Gauge, or Ga.: Shotguns are measured in gauge, or ga., instead of caliber. This old system is based on how many round balls of the bore diameter can be made from one pound of lead. A 12 gauge is 0.729 inch; a pound of lead makes twelve balls of that size. Other common gauges are 10, 16, 20, and 28. The larger the gauge number, the smaller the diameter—a 10 gauge is 0.775 inch and a 28 gauge is 0.550 inch. The shotgun exception to this rule is the .410, which is a caliber measurement—it would be about a 68 gauge. Shotguns are also capable of firing single projectiles, commonly referred to as "deer slugs," that must match the gauge of the shotgun being used.

Gobble call: A device or sound that is designed to duplicate the sound of a male, "tom," turkey.

Hammock: A term used in the southeastern United States to describe an elevated island area of trees in a swamp/wetlands. This elevation can be from a few inches to several feet above the wetlands surrounding it.

Huffer: A tubular device you blow or huff through while directing your breath over a surface that is suspected to have latent fingerprints. The moisture from your mouth and breath causes the fingerprint powder to better adhere to latent fingerprints on certain surfaces.

Hummock: Higher ground within a swamp or wetland, usually formed by fallen limbs or tree roots and most often covered with grass and moss. This term is more commonly used in the northeastern United States. It is our understanding that the terms "hammock" and "hummock" are usually not used to describe wetland area rises of the Midwest or West.

Hunting club: A property that is leased by one or more hunters for the purpose of hunting wildlife.

Laser trajectory device: A tool that uses a laser to re-create the trajectory of a bullet. Incident scene investigators use it to determine the line of sight the projectile/bullet took when it was fired from a firearm. The device can be attached to a tripod, firearm, or a protrusion rod that is pushed through a hole created by the bullet path. It is useful in determining where a shooter or victim might have been located when a shot took place. The device is invaluable in finding locations of fired projectiles/bullets and shell/cartridge casings.

Line of fire: (1) The direction a person shoots; the direction the firearm is pointed in when the trigger is pulled. (2) The person injured was between the shooter and the intended target. For example, if a rabbit runs behind another hunter and the hunter is hit with some of the shotgun pellets, then the victim was in the line of fire.

Magazine: The part of a firearm where ammunition is stored prior to loading it into the chamber. This may be a removable device (often incorrectly called a clip) or may be a fixed part of the firearm, such as the tube under the barrel of a pump-action shotgun or lever-action rifle. Technically, a clip holds cartridges to be loaded into the magazine; the magazine holds the cartridges to be loaded into the chamber prior to firing.

Measurement of visibility device, or MVD: A blaze orange device with specific markings used to measure and document how well a hunter could or should have been able to see through the woods or brush. It is most often placed where the victim was when the injury happened; a reading or measurement is then taken from the location of the shooter. Measured in percentages, 100 percent means that nothing was physically blocking the view; 0 percent means none of the device was visible, and therefore the shooter could not see what was there and could not identify what he or she was shooting at.

Methodology of the hunt: The manner in which a particular game species is pursued or the manner in which the hunt is deployed. This can include a drive, still-hunting, stalking, or calling.

Projectile: The bullet/slug/pellets that leave the barrel of a firearm. Rifles and handguns fire a single projectile—a bullet. Shotguns can fire either a single projectile (a slug) for hunting big game such as deer or multiple projectiles (pellets) for hunting small game such as turkeys or pheasants.

Push: This does not mean to place your hands on the rear end of a deer to get it to move. It does mean to walk through the woods and fields with a plan of getting the deer to go in the direction of other hunters. See also *drive*.

Rimfire: Any ammunition that does not use a primer in the center of the cartridge to ignite the powder. The priming powder is instead located in the rim of the cartridge case. Rimfire calibers range from .17 to .22 magnums and 5 millimeter.

Setup: Where a turkey hunter makes the decision to sit down and start calling to a turkey. This can be from a built blind, but more often a turkey hunter will sit down at the base of a tree that is wider than his or her shoulders and call. This is known as the hunter's set-up position.

Shell: Shotgun ammunition, also called a shot shell. Most have a high or a low brass base and a plastic upper section, but some are all plastic. Older shot shells are paper instead of plastic, and there are some all-brass shot shells. Each shell holds a primer in the bottom and contains powder and projectiles with various kinds of wads between the two. Shells are most often loaded with small pellets called birdshot or buckshot but can also be loaded with a single projectile, or slug. Used or empty shot shells are sometimes called "hulls."

Shot shell nomenclature: The pellets, sometimes called BBs, contained within a shotgun shell are categorized in different spherical sizes. Common sizes are 2s, the largest, up to 8s, which are the smallest, and in some cases a letter such as F or T. Buckshot are the largest pellets and range in size from 0, the largest, to 0000. The standard length of a 12-gauge shotgun shell is 2¾ inches. That is the length that will fit in the chamber, where the shotgun shell is inserted or loaded with the intention of being fired. The chambers in a 12-gauge shotgun range from 2¾ inches to 3½ inches. If your shotgun has a 3- or 3½-inch chamber, you can insert a 2¾-inch shell. However, you cannot place a longer shell, such as a 3- or 3½-inch, in a 2¾-inch chamber. The gun's action will not close properly and may cause a dangerous explosion, resulting in injury. "No. 5, three-inch magnum" is then a shotgun shell that is three inches long and is loaded with number 5 size shot.

Slate call and striker: A hard slate surface. The end of a dowel or a hard small-diameter rod is rubbed across the face of the slate, which causes friction in a circle or line, replicating the sounds of a hen turkey.

Slough: In a southern river swamp, a slough is a usually a river or creek-like inlet/spur of water that flows through the swamp at high water levels. At low water levels, sloughs can hold water only until it is absorbed by the earth, evaporates, or is taken up by the trees when the sap rises in spring. In dry times, sloughs are like dry river- or creekbeds.

Still-hunting: A method of hunting in which a hunter may remain in one place or choose to slowly stalk through an area in order to detect the wildlife species being hunted. When done correctly, it may take a hunter thirty minutes to an hour to stalk a distance of one hundred yards. The concept is to move slowly and walk only a step or two at a time, stopping often to scan the area for game. This is done in hopes of slipping up on quarry and seeing the game before the hunter is detected.

Trajectory: The path that a bullet/slug/pellet/arrow, also known as the projectile, takes after being fired.

Tree clips/limb clips/pellet strikes: Any marks left when a projectile strikes vegetation. Finding these allows the investigator to document the path of the projectile(s).

Two-path road: A small road that runs through the woods. The two paths are caused by the tires of a motor vehicle, creating a single-lane roadway with grass growing between the tire tracks. Commonly known and sometimes referred to as a "woods road."

Unsafe backstop: This happens when a person fails to properly safeguard against any risks behind the intended target. If a rabbit runs between two hunters and one hunter shoots at the rabbit and strikes the hunter beyond, the shooter fired when he had an unsafe backstop. This also refers to situations when there may not be any type of backstop, such as a horizon shot where the shooter is unable to see beyond the target.

Wad or cup: Shot shells contain various materials to protect and separate the powder from the pellets or slug. These can be made of fiber, cardboard, or plastic and may be a thin flat wafer or an actual cup-shaped plastic device that holds the pellets until they leave the barrel. Each component will travel different distances from the muzzle, and finding all the parts can determine the location of the shooter as well as the line of fire.

Zone of fire: A term typically used when two or more people are hunting upland game or waterfowl. A person's "safe zone of fire" can easily be determined as follows: When facing forward, raise both arms straight out in front you. Next move both arms out forty-five degrees. This V creates your safe zone of fire. This self-imposed rule prohibits a hunter from swinging beyond these boundaries, restricting the muzzle of the firearm being pointed toward hunting companions or other nontargets. For example, say that a pheasant gets up and flies to your right and back behind you and your hunting companion is thirty yards directly to your right. You do not swing beyond that forty-five-degree V, which is your safe zone of fire. Most upland game injuries occur when hunters swing their firearm beyond their safe zone of fire and discharge in an attempt to harvest a game bird. Each hunter's zone of fire, or safe zone of fire, changes as the group moves. A person in the middle of a group will have a much smaller zone of fire than the hunters at the ends of the line.

Many sources list the most important rules of firearms safety, including the NRA, IHEA, NSSF, and others. These rules are often referred to as the Four Rules or the Ten Commandments of Firearms Safety.

The Four Rules of Firearms Safety:

1. All guns are always loaded.
2. Never point the gun at anything you are not willing to destroy.
3. Keep your finger off the trigger until your sights are on target (and you have made the decision to shoot).
4. Be sure of your target and what is beyond it.

The Ten Commandments of Firearms Safety:

1. Treat every gun as if it were loaded.
2. Watch that muzzle! Be able to control the direction of the muzzle at all times.
3. Be sure the barrel and action are clear of obstructions.
4. Be sure of your target before you pull the trigger.
5. Unload guns when not in use.
6. Never point a gun at anything you do not intend to shoot.
7. Never climb a fence or tree or jump a ditch with a loaded gun.
8. Never shoot a bullet at a flat, hard surface or water.
9. Store guns and ammunition separately, beyond the reach of children and careless adults.
10. Avoid alcoholic beverages and mind-altering drugs before or during shooting.

ACKNOWLEDGMENTS

WE WOULD LIKE TO THANK THE FOLLOWING PEOPLE AND GROUPS for their support, guidance, inspiration, technical support, and love prior to and during this project:

Dr. Leanna DePue, Bob Staton, Tom "The Wad-god" Kremer, the late Homer Moe, and the late Mike Bradshaw, Texas game warden.

Daryl Byers, Mary Van Durme, Pete and Shirley Slings, Rachel and Matthew Watkins, Anne Van Durme, Beth Clymer, Selena Hall, Susanne Landgrebe, Lon and Deb Lindenberg, and Captain Denny Hill.

Steve Hall, International Hunter Education Association–USA; Dianne Vrablic, National Shooting Sports Foundation; and the National Wild Turkey Federation.

Finally, to Tammy Sapp, the one person who made this all possible. Without her friendship and her belief in what we were doing, this book would never have happened.

BIBLIOGRAPHY

Bland, Dwain. *Turkey Hunter's Digest*, revised edition. North-
 field, IL: DBI Books, 1994.
Books LLC, Wiki Series. *Hunting Accident Deaths*. Memphis:
 Books LLC, 2011.
Byers, Keith. "Afternoon Problem Solving." *The Turkey Hunter*, 7
 March 1990: 66–68.
———. *All-Terrain Vehicle (ATV) Theft Investigations Manual*.
 Forsyth, GA: Department of Natural Resources Law
 Enforcement Section, 1997.
———. "Chasing Peach State Water Gobblers." *Georgia Sports-
 man*, 2 February 1997: 48A–48C.
———. "Close to the Vest Turkey Hunting." *Georgia Outdoor
 News (GON)*, 16 February 2002: 30–34.
———. "Comfortable Silence." *Georgia Outdoor News (GON)*,
 14 May 2000: 64–66, 68.
———. "Familiar Woods." *The Turkey Hunter*, 9 April 1992:
 78–83.
———. "Morning Lessons for Afternoon Hunting Decisions."
 Georgia Outdoor News (GON), 21 April 2007: 22–25.
———. "Planning for Your Georgia Gobbler." *Georgia Sports-
 man*, 2 February 1996: 17–18.
———. "Plan B Gobblers." *Georgia Outdoor News (GON)*, 20
 March 2006: 134–137.
———. "Plan B Gobblers." *Alabama Outdoor News (AON)*, 2
 April 2008: 64–67.

————. "Talk Softly." *Georgia Outdoor News (GON)*, 19 March 2005: 92–94, 96–97.

————. "The 15-Day Gobbler." *Georgia Outdoor News (GON)*, 15 March 2001: 48–53.

————. "The Hen Factor." *Georgia Outdoor News (GON)*, 15 February 2001: 32–34, 36–37.

————. "The Moving Hen." *Georgia Outdoor News (GON)*, 18 March 2004: 48–52.

————. "The Teacher." *Georgia Outdoor News (GON)*, 10 March 1996: 84–88, 90–91.

Di Maio, Vincent J. M. *Gunshot Wounds (Practical Aspects of Firearms, Ballistics, and Forensic Techniques)*, second edition. Boca Raton, FL: CRC Press LLC, 1999.

Donovan, Tom. *Dying to Hunt in Montana*. Great Falls, MT: Portage Meadows Publishing, 2009.

East, Wayne. "Incident vs. Accident." *Hunting and Shooting Sports Education Journal*, vol. 10, no. 4, Winter 2010: 6.

Haag, Lucien C. *Shooting Incident Reconstruction*. Burlington, VT: Elsevier Inc., 2006.

Harbour, Dave. *Advanced Wild Turkey Hunting and World Records*. El Monte, CA: New Win Publishing, 1983.

Koester, Robert J. *Lost Person Behavior (A Search and Rescue Guide on Where to Look—for Land, Air, and Water*. Charlottesville, VA: dbs Publications LLC, 2008.

Lapin, Terence W. *The Mosin-Nagant Rifle (For Collectors Only)*. Tustin, CA: North Cape Publications, 1998.

Leopold, Aldo. *A Sand County Almanac*. New York: Oxford University Press, 1968.

Lewis, Allan, with Herbert Leon MacDonell. *The Evidence Never Lies*. New York: Holt, Rinehart and Winston, 1984.

Louk, John, and Lorne Smith Jr. *Treestand Accident Investigations & Reconstruction Course.* TMA, undated.

MacDonell, Herbert Leon. *Bloodstain Patterns*, revised edition. Corning, NY: Laboratory of Forensic Science, 1997.

National Shooting Sports Foundation. "Firearms-Related Injury Statistics." Industry Intelligence Reports, 2013 edition.

———. "A Profile of Today's Hunter." Industry Intelligence Reports, 2013 edition.

Norton, Bob. *The Hunter Developmental Stages and Ethics.* Helena, MT: River Bend Press, 2007.

Posewitz, Jim. *Beyond Fair Chase.* Guilford, CT: Falcon Press Publishing, 1994.

———. *Rifle in Hand.* Helena, MT: River Bend Press, 2004.

Sears, George Washington. "Nessmuk." *Woodcraft and Camping.* New York: Dover Publications, 1963.

Shaffer, W. C. *Greed and Carelessness.* Harrisburg, PA: The Telegraph Press, 1946.

Slings, Rod. "CSI in the Georgia Woods." *Hunting and Shooting Sports Education Journal*, vol. 10, no. 4, Winter 2010: 8–9.

Slings, Rod. "Firearms Safety, a Trip Down Under." *Hunting and Shooting Sports Education Journal*, vol. 6, no. 3, Spring 2007: 32.

Slings, Rod, and Sgt. Keith Byers, Captain Michael Van Durme, et al. *Hunting Incident Investigation Manual.* Windsor Locks, CT: International Hunter Education Association, 2008.

Slings, Rod, and Tim Lawhern. "CSI in the Wild." *Hunting and Shooting Sports Education Journal*, vol. 8, no. 2, Fall 2008: 22–23.

Snell, Lt. Donald E., and Lt. Michael L. Van Durme. *Report on Hunting Related Shooting Incidents "Shooter Profile."* The

Northeast Association of Fish and Wildlife Agencies, 53rd Conference, Framingham, MA, 1997.

Staton, Robert. "Hunter Ed. (Hunting Incident Academy)." *Hunting and Shooting Sports Education Journal*, vol. 2, no. 4, Fall 2000: 17.

Stuart, James H., Paul E. Kish, and T. Paulette Sutton. *Principles of Bloodstain Pattern Analysis (Theory and Practice)*. Boca Raton, FL: Taylor & Francis Group LLC, 2005.

Swanson, Charles R., Neil C. Chamelin, and Leonard Territo. *Criminal Investigation*, sixth edition. New York: McGraw Hill Companies Inc., 1988.

Tauschek, Sam. "The Most Dangerous Game." *Sports Afield*, vol. 224, no. 2, February 2001: 68–71.

Van Durme, Lt. Michael L. "Proposed Standard Form for Investigating Hunting Related Shooting Incidents." The Northeast Association of Fish and Wildlife Agencies, 54th Conference, Camp Hill, PA, 1998.

Van Durme, Lt. Michael L., and Investigators Otto Tertinek and Wayne Jones. "I'm Sorry!! I Didn't Mean To. I Didn't See You!" *Hunter and Shooting Sports Education Journal*, vol. 3, no. 2, Fall 2003: 27–30.

Whittlesey, Lee H. *Death in Yellowstone*. Lanham, MD: Roberts Rinehart Publishers, 2014.

Resources

The following resources have more information on hunting, hunter education and firearms safety, and bow hunter safety and education:

Association of Fish and Wildlife Agencies (AFWA)
Contact: Donald MacLauchlan
444 North Capitol St. NW, Suite 544
Washington, DC 20001
(202) 624-7890 / fax: (202) 624-7891
www.sso.org/iafwa
E-mail: iafwa@sso.org

International Hunter Education Association (IHEA–USA)
800 East 73rd Ave., Unit 2
Denver, CO 80229
(303) 430-7233 / fax: (303) 430-7236
www.ihea.com

National Bowhunter Education Foundation (NBEF)
PO Box 2934
Rapid City, SD 57709
(479) 649-9036 / fax: (479) 649-3098
www.nbef.org
E-mail: info@nbef.org

National Rifle Association (NRA)
National Rifle Association of America
11250 Waples Mill Rd.
Fairfax, VA 22030-9400
(800) 672-3888
www.nra.org

National Shooting Sports Foundation, Inc. (NSSF)
Flintlock Ridge Office Center
11 Mile Hill Rd.
Newtown, CT 06470-2359
(203) 426-1320 / fax: (203) 426-1087
www.nssf.org
E-mail: info@nssf.org

National Wild Turkey Federation (NWTF)
770 Augusta Rd.
Edgefield, SC 29824-0530
(800) 843-6983 or (803) 637-3106
www.nwtf.org
E-mail: info@nwtf.net

About Hunting and Shooting Related Consultants, LLC

We are Rod Slings from Iowa, Keith Byers from Georgia, and Michael Van Durme from New York and were each leaders in our respective states when it came to investigating hunting incidents. Now we have joined forces to form Hunting and Shooting Related Consultants, LLC (HSRC). We bring over seventy-five years of law enforcement experience and more than sixty years of investigating hunting-related shooting incidents. We are also the leaders in training other wildlife officers around the world in these unique skills. We are the experts in the investigation of hunting accidents, or hunting-related shooting incidents.

Every year there are hunting accidents that result in personal injury and even, tragically, death. While it is rare that any of these are intentional criminal acts, there is often a degree of negligence or recklessness involved that can result in criminal charges against the shooter. Some of these cases are truly accidents—cases where the shooter followed all the game laws as well as the rules of safe hunting and safe firearms handling. In addition, recognizing the fact that we usually hunt with our family or our closest friends makes any accident even more challenging.

There are times when an accident results in a civil action filed by the victim against the shooter. Determining the actual facts of these cases—finding and correctly identifying all the details—makes the difference. We are experts in identifying and correctly interpreting vital details and assisting in determining where the liability—if any—lies and what criminal charges might be applicable. If finding out the facts and details of hunting- or shooting-related accidents could be compared with finding a needle in a haystack, our expertise is searching for those needles.

Services We Provide

HSRC promises our clients a complete and professional review of their individual cases. While it is always best to bring the experts in at the earliest time, we can help solve cases and bring about successful resolutions even many years later.

We will, as a team, evaluate each step of the investigation using the most recent investigative techniques. We will compare any previous efforts with the professional practices we have used and taught. Our investigation strategies and efforts and the accurate documentation of your case will be our mission. HSRC will prepare a complete, detailed final report based on these answers and the facts.

In addition, we prepare a conclusion for the case—either civil or criminal. We assist in deposition preparation, provide courtroom testimony, and are available for both lectures and conferences in the areas of hunting- and shooting-related incidents, data collection, and more. Our research and experiences can be very motivating to hunter education instructors and others in the outdoor and firearms-related industries.

Our past work has included cold case homicides while hunting, civil liability claims, tree stand falls, and acting as subject matter experts in developing training materials.

Our law enforcement backgrounds have been built on personal integrity, allowing us to become internationally recognized for our expertise. This same integrity has become the foundation for our business and beneficial in our success. We will not deviate from our principle, which, in turn, benefits our clients!